OFF
THE
PLANET

In memory of my grandfather Victor Hayward (who was employed as a cinema projectionist in London before going on to work with De Havillands on their Comet Racer plane in the 1930s – about the nearest you could get to Sci-Fi at that time)

OFF
THE
PLANET

Music, Sound and Science Fiction Cinema

Edited by
Philip Hayward

John Libbey | perfect
beat
publications

LONDON · PARIS · ROME · SYDNEY

Cataloguing in Publication Data

Off the Planet: Music, Sound and Science Fiction Cinema.

    Bibliography.
    Includes index.

1. Science Fiction Cinema   2. Film Music.   I. Hayward, Philip (1956–).

ISBN: 0 86196 644 9 (Paperback)

Design and Setting by John Libbey Publishing
Front Cover design: Ross Tesoriero

Published by
John Libbey Publishing, Box 276, Eastleigh SO50 5YS, UK
e-mail: john.libbey@libertysurf.fr; web site: www.johnlibbey.com

Distributed in North America by
Indiana University Press, 601 North Morton Street, Bloomington, IN 47404, USA.
www.iupress.indiana.edu

Printed in Malaysia by Vivar Printing Sdn. Bhd., 48000 Rawang,
Selangor Darul Ehsan.

Contents

Acknowledgements

The original idea for this book arose from my experience in teaching the course MAS/MUS 303 'Screen Soundtracks' at Macquarie University, Sydney in the late 1990s and early 2000s. My thanks to the students on the course and to my colleagues Rebecca Coyle and Mark Evans for their ideas and input.

Thanks also to Michael Hill and LINC TV (Lismore) for their various assistances and to John Libbey for running with this publication.

As ever, my immediate family – Amy, Rebecca, Rosa, Roy and Ruth – have helped this project in innumerable ways.

Introduction

SCI-FIDELITY
Music, Sound and Genre
History

PHILIP HAYWARD

1977, the Harlesden Roxy in London. The Clash is playing a sell-out gig at the peak of the early buzz around the band's edgy, energetic new wave sound. Entering the auditorium shortly before the band take the stage I'm hit by a monstrously loud, multiply echoing burst of dub reggae percussion, then the horns come in, jazzily, evoking 1960s' ska at the same time as they nail the identity of the tune. The track is the 12 inch vinyl single *Ska Wars* by Rico Rodrigues, a recording that updates the Jamaican fascination with popular western cinema previously celebrated by artists such as Prince Buster, with his tribute to Hollywood gangster movies *Al Capone* (1967), or the spaghetti western/Sergio Leone fascination explored in The Upsetter's *Return of Django* album (1969). The white punk association with a version of the *Star Wars* theme is significant in that Rodrigues's engagement with Hollywood Sci-Fi music even works in the environment of a Clash gig, in which both popular music culture ("No Elvis, Beatles or Rolling Stones in 1977" [1977]) and American cultural imperialism ("I'm so bored with the USA" [eponymous]) are triumphantly disavowed in favour of cultural allusions and affinities to Jamaican roots reggae and Rastafarianism. As ever, the loops and transmutations of popular culture are nothing if not complex.

Star Wars' release in 1977 marked the beginning of a new wave of big budget Sci-Fi films that rejuvenated the genre by revisiting an earlier era of cinematic wonderment. The film involved an ultra-realist updating premised on cinematic special effects that recreated a sense of fantasy largely absent from a decade of Hollywood films in which gritty naturalism had been prominent. The 'updating and revisiting' approach was nowhere so evident as in John Williams' *Star Wars* score, which exemplified the classic Hollywood music tendency identified by Caryl Flinn (1992) in terms of its nostalgicist use of

1

previous western art music traditions to create immediately recognisable affects. Williams' score was thus doubly nostalgicist, both to classic Hollywood cinema music and the fine music traditions that this drew upon. Rico Rodrigues's reggaefication of Williams' main theme, similarly, acknowledged and playfully refigured this series of precedents. 1977 marked the beginning of a new period in Sci-Fi cinema that revived earlier approaches to the genre. The music for films such as *Star Wars* (and its sequels) and *Close Encounters of the Third Kind* were premised on classic Hollywood approaches to cinematic scoring[1] (albeit in combination with various popular music instrumentations and sound production techniques), and established these as a major strand in subsequent Sci-Fi cinema, particularly big-budget productions. Identifying 1977 as a period marker, it is possible to characterise Hollywood, European and Japanese Sci-Fi film music history as comprising five principal phases[2]:

I. 1902–27
The pre synch-sound period

II. 1927–45
Exploration of various western orchestral styles (while strands of the cinematic genre coalesced)

III. 1945–60
The prominence of discordant and/or unusual aspects of orchestration/instrumentation to convey otherworldly/futuristic themes

IV. 1960–77
The continuation of otherworldly/futuristic styles alongside a variety of musical approaches

V. 1977 –
The prominence of classic Hollywood-derived orchestral scores in big-budget films together with otherworldly/futuristic styles and, increasingly, rock and, later, disco/techno music + the rise in integrated music/sound scores

With regard to non-musical sound[3], the second strand of consideration in this anthology, the periodisation is less marked and can be characterised in terms of intermittent engagements with sound effects and sound design to convey otherworldly/futuristic elements that become more marked and complex with the revival of big-budget Sci-Fi cinema in the late 1970s and the introduction and upgrading of a series of sound production and processing technologies in the 1980s and 1990s. The interweaving and blurring of these two sonic fields provides a third historical strand that weaves through the anthology.

[NB While the following sections discuss a number of notable Science Fiction film scores and Sci-Fi influenced music recordings, this Introduction does not attempt to provide an exhaustive catalogue of SF films and music releases. Rather, it attempts to establish an historical framework for the films analysed by contributing authors and to complement individual studies with discussions of related phenomena. There are, inevitably, other films, film sub-genres, musical styles and/or composers that also merit detailed analyses in future publications on this area[4].]

I. The pre-synch sound era and the establishment of Sci-Fi cinema

At its simplest, Science Fiction (also referred to in this book as Sci-Fi and SF) is a cultural genre concerned with aspects of futurism, imagined technologies and/or inter-planetarism. These points of orientation allow for a wide range of inflections and speculations as to the dystopic or utopic aspects of future (and/or alternative) lives or realities, including, in many instances, contact with alien 'others'[5]. It has been most prevalent as a literary form but has also manifested itself in visual art, radio, theatre, cinema and music. As with any genre, it overlaps and shares characteristics with others. Referring to Susan Sontag's 1965 essay 'The Imagination of Disaster', I.Q. Hunter has identified that "SF as a cinematic genre is ... difficult to distinguish from horror" (1995: 5). (As Paul Théberge details in Chapter 7 of this anthology, the work of contemporary director David Cronenberg exemplifies this characterisation.) Hunter also argues that Sci-Fi cinema deviates from "more optimistic and technologically gung-ho" strands of SF literature by drawing on Gothic themes and "often complements horror's fearful attitudes to science and the future" (ibid). With the exception of the ambiguous idealism of *Space is the place* (1972 – discussed in Chapter 4), the selection of post-War cinematic works analysed in this book certainly conform to this categorisation (and Sontag's earlier identification of disaster as a key element in the genre). While there cannot be said to be a musical genre of SF as such, Maxim Jakubowski (1999) has provided a short survey of uses of Science Fiction themes and settings in 18th–20th Century western art music that shows that Sci-Fi's exotic elements have attracted a series of composers to write material that variously references and/or is imaginatively inspired by futurism and/or other-worldliness. (While no clear generic conventions appear to have emerged out of this work, or influenced cinema music to any appreciable extent, this body of music merits further analysis in its own right).

Although the starting point of the contemporary genre of Science Fiction has been the subject of dispute, the work of the European writers Jules Verne and H.G. Wells is usually regarded as pioneering its emergence as a popular genre. Verne's novels 'De la terre a la Lune' ('From the Earth to the Moon') (1869) and 'Autour de la Lune' ('A Trip around the Moon') (1870) provided themes that were interpreted in the earliest example of Sci-Fi cinema, George Méliès's *Le Voyage dans la Lune* ('A Trip to the Moon') (1902)[6] and can be seen to have influenced productions such as Fritz Lang's *Die Frau im Mond* ('The Woman in the Moon'[7]) (1928) and a series of subsequent, synch-sound era films. Lang's 1926 film, *Metropolis* – a cautionary story of a future, industrially dominated dystopia – is generally regarded as the most spectacular production of the pre-WW2 era. Made on a large budget over two-year period by the German state-operated film company UFA, the original (German-release) version was over three hour in length and featured dramatic futuristic city sets and mechanical technologies together with a special effects sequence showing the creation of a robotic female. As befits such a costly project, souvenir brochures, publicity stunts and extensive press coverage accompanied the international release of the film. As with many major films of the period, a music score was commissioned for performance by a small orchestral ensemble at major first-run theatres (with a single piano version available for smaller venues[8]). The music for the film was written by German composer Gottfried Huppertz and drew on established scoring traditions to emphasise dramatic and narrative aspects of the film (rather than the futuristic strangeness of its scenarios). Extracts from the orchestral score were recorded for what appears to have been the first Sci-Fi film music released on record, in the form of two 78rpm disks put out on the Vox label. Emphasising its promotion function, the first disk featured Lang speaking about the film on the a-side, with the main theme from *Metropolis* on the b. A second disk features a waltz from *Metropolis* on the a-side and 'phantastic' dance and a 'dance macabre' on the b. These disks do not appear to have been produced in any sizeable volume and have not been subsequently reissued[9].

In addition to the musical score and disks, the film also spawned a series of ancillary musical texts that extended the film and promoted it in a wider public sphere. In London, for instance, the British songwriter William Helmore wrote a song entitled 'City of Dreams' that was published in sheet music form shortly after the film's UK premiere (with a front cover that declared it "inspired by the UFA masterpiece 'Metropolis'") and featured a city image from the film and insert of the film's heroine, Brigitte Helm. In Australia, a shortened version of the original film was premiered in Sydney and Melbourne in 1928 (in a double bill with the Charlie Chaplin feature *The Circus*), with full orchestral accompaniment and – in the later city – by a twenty item song and dance presentation entitled '1928'[10]. But while *Metropolis* was significant in having a series of associated musical texts (and spawning another series through subsequent revivals and film, video and DVD re-packages[11]), the original score was not influential on the styles of Sci-Fi film music that were to emerge in the post-synch sound era.

The other major Sci-Fi film of the pre-synch sound era was Yakov Protazanov's *Aelita* (1924). Like *Metropolis*, the film was a big-budget production that was extensively promoted upon release. The film's narrative is split between contemporary Russia and Mars, with the film's hero, an engineer, encountering Aelita, the Martian queen, after travelling to the planet in a self-designed spacecraft. The original score for the film, performed in an orchestral version during its premiere run in Moscow, only exists in fragments and it cannot be ascertained to what degree the Martian sequences were accompanied by music that attempted to communicate alien culture through stylistic markers[12].

Following Méliès's pioneering Verne-influenced productions, there appear to have been only two French Sci-Fi films produced in the 1920s. Both were experimental shorts that used similar 'trick film' techniques to those exploited by Méliès to create their fantastic scenarios – Abel Gance's *La folie du Docteur Tube* (1915) and René Clair's *Paris qui dort* (1923). The only feature-length production of the decade was another film directed by Gance, *La fin du monde*, which began pre-production in 1929 and opened in Paris in January 1931. The film's scenario fitted Sontag's characterisation of the SF form as intertwined with disaster. Its narrative concerns the social trauma caused by the (apparent) imminence of Earth's collision with a comet. For all its ambition and budget (18 million francs), the film was a critical flop and box office failure and has largely disappeared from the map of Sci-Fi cinema history. One of the problems with the film noted by reviewers was its sound, which they characterised as harsh and grating[13]. This was salutary, since the director's 1929 pre-production 'manifesto' to his crew both emphasised the potential of sound (in this, his first synch sound film) and the necessity of effective technologies in competing with Hollywood cinema:

> La fin du monde *relies to a considerable extent on the use of sound ... The whole of the cataclysm sequence, in particular, can be orchestrated, organised in terms of sound, making it possible to achieve some extraordinary effects. But, I repeat, these effects will only be possible if I am given the same facilities as the Americans.* (Gance, 1929, translated in King [1984: 108])

Gance's failure to secure the sophisticated sound technologies he desired appears to have contributed to the film's box office demise. Although the extraordinary success of US synch-sound Sci-Fi film did not occur until the post-War era, Gance's assessment of competition with the US in this genre was to prove prophetic in the long run.

II. The 1930s

Along with Verne's work, H.G. Wells's novella 'War of the Worlds' (1898) was also a significant influence on later cinema, being adapted for film by Byron Haskin in 1953 and pre-dating a series of post-War alien-invasion features[14]. It was however a cinema adaptation of Wells's novel 'The Shape of Things to Come' (1933) that featured the most accomplished and sophisticated Science Fiction film music score of the early synch-sound period. The film, released under the abbreviated title *Things to come* in 1936, was adapted for the screen by Wells, produced by Alexander Korda and directed by Cameron Menzies. The production was an ambitious endeavour, shot at Denham Studios on the largest budget of any pre-War British feature in an attempt to match and compete with Hollywood's high-cost epics[15]. Wells secured the services of English composer Arthur Bliss to provide the score. Born in 1891, Bliss was initially influenced by early 20th Century French avant gardists (such as Francis Poulenc and Georges Auric) before moving to a more traditional British symphonic style, inspired by composers such as Edgar Elgar. Bliss undertook the film project on the condition that he played a central role in the film's creation and the resultant score is a striking example of music providing an integrated enhancement to the thematic core and narrative effect of a film. Wells later discussed the production and its score in the following terms:

> The music is a part of the constructive scheme of the film, and the composer, Mr. Arthur Bliss, was practically a collaborator in its production. In this, as in so many respects, this film, so far at least as its intention goes, is boldly experimental. Sound sequences and picture sequences were made to be closely interwoven. The Bliss music is not intended to be tacked on; it is part of the design[16]. (quoted in Manvell and Huntley, 1957: 54)

For the film score Bliss wrote a concert suite recorded by the London Symphony Orchestra with an extra percussion section and a large choir in several sections. In addition to the well-known march theme that introduces and accompanies the sequences of the outbreak of war, the film's most obviously SF/futuristic music sequences are those that accompany the rebuilding of cities (through massive rumbling string sounds alternated with sharper pizzicato passages) and the final sequence where the firing of the 'space gun' launches a rocket into space carrying fresh hope for the human race (signaled by an uplifting vocable choral passage). The accomplishment of the film score – and particularly techniques such as the use of increasing dissonance to signify imminent drama and violence – was later acknowledged by noted post-War screen composer Bernard Herrmann, who included a section from the *Things to come* score on an album entitled *Great British Film Music*, recorded by the National Philharmonic Orchestra under his direction in 1974.

Along with Bliss's work the other most notable contribution to Science Fiction cinema music in the immediate post-synch-sound period was that of the German composer Franz Waxman. Waxman was conversant with the traditions of western art music and those of newer, popular forms such as jazz. In the late 1920s he studied piano at the Dresden Music Academy and the Berlin Conservatory of Music. During this period (and after) he also performed in jazz bands in Berlin. His initial involvement with film music arose after a jazz ensemble he performed in was employed to perform composer Freidrich Hollaender's score for von Sternberg's 1930 film *Der Blaue Engel*[17], starring Marlene Dietrich. During the course of the film his skills in arranging became apparent and he was subsequently engaged by Fritz Lang to write the score for his 1933 film *Liliom* before migrating to the USA in 1934. His score for James Whale's Sci-Fi/horror film *Bride of*

Frankenstein (1935), written shortly after arriving in Hollywood, invites comparison with Max Steiner's seminal score for *King Kong* (1933) through its prominent use of striking leitmotifs[18] for the main characters. The Sci-Fi/horror aspects of *Bride of Frankenstein's* music involve use of atmospheric chromaticist passages to suggest unease and to create tension and the use of dynamic refinements of conventions of cinema 'chase music' (established in the pre-synch sound era) to enhance narrative drive and excitement. Mark Walker has claimed, with some justification, that Waxman's music for *Bride of Frankenstein* was "one of the first fully developed film scores ever written for a Hollywood movie"[19] and has also identified that it was "so successful... that Universal constantly recycled portions of it in innumerable B-movies and serials like *Flash Gordon*[20] thereafter" (1998: 210)[21].

With regard to serials, one of the more surprising juxtapositions of musical style and Sci-Fi theme in pre-War cinema occurred in the 1935 serial film *Phantom Empire*. The series featured emerging singing cowboy star Gene Autry as the male lead/hero and his friend, composer and accordion accompanist Smiley Burnette as his sidekick. In *Phantom Empire* Autry's character runs a ranch and also appears on a daily radio show. Normal life is soon disrupted by the arrival of mysterious riders from the subterranean high-tech city of Murania. Torn between exploring the city and returning to perform on radio (where he sings novelty songs such as *Uncle Noah's Ark*), Autry encounters the conniving queen Tika[22] and faces off hostile robots armed with flamethrowers before escaping to sing on. Here the emergent hillbilly/singing cowboy ballad tradition contrasts to the technological threat of the subterranean culture and provides an anchor to the surface world and a sense of cultural 'normality'.

Another film that combined a Sci-Fi theme with pre-existing musical styles was *Just Imagine* (1930). Directed by David Butler, the film represents an attempt to diversify the then-popular Hollywood Musical genre by setting the narrative and song and dance numbers in a futuristic scenario – ostensibly New York in 1980 – which allows the hero to leave the planet in a spaceship and get up-close and amorous with an attractive Martian humanoid. One of the most distinct aspects of the film was its elaborate sets (a feature of many big-budget musicals of the period) and its model of a futuristic New York. The musical items were written by Lew Brown, Buddy DeSylva and Ray Henderson – writers of well-known songs such as *You're the cream in my coffee* (1928) and the music for the Broadway shows 'Hold Everything' (1928) and 'Flying High' (1930) – and were not perceived by contemporary critics and audiences as deviating from the songwriters' established formula.

For all their varied accomplishments, the scores for pre-War Sci-Fi films such as those discussed above were essentially conservative in that they drew on conventions of orchestral music rather than attempting to find musical – or other sonic – signifiers that could evoke the various futuristic, scientistic and/or alien themes, narratives and associations of the SF genre. The conservatism of many 1930s' film scores is all the more marked given that the early 20th Century was a period of considerable experimentation in sound and music in both the 'fine' and popular fields. During the 1910s and 1920s, for instance, Italian Futurist Luigi Russolo experimented with various noisemaking devices (named *intonarumori*) and ensembles to stage perform-ances of *concerto futuristicas*; Erik Satie used devices such as a dynamo, morse code machine and a typewriter in performances of his *Parade* in Paris 1917; and George Antheil featured an aeroplane engine in 1926 presentations of his *Ballet Mechanique*. More profoundly still, the range of musical instru-ments available to composers and performers was widened with the intro-duction of the first wave of analogue synthesisers, most notably the theremin. The theremin was a contact-free synthesiser that allowed modifi-cation of the pitch and volume of an electrically generated sound signal by moving a hand between two aerials. The most distinct musical properties of the instrument were its capacity to provide endless glissandos (slides between notes) and subtle vibratos (moving around the central pitch of the note) and a tone that was often suggestive of the human voice. The theremin enjoyed a novelty vogue as a concert instrument in the 1920s and 1930s[23] and was also used as a (barely discernible) background element at climactic moments in the scores to pre-War films such as *King Kong*. The only apparent use of the instrument in a SF film of this period was in Waxman's *Bride of Frankenstein* score (discussed above) where its tones are blended with the general orchestration.

The most significant exception to the relative conservatism of pre-War Sci-Fi cinema sound occurred in Rouben Mamoulian's eponymous adaptation of Robert Louis Stevenson's story 'Dr Jekyll and Mr Hyde' (1932)[24]. Signifi-cantly, this did not feature in the film's (relatively conventional) score but rather in its sound effects sequences. The most striking of these were the discordantly eerie sounds that accompanied the scenes where the urbane Dr Jekyll transforms to the savage Hyde. The sounds for these sequences were produced under Mamoulian's direction through a highly original mixture of what Arthur Knight has identified as "exaggerated heartbeats mingled with reverberations of gongs played backwards, bells heard through echo cham-bers, and completely artificial sounds created by photographing light fre-quencies directly on to the soundtrack" (1985: 219)[25].

III. The Cold War Era

The production of SF films largely went into abeyance with the outbreak of World War Two. During the War, western, Japanese and many other cultures experienced a series of profound shocks. One set of shocks was produced by the development of new technologies of mass destruction (such as flying bombs, rocket bombs and nuclear devices) and communication and remote sensing media (such as radar). The speed at which these were delivered and applied was such that the War years appeared to effectively deliver on the promise of Science Fiction, which foresaw that new technolo-gies would profoundly alter human existence. The Martian death rays that had so shocked US radio audiences in 1938[26] were even more credible when viewed against the rapid profusion of such extreme weapons as nuclear bombs. The rapid switch from the 'hot' War of 1939–45 to the Cold War of the immediate post-War decades, with its own high-tech arms and communication races, established Science Fiction of the 1940s–1960s as a form premised on and exploitative of various anxieties.

In the late 1940s, a series of film scores used the fluid vibratos and glissandi of the theremin synthesiser to signify otherworldliness and/or threat. The former quality was also developed in a collaborative musical project entitled *Music out of the Moon* (originally issued as three 78rpm disks in 1947 and repackaged and re-released as a single vinyl album in 1950). Its six compositions (entitled *Lunar Rhapsody, Moon Moods, Lunette, Celestial Nocturne, Mist O' the Moon* and *Radar Blues)* were written by British stage and film composer Harry Revel and arranged and produced by Les Baxter. Baxter was a popular composer and arranger who pioneered post-War musical exotica in the 1950s before becoming a prolific film composer in the 1960s and 1970s[27]. The featured instrumentalist was theremin player Samuel Hoffman. Hoffman began performing on the theremin in New York in the mid-1930s, leading an ensemble named the Hal Hope Orchestra. In 1941 he relocated to Los Angeles with the intention of retiring from the music business to concentrate on a medical career. His retirement was interrupted in 1944 when composer Miklos Rosza, employed to write the score for Alfred Hitchcock's thriller *Spellbound*, contacted him to try out a theremin part in order to achieve Hitchcock's instruction to find a "new sound" to convey the film's intense paranoia (Glinsky, 1999: 11). The film and its music were widely acclaimed and Rosza received an Oscar for his score in 1945. Hoffman's skills on the theremin became suddenly in-demand and he was featured in the orchestral scores for *The Lost Weekend* (1945) and *The Spiral Staircase* (1945). *Music out of the Moon* attempted to capitalise on this profile, received enthusiastic reviews in publications such as *Variety* and sold well in the USA (ibid).

The connection between the theremin and alien places and life forms was cemented through the instrument's use in the scores of a series of post-War Sci-Fi films. The post-War SF cycle was initiated by two releases in 1950, *Destination Moon* and *Rocketship X-M*. The former, a sober, scientistic narrative about the construction of a rocket to the moon, directed by Irving Pichel, began pre-production in 1949. When news spread through the film community, a competitor, entitled *Rocketship X-M*, was hurriedly written, produced and directed by Kurt Neumann (eventually opening at US cinemas prior to the release of its rival). In terms of scores, *Destination Moon's* music, composed by Leith Stevens[28], was relatively conventional in its mood-scoring[29] (although music accompanying its moon surface sequences featured a sonovox – an early sound processor – to provide an alien 'edge'). To mark it out from its rival, *Rocketship X-M* had its crew deflected off-course to Mars, a planet inhabited by aggressive caveman-like survivors of a nuclear war. Neumann's film was scored by Ferde Grofé and orchestrated by Albert

Glasser and featured a theremin as an audio marker of the otherness of Outer Space and the hostile Martian environment and populace. This approach was refined in a film released in the following year, Robert Wise's *The Day the Earth stood still* (1951). As Rebecca Leydon discusses in Chapter 1, this film addressed aspects of the social anxieties of the Cold War era through its theme of a representative of an alien superpower visiting Earth in an attempt to impose peace upon the planet. Bernard Herrmann's trademark 'edgy' compositions and arrangements used the theremin in combination with other unusual electrified instruments and percussion sounds to evoke alienness. Russian émigré composer Dmitri Tiomkin[30], also drew on unusual orchestrations and the theremin to create tension and menace in another 1951 film, *The Thing from Another World*, directed by Christian Nyby. The "thing" referred to in the film's title is an intelligent, hyper-adaptive, vegetable alien that arrives in Alaska and begins eating terrestrials to grow and multiply before it is electrocuted and killed. Tiomkin's score creates unease through its eschewal of strings and features harsh, explosive dissonance in its climactic electrocution scene. Irving Pichel's big-budget version of Wells's *War of the Worlds* (1953) was also notable for its high-impact soundtrack. In addition to Leith Steven's score, the most dramatic audio moments were provided by Harry Lindgren and Gene Garvin, who created startling sound effects for Martian screams and death-rays from processed analogue sounds (and secured an Academy Award nomination for 'Best Sound Recording' for their efforts).

Similarly to *The Day the Earth stood still*, the series of *Godzilla* films that commenced in Japan in 1954 with *Gojira* (directed by Ishirô Honda) expressed contemporary anxieties about nuclear power and new technologies (and the continuing trauma arising from the US nuclear attacks on Hiroshima and Nagasaki in 1945). Unlike Wise's film, however, these anxieties found expression in a scenario that drew on aspects of Japanese folklore and mythology to construct a monstrous 'other' – the mega-reptile Godzilla. As Shuhei Hosokawa identifies in Chapter 2, these elements were strongly inscribed in *Gojira*'s soundtrack, where both Akira Ifukube's orchestral score and Godzilla's electronic roar attempted to express the primitive-primeval aspect of the narrative. Between the mid-1950s and mid-1970s Ifukube was a prolific composer for Japanese cinema, writing music for eleven further Godzilla features and several other SF films, such as *The Mysterians* (1957), *Battle in Outer Space* (1960), *Dagora* (1965) and *Gezora* (1970).

However, as ambitiously futuristic as aspects of Ifukube's music and the work of those post-War Hollywood composers discussed above may have sounded in the late 1940s and early 1950s, it was Bebe and Louis Barron's electronic score for *Forbidden Planet* in 1956 that marked the first connection between the electronic music experiments pursued in the US, Western Europe and Japan from the 1950s on (chronicled by writers such as Chadabe [1997]) and western commercial film making. As Rebecca Leydon discusses in detail in Chapter 3, the Barrons' score explored the limits of available sound making technologies and created a highly distinctive audio track which attempted to express thematic aspects of the narrative by developing new sonic signifiers for mood, drama and effect. Along with *Forbidden Planet*, another notable early Sci-Fi film that explored "electronic tonalities"[31] – apparently independent of any influence from the Barrons' score – was the (critically neglected) East German/Polish co-production *Der Schweigende Stern/ Milczaca Gwiazda* (1959), directed by Kurt Maetzig (and released in a much abbreviated and modified English language version as *211 First Spaceship On Venus*[32]). The film is notable for its bleak, hellish depiction of a Venusian landscape devastated by nuclear explosion and for its striking music and sound effects. Along with dialogue, the film's soundtrack combines conventional thriller-style orchestral scoring with frequent extended passages of sound effects (such as rocket launches) and lengthy passages of electronic music that often overlap and merge with the orchestral score. The electronic music has a diegetic source in the film in the form of a large computer (complete with oscilloscope) that attempts to translate a Venusian 'spool' found on Earth. The machine's bleeping, burbling electronic noises are eventually translated into English language as a declaration of hostile intent. Harsher electronic sounds and dissonant orchestration and effects also mark the planet's surface (together will a theremin-like melodic line played on an electronic oscillator[33]). Polish composer Andrzej Markowski produced the highly original score with the assistance of sound engineer Krzysztof Szlifirski, working at Polish Radio's Experimental Studio[34]. In its combination and overlaps of orchestral music, electronic sound and sound effects, the film anticipates both the integrated ambience and score of *Blade Runner* (discussed in Chapter 8) and the harsher sounds worlds of the *Terminator* films (discussed in Chapter 9).

Along with sound experimentation in Sci-Fi cinema, the late 1950s and early 1960s saw the release of a series of space theme albums aimed at the crossover hi-fi/Sci-Fi enthusiast market (which appears to have been considerable in this period)[35]. As Timothy Taylor has characterised it, "commodity scientism in the domestic scene for men [was] best represented by the hi-fi craze of the late 1940s and 1950s" (2001:79) and, following *Music of the Moon*, albums such as Andre Montero and Warren Baker's *Music for Heavenly Bodies* and Bobby Christian's *Strings for a Space Age* (1959) tapped into one vein of the craze, a desire for the invocation of exotic inter-planetariness in the earthly living-room. As Taylor (2001) and Leydon (1999) have emphasised, such invocations mainly relied on techniques drawn from modern western art music to which were added new electronic instruments, production techniques and stereo effects.

The first wave of 1950s' alien visitation movies also prompted the production of a series of novelty rock n' roll and pop singles in the US, from the Mello-Tones' *Flying Saucers* (1951) through to Sheb Wooley's *Purple People Eater* (1958)[36]. One of the best known of these songs, *Flying Saucer Rock and Roll*, was written after its composer, Ray Scott, observed what he took to be a UFO (Morrison, 1988: 88). Opening with an arresting, 'alien' sounding, tremeloed guitar line (played by Sun Records session player Roland Janes), the hit version recorded by Billy Riley and his Little Green Men in 1957, tells of an encounter with humanoids that are "ready to rock"[37]. While the SF references of most of these singles were almost exclusively lyrical, the first wave of orbital satellites prompted records such as The Tornados' instrumental *Telstar* (produced by Joe Meek, complete with rocket launch effects, in 1962) which prefigured the futuristic, effects-laden rock-pop sound pursued by performers during the psychedelic era of the 1960s–70s (discussed in Section V below).

The 1950s also saw the development of new style of SF themed song that has continued to the present as a flourishing subcultural form. This form has come to be known as the filk song[38] and is premised on the substitution of words to existing songs with new SF themed lyrics. The practice first emerged at SF conventions in the US in the 1940s, usually as an after-hours party activity, performed by 'filkers' to guitar or piano accompaniment, often with roneod copies of the lyrics distributed to fellow delegates to enable them to sing along. Most filk songs written in the 1940s–1950s alluded to popular magazines, novels or writers but with the increase in TV Sci-Fi series in the 1960s (discussed below), programs such as *Star Trek* prompted aficionados to pen lyrics about various characters and scenarios. Filking has now grown to be an international practice that has been represented in a series of filk songbooks, private tapes, records, cassettes and, most recently, commercially manufactured and retailed music CDs. With the advent of video (and subsequently DVD) re-releases of classic SF movies from the mid-1970s on, these films also became regular subjects for filk songwriters, who provided a low-fi, shadowy commentary on the productions discussed below[39].

IV. 1960s – mid-1970s

a. Screen Sci-Fi in the 1960s

In the 1960s, SF cinema's monopoly over screen images, dramas and fantasies of technological progress was increasingly countered by two strands of television programming. The first comprised the series of manned space missions that culminated in the 1969 lunar landing (and which, in classic cinema style, was followed by several sequels before the series declined in popularity). The coverage of these in TV news and live-to-air coverage facilitated by NASA[40] provided an intense drama that attracted a broad audience. Through its blurry, grainy video images and harsh-toned two way radio dialogues it also created a new set of styles and realist signifiers for later film makers to exploit and formularise (from *Alien* [1979] on). While TV space exploration coverage departed from its cinema predecessors by being music-free, a second strand of TV programming developed a new set of powerful and popular expressions of Sci-Fi. Popular television series such as *Dr Who*, which commenced in 1963 in the UK, and *The Twilight Zone* (1959–64), *The Outer Limits* (1963–65), *Lost in Space* (1965–68) and *Star Trek*

(1966–69) in the US, all had signature tunes and incidental music that were strongly evocative of their genre. The signature tune for *Doctor Who*, in particular, produced by the BBC's radiophonic workshop, had a strikingly futuristic sound (which was revised in subsequent years to keep its modernist edge). Along with established professionals such as Herrmann, *The Twilight Zone* also gave relative newcomers such as Jerry Goldsmith and Leonard Rosenman the opportunity to explore Sci-Fi scoring before going to produce the music for big-screen SF features.

In terms of original orchestral composition, Goldsmith's music for the 1968 film *Planet of the Apes* (the first in the series) was a notable achievement. His music recalled Herrmann's work on features such as *The Day the Earth stood still*, mixing abrasive rhythmic scoring (that recalled aspects of Stravinsky's work) with atmospheric textural cues and unnerving sustained treble passages[41]. Reversing the interplanetary themes of much 1960s SF, Richard Fleischer's 1968 film *Fantastic Voyage* followed the adventures of a medical team who are miniaturised and injected into the injured body of a top scientist. The film's impressive score was written and conducted by Rosenman, audiating the fluid inner-space of the human bloodstream with percussion parts that blur between music and sound effects and atonal orchestral passages. Rosenman had previously pioneered the use of atonal elements in Hollywood cinema with his music for the Freudianesque melodrama *The Cobweb* (1955). However, his *Fantastic Voyage* score is more complex than his earlier work in the style and is premised on complex layering and dissonances and alternating crescendos and decrescendos. As if to underline the music's signification of another space, the score returns to conventional melodic structure and orchestration in the final stage of the film, where the miniaturised submarine and its crew exit the human body and return to their usual size.

Along with Hollywood productions (and the Japanese films discussed in Section IV), a number of other Sci-Fi films were made in Western Europe during the 1950s and 1960s. Several dozen of these were made in the United Kingdom. Productions ranged from micro budget curios such as *Devil Girl from Mars* (1964), disaster movies such as *The Day the Earth caught fire* (1962) and literary adaptations such as *Village of the Damned* (1960). Although veteran composer Ron Goodwin provided notably eerie choral sequences for the latter, arguably the most distinctive scores to emerge from this body of films were those written by British composer James Barnard for The *Quatermass Experiment* (1955), its sequel *Quatermass II* (1957) and the similarly themed *X the Unknown* (1956). In these films, the composer used a combination of string and percussion parts to create an eerie, jarring tension. Hammer Films commissioned composer Tristram Cary to score the (delayed) third film in the Dr Quatermass series, *Quatermass and the Pit* (1967). Somewhat unusually, the producers hedged their bets by asking Cary to submit an orchestral and an electronic score. The final film used extracts of both versions plus extracts of music by Carlo Martelli. Cary's surviving electronic sequences mainly comprise harsh drones and blasts that reinforce the alien and technological theme of the film and suggest how innovative (and perhaps abrasive) his full electronic score would have been if adopted.

Two (distinctly different) Sci-Fi films produced in France in the mid-late 1960s also had notable soundtracks. Jean Luc Godard's *Alphaville*, released in 1965, was an ambitious low-budget venture that made impressive use of Parisian locations for its futurist dystopia. At the centre of Godard's city is a governing brain (Alpha 60) whose flat, unvarying voice occurs throughout the soundtrack, offset by the ambivalent and relatively disconnected mood of veteran composer Paul Misraki's score[42]. By contrast, Roger Vadim's film *Barbarella*, featuring Jane Fonda as an alluring astronaut battling the evil Durand Durand[43], was released, with a swinging title song sung by Mike Gale, in 1967. The film's score (now regarded as something of as kitsch classic) was written by Charles Fox and Bob Crewe (best known for his 1966 hit single *Music to watch girls by*) and was performed by an orchestra augmented by members of US band Glitterbox. The film's music comprises orchestral pop pieces that range from Ennio Morriconesque atmospheric tracks (often featuring twangy, fuzzed guitar) to more uptempo pop-funk numbers and jazzy cues. The sound design of the film combined this music and the film's dialogue with an underscore comprising sustained tones, echoed and processed voices and musical burbles (to suggest the otherworldliness of its location) and an electronic leitmotif to indicate the arrival of the 'great tyrant's' threatening 'black guards'. In one of the stranger climaxes to a SF film, the overthrow of the planet's tyrannical dystopia is precipitated by Barbarella's striking capacity to survive the stimulation of a device named the 'excessive machine'. This apparatus is one in which women are enclosed and 'played' by large mechanical keys activated by a keyboard. The film shows Durand Durand playing a gentle fugue on Barbarella's body, to her evident delight, before breaking into an uptempo rock-funk piece which accelerates in speed and intensity *almost* overwhelming Barbarella until her (implicit) multi-orgasmic capacities cause it to burn out.

A similar kitsch/futuristic cult status has also accrued to five low-budget SF films made by the Italian director Antonio Marghereti (under the pseudonym Anthony Dawson), commencing with *Assignment Outer Space* (1960) and ending with *Wild, Wild Planet* (1965). Released in the United States in 1967, the latter achieved some success – apparently due to a 'trippy' psychedelic visual sense that seemed in accord with the mood of the times (as also manifest in *Barbarella*). The scores for Marghereti's films were written by veteran Italian composer Angelo Francesco Lavagnino, who drew on the exoticist orchestral music styles of composers such as Les Baxter[44] to support the film's lurid visuals and themes. Two other Italian films of the period featured notable scores, Mario Bava's *Terrore nello spazio* (1965) (released as *Planet of the Vampires* in its English language version) and Paulo Zeglio's *...4 ...3 ...2 ...1 Morte* (1967). Bava's gothic/SF thriller was scored by American-born Italian film composer Gino Marinuzzi, who had gained an interest in avant garde music while studying in Milan in the 1940s. The film occupies an interesting historical position between the 1950s resurgence of SF and its late 1970s revival – its images and scenario strongly resembling those of 1979's *Alien* while the use of electronic effects in its score echoed the Barrons' (entirely synthesised) soundtrack to *Forbidden Planet* (1956). Although less well-known, Giombini Abril's score for Zeglio's film is also notable as a Sci-Fi score for its combination of unusual accapella pieces, electronic tonal passages and up-tempo jazz-rock grooves[45].

One of the most unusual musical scores of the decade was that of Kubrick's 1968 screen adaptation of Arthur C. Clarke's novel '2001: A Space Odyssey'. Kubrick rejected a score commissioned from Alex North in favour of the original 'temp track' material, overseeing production of a music soundtrack that included a range of European art music pieces used imaginatively and highly effectively. One of the most memorable sequences utilises the opening section of Richard Strauss's composition 'Also Sprach Zarathustra', to give epic depth to the film's opening montage of human development. Extracts from Gyorgy Ligeti's 'Requiem' and 'Lux Aeterna' are also used to create tension and unease in a similar manner to many 1950s Sci-Fi scores. One of the most unexpected musical sequences is that which accompanies an astronaut's weightless exercise in a space station. Reversing expectations of futuristic accompaniment here, the soundtrack uses Johann Strauss Junior's 'Blue Danube' waltz to both dignify the action shown on-screen and suggest the socio-cultural history that has enabled technological progress. The use of this music at the end of the film, while the credits roll, also revisits these associations after the ambiguous ending. A similar set of unexpected juxtapositions of music and film were present in Kubrick's 1971 screen version of Anthony Burgess's 1961 novel 'A Clockwork Orange', in which the ultra-violent anti-hero, Alex, has an infatuation with the music of Beethoven (which is made suitably manifest in the soundtrack). Along with Beethoven, the film also offers a series of other incongruous combinations, such as Alex's whistling of the title song of *Singing in the Rain* during his gang's attack on the Alexander family. Although the radical juxtapositions of well-established music and unexpected screen action and images in Kubrick's films are notable, in terms of stylistic innovation the majority of action in the Sci-Fi music nexus was happening *off-screen* in the 1960s.

b. The Vinyl Frontier – Sci-Fi, Psychedelia, Progressive Rock and Jazz

As Nabeel Zuberi discusses in Chapter 4, Science Fiction and psychedelia had a marked impact on the work of Afro-American avant-garde jazz performer Sun Ra. Ra's work provides one of the most sustained engagements with Sci-Fi themes and images by a musician. From the 1950s on, Sun Ra explored and, indeed, personified aspects of the radical black interpretation of Science Fiction known as 'Afrofuturism'. Musically, his work with various line-ups of his Intergalactic Myth-Science Solar Arkestra combined modern jazz styles with ambitious explorations of emergent musical technologies such as synthesisers. The 1972 feature film *Space is the Place* features Ra (effectively as himself) in a narrative that involves him as an alien, working in California as a musician, trying to establish a space colony for Afro-Americans. The

15

opportunities this scenario gives for Ra and his band to perform on-screen further cement the associations between his musical style and alien/inter-planetariness. Several other leading Afro-American jazz exponents also explored Science Fiction themes, Eric Dolphy, for instance, entitled one of his pioneering early 1960s twelve-tone compositions *The Red Planet* (a composition which was later recorded by John Coltrane under the title *Miles' Mode*). Coltrane himself frequently used SF names as track and album titles for his explorative music and recorded a duet album in 1967 with drummer Rashied Ali entitled *Interstellar Space*. On a group of tracks named after the middle planets of the solar system, he pursued extreme improvisational leaps that suggested how his work may have developed had he lived. The Art Ensemble of Chicago, formed in 1968 also incorporated Afrofuturist aspects in their work and, inspired by a similar sensibility, Ornette Coleman recorded his *Science Fiction* album in 1971, combining free jazz and bebop styles with the poetry of David Henderson. Seminal funk musician George Clinton also explored a number of Afrofuturist themes on albums such as Parliament's 1976 release *The Clones of Dr Funkenstein* and his 1982 solo album *Computer Games*. During the 1970s, in particular, Clinton's work was typified by its hard funk rhythms, processed guitar sounds and Sci-Fi/cosmological lyrics. Yet despite this emphasis, also explored by later Afro-American and Afro-European artists – such as Roni Size, who contributed to the soundtrack of *Blade 2* (2002) – *Space is the Place* remains (to date) the principal point of connection between Sci-Fi cinema and Afrofuturist music – reflecting the continuing Eurocentricism of Hollywood as the major producer of western feature films.

During the 1960s and 1970s, Western Europe was also the location of a number of significant engagements between Sci-Fi and psychedelia. In mid-1960s London one of the most significant centres was the UFO Club, the venue for many an all night 'happening' in which LSD, marijuana and other drugs aided patrons in engaging with the psychedelic impressions the music and light shows presented. One of the hottest bands associated with the club was the early Pink Floyd line-up led by Syd Barrett. Their futuristic music, featuring heavy use of echo and other sound effects, not only evoked the type of 'otherworldly' sounds associated with SF cinema scores in the 1950s and 1960s, it also made direct thematic allusions through compositions entitled *Interstellar Overdrive* and *Astronomy Domine* (both included on the 1967 album *Piper at the Gates of Dawn*) and their subsequent live favourite *Set Controls for the Heart of the Sun* (1968). Interviewed in 1967, Barrett suggested his teenage interest in the British *Quatermass* films[46] as an inspiration for the Science Fiction orientation (quoted in Watkinson and Anderson, 1991: 68). While the explicit SF aspect of their music declined with Barrett's exit from the band in 1969, several other bands took up the torch. The most notable of these was the Moody Blues, a melodic progressive rock band that had formed in the early 1960s and adopted a number of psychedelic elements as the decade progressed. At the instigation of producer Tony Clarke, an amateur astronomer[47], the band's fourth album, *To our Children's*

Children, had a strong SF theme and was originally intended to be released to coincide with the Apollo 7 manned moon landing. The album incorporated audio effects, such as the rocket launch take-off that opens *Higher and Higher*, and SF themed lyrics into their progressive soft-rock sound. Although it failed to generate the hit singles the band had previously enjoyed, the album was critically acclaimed and was adopted by NASA as recommended in-flight entertainment on subsequent space missions[48].

Another significant contributor to the Sci-Fi/psychedelia nexus was the ensemble Gong. Formed by Australian guitarist/vocalist Daevid Allen in Paris in 1968, various line-ups have continued to perform until the present[49]. Allen has claimed that inspiration for the band came from seeing Pink Floyd perform in 1966, through consumption of various illicit drugs and through his being contacted by alien intelligences he later referred to as 'the octave doctors'. Gong's music developed as a mixture of extended instrumental passages, wordless vocal parts (referred to as 'space whispers') and passages of intelligible vocals referring to entities such as 'pothead pixies'. In the early 1970s the band was augmented by guitarist Steve Hillage (from the British band Kahn, who had recorded an album entitled *Space Shanty* in 1972) and achieved a high profile on the UK alternative/student circuit after being signed to Virgin Records and releasing the albums *Radio Gnome Invisible Pt 1* (1973) and *Angel Egg* (1974). A similar SF focus was prominent in the work of alternative circuit orientated British band Hawkwind, founded in 1969, who toured their 'Space Ritual' stage show extensively in the early 1970s and secured a UK chart hit with their single *Silver Machine* in 1972. The band's sound relied on mystic lyrics, driving riffs, a hard 'wall-of-sound', synthesiser swoops and a dramatic stage show featuring costumes, dancers and visual effects. During the 1970s Christian Vander's ensemble Magma took the SF theme further by making it the centre of their songs, imagery and mystique. Vander founded the ensemble to perform and record an extended allegorical work concerned with interplanetary conflict between a declining, decaying Earth and the idealistic human colony world of Kobaia. The music of the French ensemble was heavily influenced by John Coltrane's improvisational style, Carl Orff's approach to choral work and Stravinsky's orchestrations and the band recorded Vander's work over ten albums recorded between 1970–81.

While Sci-Fi influenced psychedelic rock music was primarily an Anglo-French pursuit in the 1960s, some related strands developed in West Germany. Inspired by radical composers such as Karlheinz Stockhausen and the activities of the Fluxus group, a number of young musicians formed avant garde rock ensembles. The first band to emerge was Can, in 1968. Composer Edgar Froese, who had previously scored experimental films, formed another ensemble named Tangerine Dream in 1968 that experimented with synthesisers, rock rhythms and ambience. The ensemble began a sustained engagement with SF themes on their 1971 album *Alpha Centauri* and, following a series of line-up changes recorded soundtracks for films such as Ridley Scott's fantasy feature *Legend* (1985). Florian Schneider-Esleben and Ralf Hütter formed the third notable German band of the period in 1969. Initially named The Organisation, this group performed at various gallery events and happenings before renaming themselves Kraftwerk in 1970. Kraftwerk pioneered a sound based on drum machines, moog synthesisers and detached vocal parts in the early 1970s and achieved an international breakthrough with their *Autobahn* single and album in 1974. Their 1976 album *Radioactivity* had Sci-Fi/technology themed titles and lyrics, and this aspect of the band was intensified on their 1978 album *The Man Machine*, its accompanying single, *The Robots*, and the band's use of robotics in subsequent stage shows.

One performer who began a sustained engagement with SF themes in the late 1960s was David Bowie. The Apollo missions prompted him to write his first hit single, *Space Oddity* (1969), about an astronaut's otherworldly experiences. The SF element of his work was given full reign in the overall concept and personae of his album *The Rise and fall of Ziggy Stardust and the Spiders from Mars* (1972), its associated stage show and singles such as *Starman* (1972) and *Life on Mars* (1973). Bowie's interests, music and persona led him to be cast in *The Man who fell to Earth* (1976) directed by Nick Roeg, playing the part of an alien. Despite the apparently fortuitous combination of Sci-Fi film and Sci-Fi sympathetic rock star, the film met with a mixed response and, due to disputes between Roeg and Bowie over the contents and authorship of the production, a soundtrack album did not eventuate[50].

Along with the European performers and ensembles discussed above, several US bands explored SF themes in the late 1960s. The Grateful Dead wrote and recorded one of the most notable tracks from the era in the form of the poetic and instrumentally intense song *Dark Star* (1968)[51]. Jefferson Airplane composer/singer/guitarist Paul Kantner was a particular devotee of the genre. His 1969 song, *Wooden Ships*, co-written with David Crosby and Steven Stills (and recorded by both Jefferson Airplane and Crosby, Stills and Nash) described a small group of people escaping from a future authoritarian dystopia. Kantner's similarly themed ecological protest song *Have you seen the Saucers?* was also recorded by Jefferson Airplane in the following year. In 1971 Kantner teamed up with Grateful Dead guitarist Jerry Garcia and Crosby to record a project album entitled *Blows Against the Empire*, which included a suite of SF inspired songs on the A-side. Credited to a new band entity, Jefferson Starship[52], the album was a commercial and critical success (winning a SF 'Nebula' fiction award, the first awarded to a music recording). Like Kantner's earlier compositions, the *Blows Against the Empire* suite depicted dissidents in a future dystopia (a topic also tackled by Canadian band Rush on the central track of their 1976 album *2112*).

The only Sci-Fi film score of the 1960s and 1970s to have any affinity with the types of experimental music discussed in this section was that written by Eduard Artemiev for Andrei Tarkovski's epic *Solaris*, released in 1972. Artemiev was a member of the Moscow Experimental Studio of Electronic Music and had begun working with synthesisers and tape composition in the 1950s. In 1960 he began working with the (sole model) of the newly developed Russian ANS Synthi-100 synthesiser[53] and, during the mid-late 1960s, became aware of the work of a range of western avant garde and progressive rock artists[54]. Artemiev provided an unobtrusive synthesiser-based score for Tarkovski's lengthy, looping narrative, set on a mysterious, sentient oceanic planet. The music was mixed relatively low in the final release version, reinforcing the film's themes and moods as ambient under-score – using vocal samples in the 'Dream' sequence to give an emotive ethereal feel and producing dark, clashing timbres and textures to express complexity and mystery in 'Ocean'[55].

At some distance from the mood and ambition of Tarkovski's *Solaris*, the mid-late 1970s saw the production of a cluster of British Sci-Fi concept rock albums (and related products). Markedly more mainstream than the albums discussed above, the first of these was released in 1974. Yes keyboard player Rick Wakeman chose Jules Verne as the inspiration for a solo LP entitled *Journey to the Centre of the Earth*. The album comprised a series of keyboard-based instrumental and vocal pieces accompanied by the London Symphony Orchestra and a narration of portions of Verne's text by actor David Hemmings. The album was a success in the UK and US markets and was toured internationally with an ambitious stage show[56]. A more direct SF cinema connection was evident in the 1975 release *Flash Fearless v the Zorg Women: Parts 5 and 6*, an affectionate tribute to 1930s SF serial films. Produced and arranged by John Allcock, the album featured Alice Cooper, Elkie Brooks and Maddy Prior on vocals and musicians such as John Entwistle and Nicky Hopkins. Despite low sales and a mixed critical reaction, a live version was also mounted in 1981 but met with similar indifference. A second SF concept album, *I Robot*, released in 1977, achieved considerably greater commercial success in the UK and US. Produced by Alan Parsons, with lower-profile guest vocalists and musicians, the album's ambitious theme was "the rise of the machine and decline of man" (album notes). The album included a range of soft-rock, rock-funk and ambient synthesiser pieces and final orchestral tracks that recalled 1950s SF film scores. The fourth and best known of this cycle of British productions was Jeff Wayne's *War of the Worlds* (1978), an adaptation of Wells's novella that included text extracts narrated by Richard Burton and musical compositions performed by prominent pop and rock performers such as Moody Blues member Justin Hayward, singer Julie Covington and guitarist Chris Spedding. The album covered a range of pop-rock styles and lodged in the British album charts for over two years[57].

This concept album cycle culminated in a direct crossover between Holly-wood cinema and British rock when Queen released their *Flash Gordon* LP in 1980. The album resulted from producer Dino de Laurentiis's invitation to the band to contribute songs and instrumental music to the soundtrack of his big-budget feature update of *Flash Gordon* (1980, d Mike Hodges). In one of the most successful aspects of the film's production, Queen's contributions were acknowledged and accommodated by composer Howard Blake, who

19

echoed aspects of the band's rock approach and the arrangement and hooks of their film title song in his orchestral music. Queen's album included material written for the soundtrack, new material and dialogue sequences from the film (omitting much of Blake's music), resulting in a product that was at one remove from the film and its original audio track.

During the 1970s a number of individual pop songs also engaged with space/Sci-Fi themes. In Japan, the highly successful late Seventies pop duo Pink Lady had hits with *UFO* (1977) and *Tomei Ningen* ('Invisible Man') (1978). Several Japanese synth-pop bands recorded SF themed singles late in the decade, Shigeru Matsuzaki releasing *Kinga Tokkyu* ('Galaxy Express') in 1978 and Maki Ueda releasing *Aitsuwa Invader* ('He's an Invader') in 1979. The Filipino band Passionata also achieved Japanese chart success in 1979 with their single *Kasei to Kinsei no Inbo* ('The Plot between Mars and Venus')[58]. Notable western songs of the period include Elton John's *Rocket man* (1972), Sarah Brightman and Hot Gossip's *I lost my heart to a starship trooper* (1978) and the Carpenters' version of *Calling occupants of interplanetary craft* (1977). The latter track revisited the theme of one of the seminal post-War SF films, *The Day the Earth stood still*. The song was written by the Canadian band Klaatu, which formed in Toronto in 1973, taking its name from the alien character featured in the 1951 film. Unlike Herrmann's moody, dissonant score for the original, the song is a melodic ballad (which was given a plaintive, yearning feel in the Carpenters' cover through Karen Carpenter's light vocal delivery). Subtitled 'The Recognised Anthem of World Contact Day', the song prefigured the sense of optimism and wonder captured in Spielberg's 1977 film *Close Encounters of the Third Kind*[59].

The rise of SF influenced rock also influenced the filk song sector (described in Section III) from the mid-1970s on, inspiring some filkers to work towards professional standard audio recordings[60]. The best-known early work of this type was Julia Ecklar's album *Divine Intervention*, recorded with keyboard player Michael Moricz in 1986. The recording featuring soft-rock arrangements of songs inspired by films such as *Star Trek III* (1984) and the fantasy feature *Ladyhawke* (1985). As a result of twinning the SF influenced rock tradition (discussed above) with filking, the cassette album remained a cult-classic among filkers through the 1990s and was re-released in CD format (with additional tracks) in early 2003.

V. The Revival of SF Cinema

The Hollywood Sci-Fi cinema revival of the late 1970s coincided with and was enhanced by the arrival of new, improved sound recording and playback technologies. These were provided by the British Dolby company, which had first developed a noise reduction system for the music recording industry in the mid-1960s. In the early 1970s it originated a stereo optical (SO) film print format that it pitched at film producers and exhibitors. Ken Russell's *Lisztomania* (1975) – scored by rock keyboardist Rick Wakeman and starring Who singer Roger Daltrey – was the first film with a Dolby SO soundtrack to go on general release and was followed by productions such as *The Grateful Dead Movie* (1976). The rock focus of these films was far from accidental. One attraction of the format was that it enabled the films' music tracks to approach the sound quality of vinyl albums played on domestic stereo systems. A further innovation followed, the production of film prints with encoded surround sound effects[61]. While it wasn't the first commercially released film to include these elements[62], *Star Wars* received industry acclaim, winning an Academy Award for Best Achievement in Sound at the 1978 Oscars. Philip Brophy has characterised *Star Wars* as a "virtual showcase for the Dolby stereo process" that set a benchmark and agenda for future productions (1991: 106 fn1). This is a view shared by Dolby on its official website, which states that:

> *One further element was needed to ensure Dolby's lasting presence in the field of film sound: audience awareness. This came in 1977, with the release of two immensely popular films that were recorded with the new Dolby technology:* Star Wars *and* Close Encounters of the Third Kind. *These blockbusters were exhibited in enough theatres that had the new Dolby equipment for audiences and industry alike to sit up and take notice. Marketing research soon showed that moviegoers would seek out theatres exhibiting in the Dolby stereo format, and avoid mono presentations of the same films.* (http://www.dolby.com/company/is.ot.0009.History.11.html: np – accessed July 2003)

As Dolby's promotional text goes on to emphasise:

> *While "big" films were early adopters of the new Dolby technology, it wasn't long before films of all types were released with stereo optical soundtracks. This created a profound change in the moviegoing experience.* (ibid)

While the degree of profundity of the change is open to debate (and continues to depend on the playback environments of individual venues[63]), the 1980s and 1990s undeniably brought an increase in the technical sophistication of film soundtracks and a more complex and intense audio experience that had previously been possible.

Despite the various explorations of musical style discussed in Section V, the western Sci-Fi cinema revival of the late 1970s, in the main, embraced those classic Hollywood film score traditions that had been maintained by composers such as Jerry Goldsmith during the preceding decade. As Neil Lerner discusses in Chapter 5, John Williams' musical scores for the two key revival films, *Star Wars* and *Close Encounters* were highly conservative and nostalgicist. This aspect has also been discussed by Carryl Flinn, who has identified how, in *Star Wars*, in particular, "the film's nostalgia for a lost golden era is revealed with special particularity by the score" (1992: 153). The increased clarity provided by the Dolby system gave added richness and punch to

21

orchestral scores, refreshing their impact with audiences and rendering their music a simulacrum, a 'more perfect copy', of their models.

Along with music, 'atmos'[64] and sound effects were also obvious beneficiaries of new technologies. While the music of the early Sci-Fi revival may have been essentially conservative, films such as *Star Wars*, *Close Encounters* and the *Star Trek* series shared another notable aspect. The soundtracks of these films featured audio effects that have come to serve as sound signatures for the productions. *Star Wars*, in particular, not only set a technical benchmark for modern cinema but also elevated the role the sound designer- a figure responsible for the *design* (rather than *assembly*) of a film's audio effects and overall sonic environment[65] – to a new prominence[66]. This rise in status did not simply arise from the technological facilities made available by Lucas; it resulted from his particular creative vision for *Star Wars*. Often summarised (aphoristically) as a "used future" aesthetic, it was one that imagined the future as a working, mechanistic extension of the present (rather than a high-sheen fantasy world). Lucas provided the aesthetic agenda, budget and directorial support that enabled sound specialist Ben Burtt to create the film's rich, highly charactered sound design. The results of this enterprise were the film's distinct – and, now, near-iconic – audio images, such as R2D2's electronic burbling 'speech', the sound of clashing light-sabres and the screech of the X-wing fighter in flight (all of which were produced by processing analogue sound recordings, to give them a realist quality[67]).

The combination of score, sound effects and overall sound design within the enhanced fidelity environment provided by Dolby systems allowed a greater integration of these elements than in preceding SF film practice. Responding to the harsh 'tech-noir' visual style of Ridley Scott's *Alien* (1979), with its fragmented, dark images, for instance, composer Jerry Goldsmith and orchestrator Arthur Morton produced music that included shrill, processed treble sounds and percussion effects blended in with atmospheric score, blurring the lines between music, sound effect and diegetic noise. As Michael Hannan and Melissa Carey detail in Chapter 8, the integration of sound effects within Vangelis's score for *Blade Runner* (1982) also created an innovative mix of sonic ambiences and music. The majority of *Blade Runner's* score blends so seamlessly between (extra-diegetic) music and (infra-diegetic) sounds that their differentiation is ambiguous. Paul Théberge also identifies a similar integration of score, sound effects and ambience in director David Cronenberg's work with composer Howard Shore (and various sound designers) from the late 1970s on (Chapter 8).

As Rebecca Coyle's analysis of the 2nd and 3rd *Mad Max* films in Chapter 6 and Karen Collins' discussion of the first two *Terminators* (1984 and 1991) in Chapter 9 elaborate, the increasing sophistication of sound production and mixing technologies has allowed for complex significations of sound, music and effects that match the post-Apocalyptic worlds represented in both their case study films (and similar 1980s/1990s productions). In this regard, it is significant to note the continuing association between big-budget

SF cinema and the development and showcasing of new audio technologies: Dolby's spectral (multi-positional) recording format was introduced to cinema audiences with the release of *Innerspace* and *Robocop* in 1987; Eastman Kodak trialed their (subsequently abandoned) Cinema Digital Sound format with *Terminator II: Judgement Day* in 1991; and Dolby introduced their rival (and successful) digital format with *Star Trek 6: The Undiscovered Country* (1991) and *Batman Returns* (1992).

Developing the sonic potential of the genre further, several recent films have used advanced digital sound production, editing and mixing techniques to create complex audio environments for their narratives. The emerging (sub)genre of virtual reality/cyberpunk Sci-Fi cinema has been particularly notable in this regard, particularly in the Wachowski Brothers' films *The Matrix* (1999) and *Matrix Reloaded* (2003). As Mark Evans discusses in Chapter 11, while there is some use of orchestral underscore, the various spaces of the digital world of the original *Matrix* are primarily marked and complemented by a differentiated sound design and use of effects and ambiences. In the Wachowski Brothers' representation of a digital inner-space, the epic orchestralism of the revived 'space operas' of interplanetary adventure are sidelined by intricate sound planes and mixes. In the *Matrix* films changes in ambience and sound design indicate and mark the transitions between various digital and actual diegeses that are central to the films' narratives and themes.

Conservatism and nostalgicism continue to be present in SF film scores but, more significantly, the 1990s and early 2000s has been a period in which innovation, classicism, homage and pastiche have interwoven to create a pluralist character for the genre. As I discuss in the introduction to Chapter 10, the work of composer Danny Elfman has exemplified this tendency. Elfman has produced scores that draw on Herrmann's classic SF work and combine this with various strands of popular music (such as those Elfman pursued with his band Oingo Boingo in the early 1980s). Another element that has contributed to the sound mix of recent cinema has been the insertion of (existing or commissioned) pop/rock songs into the narrative (as in the use of Slim Whitman's *Indian Love Call* in *Mars Attacks!*) and/or concluding credit sequences (as in the case of Tina Turner's opening and closing songs in the third *Mad Max* film – *Beyond Thunderdome* [1985]). While, to date, there have been no developments in this usage specific to the SF genre, one of the more integrated approaches has been in *Batman* (1989). In this film, Elfman's contributions were complemented by music provided by Prince[68], a venture that led to the issue of two separate CDs, the first containing Elfman's theme and cues, the second, Prince's songs and instrumental pieces[69].

Although there was a revival of 1960s/1970s styles of 'space rock' in the mid-1980s, led by bands such as Spaceman 3[70], direct engagement between rock artists and SF film music production was curiously muted during the decade. Aside from the simple insertion of rock songs into soundtracks (as in Russell Mulcahy's *Highlander* [1986]), the most notable rock input into SF cinema has come in the 1990s and early 2000s, in films such as Shinya Tsukamoto's *Tetsuo – the Iron Man* (1994) and *Tetsuo II: Body Hammer* (1997) and John Carpenter's *Ghosts of Mars* (2001). The music for *Tetsuo – the Iron Man* was written and produced by percussionist-composer Chu Ishikawa. The film's repetitive 'industrial' rock-techno score (similar in style to the work of German band Einstürzende Neubauten)[71] is effective in prefiguring and complementing its narrative scenario of a frustrated 'salary man' who is transformed into a metallic cyborg. Ishikawa also wrote similarly styled music for the follow-up, *Tetsuo II*, financed by the Japanese music company Toshiba-EMI, which also featured a theme song written and performed by popular Japanese rock guitarist Tomoyasu Hotei[72]. Unlike many of his previous films, which he has self-scored with atmospheric synthesiser parts, Carpenter's *Ghosts of Mars* (2001) featured music developed by the director in collaboration with members of the rock band Anthrax, Buckethead and Steve Vai. These musicians provided a series of hard, abrasive riffing tracks that gave further edge and intensity to the film's narrative of a small group of police under unrelenting attack from murderous humans possessed by Martian spirits. Aided by the gothic/heavy metal visual stylings of the renegades, the score is a highly successful demonstration of the possibilities of rock in the SF medium.

Another notable aspect of SF cinema has been the minimal use of non-western musical styles and instrumentations to provide atmosphere and sound colour[73]. Aside from Ifukube's passing references to Ainu music in *Gojira* (1954) and his use of an actual Ainu chant in *Godzilla v Mechagodzilla* (1974), the principal use of non-western musical styles in a Sci-Fi film to date has been in Katsuhiro Ôtomo's *anime* (animated) feature *Akira*, set in a post-nuclear ravaged (Neo-)Tokyo. The music for this film was written and performed by Shoji Yamashiro and the Geinoh Yamashiro Gumi ensemble, drawing on Balinese gamelan music and using bamboo instrumentation in conjunction with massed choral parts. Given an unusually free reign by the director, Yamashiro produced a score that was based on a computer database of modular units that could be assembled in various combinations to fit the final visual and narrative form of the film[74]. While the music has been widely acclaimed, it has not spawned similar engagements with non-western musical styles within the SF genre (in Japan or internationally).

Conclusion: Associated Music and Sound

In common with the 'retro-futurism' of films such as *Star Wars* and their music, many contemporary Sci-Fi film scores also draw on the western film music tradition of expressing futurist/alien themes through use of dissonance and/or electronic sounds. This latter strand can be regarded as a form of musical exoticism (and it is no accident that there was a blurring of the exoticist and SF genres in the 1940s and 1950s in the work of artists such as Hoffman and Baxter[75]). Indeed, it is fitting that one of the few moments of infra-diegetic music in *Star Wars* is the cantina scene in which aliens play a form of 'weird jazz' on weird instruments (and sound much like a cross between the musical styles of key 1960s exoticists Martin Denny and Esquivel in the process[76]). The juxtaposition of musical exoticism (a style that is premised on evocations of otherness and/or primitivism[77]) and futurism also informs deeper levels of cinematic themes and imagery. Shuhei Hosokawa's discussion of the original *Godzilla* film identifies a futuristic-folkloric theme as central to the film and analyses Ifukube's evocation of an (imagined) Ainu aboriginality as a key musical reference point. As in musical exotica, alienness and otherworldliness are expressed through selective 'othering' of cultural conventions. Extremely radical departures in musical style risk alienating audiences. However appropriate this might seem – in one sense – for Sci-Fi, this is not the aim of the genre.

The creative space of SF allows for representations of and reflections on the future, new technologies and/or alien worlds and life forms *within* established fictional frameworks and conventions. In a similar manner to the convenient 'defaulting' of aliens to humanoid forms in film narratives, the music used in SF cinema overwhelmingly draws on recognisable and well-known conventions and associations. While this may limit any radical claims we might wish to make for the musical attributes of the genre, SF cinema has produced the rich and often ingenious set of audio-visual texts that this anthology begins to excavate and analyse. In those works that attempt to auralise the otherworldliness of outer or cyber space through the combination of music and sound design, we can begin to see the development of an approach that marks a new edge of accomplishment and originality for the genre. Enabled by the imaginative frame and scope of SF, this might also allow for a flowering of the *audio*-visual potential of cinema that has been under-developed since its inception, one where the primacy of vision in the cinematic experience can (at least) be balanced.

Thanks to Rebecca Coyle, Rebecca Leydon and Nabeel Zuberi for comments on earlier drafts of this Introduction and to Shuhei Hosokawa and Jeff Berkwits[78] for research assistance.

Notes

1. Of the kind analysed in Flinn (1992).

2. Although, as with any other such attempts at periodisation, they all contain various elements that do not entirely conform to this characterisation.

3. Here these are posed as separate. However, as several chapters in this anthology argue, the elements are often combined, crossed-over and/or interactive.

4. Readers can identify such omissions for themselves but, should funding and opportunity permit, *Off The Planet* Part II would aim to discuss the *Star Trek* series, *Star Wars'* various sequels and prequels, the *Alien* series, and animated Sci-Fi films. Similarly, 1980s–2000s styles of space rock and techno would also warrant extended analysis.

5. For a series of contrasting 'Definitions of Science Fiction' visit: http://www.panix.com/~gokce/sf_defn.html#AT – accessed May 2003.

6. While there is no evidence that this film had any musical accompaniment specifically

written for it upon first release, the film had a musical aspect in that its lead actors were Parisian music hall singers and the 'stars' were ballet dancers.

7. Also known in English as *By Rocket to the Moon*.

8. This music was subsequently adapted for the shortened version of the film released in the United States in 1927.

9. Huppertz's score has however been substantially reconstructed for a new extended print of the film that was assembled by archivist Martin Koeber and released in 2003 (but which I was unable to access prior to completing this chapter).

10. This discussion of *Metropolis* and early musical presentations draws on the excellent web resource '*Metropolis* 1927 – Film Archive' – http://www.uow.edu.au-morgan/Metroe.html

11. Various musical accompaniments have been written for post-War screenings of the film and video and DVD release versions. The best known of these is Austrian producer/composer Giorgio Moroder's 1984 version, featuring contributions by rock performers such as Jon Anderson and Freddie Mercury.

12. Alexander Rennie's score for the 1999 US DVD release incorporates these but the score is largely an original one that draws on various aspects of early 20th Century modernist music.

13. Phillipe Soupault, for instance, described it as "painful to listen to" (1931, reproduced and translated in King [1984: 52]).

14. Wells's novella was also famously adapted into a radio drama by Orson Welles's Mercury Theatre Company that caused widespread panic in the United States when broadcast in 1938 – see Cantril (1940) for discussion.

15. Due to its somewhat stilted and heavy-handed moralistic orientation (and various distribution difficulties overseas) the film was not a commercial success.

16. Although it should also be noted that Wells added that it "cannot be pretended that in actual production it was possible to blend the picture and music so closely as Bliss and I had hoped at the beginning" (ibid).

17. The film, which largely takes place in and around a nightclub, features mostly infra-diegetic music, such as the songs famously sung by the nightclub singer played by Marlene Dietrich, *Falling in love again* and *Blonde women*.

18. A leitmotif is a recurring musical phrase that is identified with an element of the drama of an audio or audio-visual text.

19. Waxman followed up his work on *Bride of Frankenstein* in the Sci-Fi horror film *The Invisible Ray* (1936) and Victor Fleming's re-make of *Dr Jekyll and Mr Hyde* (1941).

20. The *Flash Gordon* film serials were adapted from the eponymous US comic strip, written by Alex Raymond, which was syndicated in the US press from 1934 onwards and first adapted into a popular radio serial in 1935 before being adapted for film. The cinema serial commenced in 1936, with a 13-episode block, and was followed up in 1938 and 1940. The serials' music featured frequent 'chase music' derived passages to mark flight sequences and discordant passages to mark crises or 'cliff hanger' endings.

21. See Bush (1989) for further discussion of the music for the *Flash Gordon* and *Buck Rogers* series.

22. To whom Autry explains, "my business is singing – I sing about horses and sunshine and the plains – well, how can anybody sing about those things here?"

23. See Hayward (1997: 33–37).

24. Which had previously been adapted for the screen by John Robertson in 1920 with Lionel Barrymore appearing in the title role(s).

25. Thanks to Paul Théberge for alerting me to uses of sound in Mamoulian's film.

26. See footnote 14.

27. See Leydon (1999).

28. Stevens went on to score the notable Sci-Fi films *War of the Worlds* and *When Worlds Collide* (both 1953) and compose the narrated space travel concept album *Exploring the Unknown* in 1955.

29. Although Jeff Berkwits has identified that its Earth-to-Moon travel sequence "marvelously emulates weightlessness" – "Soft violins waft through the work generating a comforting, easygoing serenity that's offset by erupting horns and mysterious woodwinds" (nd: np).

30. Tiomkin studied at the St Petersburg Conservatorium and worked as a silent film accompanist before leaving Russia during the revolution. After studying with Busoni in Berlin in 1919 he relocated to the US in the mid 1920s.

31. The Barrons were credited with providing "electronic tonalities" – rather than music – on the film's credits.

32. And subsequently as *The Silent Star*, *Planet of the Dead* and *Spaceship Venus Does Not Reply*.

33. According to Szliforski, the "theremin-like motif was made in fact with a measuring electronic oscillator working on the same principle as the original theremin. I adapted it to control the frequency by moving the hand nearer or away and Andrzej Markowski used it as musical instrument." (pc July 2003).

34. With post-production undertaken at the Defa studio in Berlin and additional sound effects produced at the Military Academy laboratories in Warsaw. (Thanks to Krzysztof Szlifirski for this information – pc July 2003).

35. See 'Odd Pop: Space – Orchestral (Early)' at http://www.wildscene.com/music/oddpop/ – for a list of the best known of these.

36. A selection of these is included on the German release compilation CD *Buffalo Bop* (1997).

37. Lee returned to extra-terrestrial themes in the following year, recording the single *Rockin' on the Moon*.

38. This name apparently arose from a typographical error in the description of the form as a type of folk song. It was subsequently adopted by aficionados and is the (uncontested) name for the form.

39. Thanks to Robin Holly for information on the context of filk song writing (pc July 2003). See Gold, 1997 for a detailed historical overview of the form.

40. The National Aeronautics and Space Administration.

41. Somewhat paradoxically perhaps, given the influence of his music for Wise's 1951 film, one of Herrmann's best known 1960s' SF scores was written for Francois Truffaut's eponymous adaptation of the Ray Bradbury novel 'Fahrenheit 451', made in 1966. Here, Herrmann's music eschews dissonant modernist elements and accompanies the director's interpretation of future totalitarianism with warm, almost romantic score more typical of 1930s Hollywood than the bleak scenarios adapted from Bradbury.

42. In 2000 British electronic musician and found-sound artist Scanner provided a new, more discordant music soundtrack to the film in a series of live performances in the US.

43. Whose name – in its anglophonic phonetic form – was adopted by a well-known British band formed in the 1970s.

44. See Leydon (2001) for discussion.

45. Although it is less notable within the corpus of late 20th Century low-budget Italian film making, given the ambitious, ingenious and often eclectic approach to film music pursued by various composers and performers.

46. The music for which is referred to in the previous section.

47. Moody Blues' lead singer Justin Hayward has related that:

    The whole idea for the album was really Tony Clarke's – our record producer at the time. He

27

had a bee in his bonnet about doing an album about space: he was an astronomer and followed the stars... his idea was really to try and coincide releasing an album – in our usual kind of pretentious way – with man landing on the moon... which we missed. (quoted in Barajas, 2000: np).

48. In 1993 NASA presented the band with a cassette tape copy of *To our Children's Children* that had been played on-board a series of space shuttle missions during the 1980s (ibid).

49. The ensemble has continued to the present, being known, at various stages, as Mother Gong and Planet Gong.

50. Roeg wished to combine Bowie tracks with material by other artists (in a similar style to that used on *Performance* [1970], starring Mick Jagger) while Bowie wanted to produce the entire music. The resulting impasse blocked production of a soundtrack album.

51. See Skaggs (nd) for a discussion of the "transcendental aesthetics" of this track.

52. Following the dissolution of Jefferson Airplane in 1974 this name was resurrected for Kantner's new band.

53. His son Artemiy Artemiev provides a description of his father at ESEM that recalls a classic gothic 'mad scientist' scenario that would not have been out of place in many of the films discussed in this anthology:

    Different twinkling lamps, buttons, levers, indicators. My father, surrounded by huge appara-tuses, two sound engineers always wearing black clothes and heaving beards and long hair, smoke that comes from their cigarettes, loud very strange music and the dark basement floor where this all happened – it frightened not only people who are used to this kind of music and atmosphere of the studios, but also local inhabitants and even policemen. (quoted in Weiden-baum (2003:np).

54. Artemiy Artemiev provides a list of these in Weidenbaum (ibid).

55. Titles as used in the 1999 Electroshock Records CD re-release.

56. The stage show featured elaborate visual effects and inflated green dinosaurs wobbling around on stage. An audiovisual recording of a performance in Melbourne in February 1975 was released on DVD in 2001.

57. Wayne's product was also revived in 1990s with the release of a computer game based on the album (*Jeff Wayne's War of the Worlds*, GT Interactive, 1998) and a remix album entitled *War of the Worlds: UlladubUlla* (2000).

58. Thanks to Shuhei Hosokawa for supplying this information.

59. Even more directly connected to the SF Cinema revival, Meco also had a one-off hit with his orchestral disco track *Star Wars theme* (1977).

60. Although filking continues to be a predominantly amateur practice, with a strong emphasis on live performance at social gatherings.

61. See Emery *et al.* (2001) for further discussion.

62. This honour going to the musical drama *A Star is Born* (1976).

63. Inadequate, faulty and/or inappropriately modified speaker systems can substantially undermine the quality of an audience's experience of the soundtrack.

64. Background and/or ambient sounds, often location recorded.

65. This role encompassee (and/or oversees) the activities previously carried out by the process team of production recordist, sound editor and sound mixer.

66. While Burtt was not the first sound technician credited as a film sound designer – this honour going to the acclaimed Walter Murch – he was the first to gain broader recognition for his contribution to a film production.

67. See Carlsson (ed) (nd) for details of the production of these effects.

68. Who was largely referred to as 'the artist formally known as Prince' in the 1990s.

69. The mixing of composed sequences and original and/or incorporated popular music tracks has become an increasingly prominent element (and marketing hook) in popular cinema that merits substantial research and analysis in its own right.

70. And, later, Spiritualized, the ensemble formed by Spaceman 3 co-founder Jason Pierce in 1990. Another notable British mid-1980s band was the much hyped 'trash futurist' Sigue Sigue Sputnik (who attempted an abortive relaunch in 2000).

71. With occasional softer mood passages such as that used in the scene in which Tetsuo's dead girlfriend is placed in a bath surrounded by petals.

72. Reinforcing the rock association of the films, the cyborg character of both was played by Tomoroh Taguchi, the lead singer with the Japanese band Bachikaburi.

73. The only exception that might be claimed here is the slightly SF tinged youth melodrama *Charly* (1968) which has a score by Ravi Shankar.

74. The production of *Akira's* score was documented in a short film made in 1988 that is included on disk two of the *Akira Special Edition DVD* (2001).

75. Baxter went on to write the scores for low-budget SF movies such as *Panic in Year Zero* (1962) and *The Man with the X-Ray eyes* (1963).

76. See Hayward (ed) (1999) for a discussion of post-War musical exoticism.

77. ibid.

78. Jeff Berwits's CD reviews for *Science Fiction Weekly* provided valuable reference points for this Introduction and are essential reading for any student of the area.

Chapter One

HOOKED ON AETHEROPHONICS
The Day the Earth stood still

REBECCA LEYDON

In 'Farewell to the Master' (1944), Harry Bates' short story upon which the film *The Day the Earth stood still* (1951) is based, an extra-terrestrial called Klaatu visits the Earth and is promptly killed by a deranged citizen. It is left to the robot 'Gnut' to somehow bring him back to life. The task is eventually achieved by reconstituting Klaatu's body from a tape-recording of his voice. This last intriguing plot detail was dropped in the reworking of the original story for the script of the 1951 film. In Robert Wise's adaptation, Klaatu is killed by military police, after moving covertly among the inhabitants of Washington, DC. His corpse is retrieved and reanimated by the robot, 'Gort', by means of a mysterious medical operation ("Nikto"?) conducted inside the space ship. Yet the notion of the alien being's essence as fully encrypted in pure sound remains a crucial part the film: the extra-terrestrial 'voice', as represented by Bernard Herrmann's score, plays a central role, for it is primarily through musical clues, rather than special visual effects, that Klaatu's alien nature is enacted. After all, Klaatu looks and behaves exactly like an ordinary human, as the two Medical Corps officers who examine him in the hospital observe:

> Major:
> *(studying a series of X-ray films)*
> *The skeletal structure is completely normal.*
> *(pointing)*
> *Same for the major organs – heart, liver, spleen, kidneys.*

> Captain:
> *And the lungs are the same as ours. Must mean a similar atmosphere –*
> *similar pressure.*

Klaatu blends in and moves inconspicuously among the human population. For the cinematic spectator, the only consistent evidence of his alien origins is the halo of otherworldly sounds with which the musical score envelopes him. The link between particular sonic elements and things extra-terrestrial is forged during the film's opening titles as the camera peers through celestial nebulae toward the planet Earth. But the music's defamiliarising function becomes important precisely in the unexceptional scenes, like those showing Klaatu walking through the streets of Washington. As Royal Brown might put it, Herrmann's music acts as a "fictionalizing" force against the iconicity of the cinematic visuals (Brown, 1994).

The film's score is often noted for the prominent role it assigns the theremin, a vintage electronic instrument developed by the Russian scientist Lev Sergeyevich Termen in the nineteen-teens. The instrument has always seemed highly peculiar because it is played without actually touching it: the distance of the performer's hand from an antenna controls a radio-frequency oscillator, which, combined with a second, fixed-frequency oscillator, generates a difference tone that is amplified through a loudspeaker. Movements of the hand towards and away from the antenna thus create a continuous glissando across some four or five octaves. (The lowest note on the instrument is determined by the frequency at which the two oscillators 'lock', ie when their difference approaches zero.) Volume is, likewise, controlled by movements of the performer's opposite hand, toward and away from a metal loop that projects horizontally from the side of the instrument. Skilled performers use precise adjustments in volume to mask the unavoidable 'swoop' that marks the movement from one pitch to another. The instrument is fiendishly difficult to play, not only for the physical coordination it requires to synchronise the hand movements around the two antennae, but especially for the demands made on the performer's sense of pitch. The player must be able to remember precise positions in three-dimensional space, without reference to frets or a fingerboard. Moreover, small inadvertent motions of the right arm will cause the pitch to fluctuate noticeably; in ensemble playing the performer usually compensates for flaws in the intonation with a deliberate measured vibrato produced by shaking the right hand.

By analogy with 'idiophone', 'chordophone', and other terms for instrument 'families', Termen's instrument was initially classified as an 'aetherophone', since its sounds were supposed to emanate from the *ether*, the imaginary propagating medium for electromagnetic waves. Termen and his disciples envisioned that the instrument would take its place in the concert hall along side respectable classical instruments. Much to the dismay of Clara Rockmore and other serious practitioners, however, it quickly found its way into movie music, where its 'action-at-a-distance' method of sound-production led to its use as a sonic marker for 'unseen forces': magnetism, unconscious drives, even substance abuse. As Philip Hayward describes, "it was a *virtual* instrument, one which involved the instrumentalist conjuring sounds by means of moving his/her hands in the air" (1997: 31), and this "conjuring" was

31

easily mapped onto narrative situations involving mesmerism and the supernormal.

Herrmann's inventive orchestration in *The Day the Earth stood still* is developed through the combination of electronic sounds with more conventional orchestral resources. His use of the theremin – actually *two* theremins, to accommodate polyphonic writing – is only the most conspicuous of several unusual instruments in the score: a pair of Hammond organs plus a large studio organ, electric violin, electric cello, and electric bass (one of each), a trio of vibraphones, and electric guitar. Equally unexpected are the sounds Herrmann obtains from conventional orchestral instruments, through odd combinations and additive layering: muted brass, tam-tams struck with nail-files and triangle sticks, whole families of suspended cymbals, special effects performed on multiple harps, chimes, celesta, and glockenspiel. Figure 1 shows some of these resources as they are employed in the opening measures of the densely scored overture.

What are the narrative elements that call for such extraordinary musical resources? The film opens with the sound of radio broadcasts in many languages as a UFO is tracked by radar systems around the world. The flying saucer makes a landing at the National Mall in Washington, DC where it is quickly surrounded by tanks, guns, and nervous military personnel. A solitary figure, Klaatu, emerges from the ship, announcing: "We have come to visit you in peace and with goodwill". As he extends his arm to offer a gift (a special telescope for observing life on other planets), he is shot and wounded by a jittery soldier. This misdeed brings forth Gort, the indestructible laser-firing robot, who appears bent on revenge until Klaatu calls him off ("Gort! Deglet! Ovrosco!"). Klaatu is taken to a hospital to have his wounds treated. There an advisor to the president of the United States visits him but Klaatu insists that the message he bears must be delivered to all of the Earth's people, and not to any one nation alone. Klaatu requests a meeting with the United Nations, and when this proves diplomatically impossible, he escapes from the hospital to move secretly among the city's inhabitants. Under the assumed name of 'Major Carpenter' he takes up residence in a boarding house where he meets a widow, Helen, and her son Bobby, who become his confidants. With their help he arranges for a meeting with the international scientific community, lead by Dr. Barnhardt, deemed "the smartest man in the world". To illustrate just what is at stake for the Earth's people, Klaatu disables all electronic devices on the entire planet for an hour. Meanwhile, Helen's fiancé, Tom Stevens, reveals Klaatu's whereabouts to the authorities and the spaceman is shot to death before he can address the scientists. Helen must then deliver a message to the robot Gort ("Klaatu! Barada! Nikto!") which undertakes the recovery of Klaatu's body and its reanimation. Finally the re-born Klaatu is able to deliver his message: the nations of the Earth must dismantle their nuclear arsenal or face complete annihilation by extraterrestrial law enforcement.

The film weaves together a variety of themes drawn from heterogeneous

Figure 1: Overture

sources, including Christianity, McCarthyism, the Manhattan Project and
'Big Science'. Klaatu's rebirth, his message of peace, and his adopted pseudonym plainly allude to Christian biblical events. But, as Krin Gabbard has
pointed out, these Christian references are hybridised with expressions of

33

anti-McCarthyism (Gabbard, 1982). In a parody of red-scare hysteria, one of the characters asserts that the mysterious space ship has come, not from the stars, but from the Soviet Union. Helen's fiancé plays the role of Judas when he betrays Klaatu's identity to the authorities; but the incident also clearly alludes to the 'friendly witnesses' who denounced their Hollywood colleagues at the 1947 HUAC hearings. In a different type of hybridisation, the scientist Dr. Barnhardt is presented as one of the few 'believers' in Klaatu's message. As Cyndy Hendershot has argued, the film represents atomic scientists as "mystics who impart political and ethical wisdom to a frightened American public" (Hendershot, 1997: 33).

Herrmann's electronic musical resources, then, serve several narrative goals in the film. First, they perform an alienising function – including the alienness invoked by xenophobia and anti-communist hysteria; second, they epitomise the sounds of science – including science gone horribly wrong; and finally they mark off a space of numinosity, associated with Klaatu's 'sacred' mission and that of the 'priestly' scientists. The theremin proves uniquely well adapted to all these functions. As Hayward notes:

> [T]he theremin's otherworldliness invokes another, earlier association – the mystery of interplanetary space, that of the metaphorical 'music of the spheres', the celestial harmony of the movement of the planets which Earth's factionalism and arms race threatened, and which had prompted Klaatu to be dispatched as an ambassador to Earth, to invite us to change our ways. (Hayward, 1997: 38)[1]

While the theremins are the most conspicuously 'alien' feature of Herrmann's score, some of the strangest-sounding passages are generated by other means. One example is the scene where Klaatu, masquerading as 'Mr. Carpenter', pays a nocturnal visit to his ship. The youngster Bobby follows him as he leaves the house late at night; from a safe distance, Bobby watches as Klaatu makes his way to the site and signals to Gort with a flashlight. Figure 2 shows a segment of the music that accompanies Bobby and Klaatu's passage through the streets of Washington. One consequence of this particular combination of instruments with this tessitura is that each layer is slightly mistuned with respect to the prevailing concert pitch. The harp harmonics sound a little sharp to the vibraphone, while the cup mutes on the trumpets also tend to pull the intonation noticeably sharp with respect to the same notes doubled by the Hammond organ (whose 12-tone gear train temperament approximates, but deviates very slightly from equal temperament). Next come the series of pedal glissandi in the low register of the harp combined with the sound of the chime, a naturally 'mistuned' instrument by virtue of its inharmonic overtone series[2].

This teetering ensemble nicely sets up the sonic landscape for the next scene: for the flash-light sequence, Herrmann introduces the two theremins, playing an interlocking chromatic neighbor figure, accompanied by long sustained notes on muted cello and electric bass and tam-tam. A particularly

Figure 2: "Nocturne"

weird feature of the passage in Figure 3 is that while the higher of the two theremins performs with the instrument's characteristic vibrato, the lower one plays without. Exposing the inherent instability of the theremin's intonation, Herrmann once again sets up a wide pitch 'fringe'. (This particular pairing of the two instruments, *senza*- and *con* vibrato, and the same mewling chromatic half-step figure will return later in the film to accompany the scene in which the world's electrical devices are temporarily impaired[3].)

A series of timpani glissandi, mimicking the portamento of the theremins, accompany Gort's disposal of the guards. Klaatu then makes his way inside the space ship to begin his calculations. The theremins now take on a new musical role: for the first time in the film, they play something resembling a full-blown melodic theme. Up to this point, the instrument has had very little to do in the way of thematic material, per se, mostly playing brief repetitive two-note fragments, like those shown in Figure 3. Now it is as if the theremin emerges in its 'natural environment', the interior of the spaceship, which offers a glimpse of the alien world from which Klaatu has come. The tune, shown as the upper voice in Figure 4, materialises as part of a dialogue: stated first by the solo electric guitar, it shifts to the first

35

Figure 3: "The Flashlight"

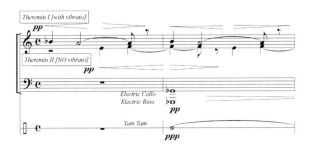

theremin, then the second, while a clockwork-like rhythmic accompaniment unfolds in the harps, glockenspiels, vibraphone, celesta and piano. The melodic imitation in this passage suggests a kind of rational communication among the voices of the musical texture. All this takes place as Klaatu speaks aloud in his mother tongue, issuing commands to the ship's controls.

Figure 4: "Space Control"

Klaatu's own movements in this scene actually mirror those of a theremin player: he waves his hand over panels as lights turn on and off and a projection screen is illuminated.

Klaatu's actions here will soon incapacitate electronic devices all over the planet, and the most elaborate orchestral effects of the film are reserved for the scene in which this event transpires. Herrmann once again employs the two theremins, along with the three organs, the electric bass and the full complement of brass; all playing dissonant sustained pianissimo chords. The most striking element in the soundtrack here, however, is a separate ensemble made up of three sets of chimes struck with steel mallets, two pianos, and crash cymbals. A series of *sforzando* chords played by this group is recorded both forward (track 1) and backward (track 2); the tracks are linked end to end in a chain of dramatic *diminuendi* and *crescendi*, articulated by the concussive chords. Figure 5 shows the first pair of these chords. Each 'stinger' corresponds to a shot in the film, showing first the streets of Washington, then London, Moscow, and Paris, all paralysed by Klaatu's stunt.

Herrmann's use of poly-triads in Figure 5 – for example, E♭ minor plus E minor (a particular juxtaposition that returns elsewhere in the film) – is a hallmark of his musical language and a technique he likely picked up from his close study of the music of Charles Ives. Like Ives, Herrmann tends to combine major or minor triads whose roots lie either a minor second or a tritone apart, for maximum contrast. (Triads of separated by other intervals tend to be less convincingly bi-tonal.) Another example of this technique is the music that accompanies Klaatu's arrival near the beginning of the film. Figure 6 shows the signature motif that is reiterated twelve times during the scene. This sonority freezes and sustains a harmony that had first occurred in the context of the overture, in a passage featuring alternating D major and A♭ major chords (reminiscent of the 'Coronation Scene' from Mussorgsky's *Boris Godunov*). The tonal centers, A♭ and D, which lie a tritone apart, are juxtaposed here in this isolated 'Klaatu' chord. The chord also represents a particular configuration known as the 'all-interval tetrachord' – a four-note sonority in which each of the six possible interval-classes is represented.[4]

	A♭	C	D	E♭
min 2nd (ic1)			*	*
maj 2nd (ic2)		*	*	
min 3rd (ic3)		*		*
maj 3rd (ic4)	*	*		
p 5th (ic5)	*			*
tritone (ic6)	*		*	

It is a particularly rich sound, and is often used by composers to evoke a

Figure 5: "The Magnetic Pull"

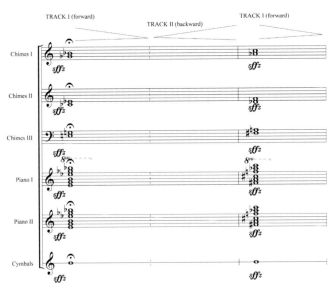

Figure 6: "Klaatu"

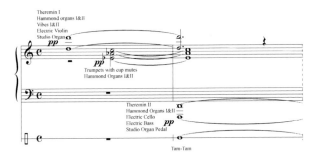

sense of chromatic saturation; in the context of Herrmann's score, it is analogous to the theremin slides, timpani glissandi, and harp pedal portamento and the way these slippery sounds allude to the complete chromatic gamut.

Herrmann went on to create similar 'slippery' effects in other film scores – for example, harp pedal glissandi (played by nine harps) for the octopus scene is Robert D. Webb's *Beneath the Twelve Mile Reef* (1953), and most famously, the shrieking violin glissandi in *Psycho*'s shower scene. The theremin is a natural choice for producing this kind of irrational pitch wandering. But after its distinctive sound was featured in a number of mid-century film scores, the instrument was eventually abandoned in favour of more versatile and user-friendly synthesisers. Herrmann himself used Moog synthesisers in place of the theremins when he conducted selections from *The Day the*

Figure 7: "Rebirth"

Earth stood still with the National Philharmonic Orchestra for a London recording in 1974. By then, the theremin had been superceded by a new generation of electronic instruments; in any case, there had only ever been a handful of truly competent players able to negotiate the theremin's slithery pitch space. Still, Herrmann's music had made the instrument's own limitations work in its favour, exacerbating its more freakish qualities through *senza vibrato* technique and through ensemble combinations with other electronic and acoustic resources to best serve the particular narrative goals of the film.

Pitch collections such as the all-interval tetrachord in Figure 7 and the superimposed triads at half-step and tritone-transpositions throughout the score attest to Herrmann's efficiency in evoking a thoroughly modern, 'Ivesian' harmonic idiom through the most succinct of gestures. Herrmann had already developed his characteristic brevity during his career in radio in the 1940s, with CBS and especially with Orson Welles' *Mercury Theatre on the Air*, where the combination of narration, dialogue, sound effects, and music demanded concision of cues and an epigrammatic approach to musical materials. In *The Day the Earth stood still*, Herrmann makes similarly economical use of his sparse melodic materials, frequently recycling his basic melodic components – like the half-step neighbour-note figure from the overture – and placing them in new narrative/musical contexts. Klaatu's 'rebirth' music, for example, shown in Figure 7, represents a subtle motivic transformation of the earlier 'flashlight' music: the interlocking half-steps of the two theremins from the flashlight scene (see Figure 3) are here reconfigured as a call-and-response pattern between the electric violin and the pair of theremins. The music thus once again suggests the secret channels of communication between Gort and Klaatu.

39

This 'rebirth' moment stands alone in the film inasmuch as the violin briefly adopts its conventional role as the primary melody-bearing instrument of the orchestra – the emotive 'voice' of the musical fabric. The three-voice texture here accommodates full triads, and the descending sequence features expressive appoggiaturas performed with conspicuous vibrato in all the instruments, so that the ensemble blends into a homogeneous string-like timbre. Elsewhere the strings are subsumed into dense and murky textures. Indeed, one of the principal means by which Herrmann evokes a sense of the paranormal in this score is by dispensing altogether with the convention of a large string section. The sound of orchestral strings may be understood as the normative, unmarked sonic term in film music practice. Caryl Flinn, Claudia Gorbman and other scholars have considered the historical contingencies that lead to the pervasive 19th Century symphonic sound of mid-20th Century film scores. In particular, they point to the wave of immigration to Hollywood by European musicians including Max Steiner, Erich Korngold, and Dmitri Tiomkin. The 'classical Hollywood score' was a genre forged by these musicians, and the entire set of musical conventions that came to characterise the genre drew heavily upon 19th Century operatic models: leitmotif technique, uninterrupted scoring, dense orchestral textures, and associative use of key-centers. By the late 1930s, such techniques constituted a powerfully institutionalised model, one strenuously maintained by the Hollywood studio system. More specifically, Caryl Flinn identifies a pronounced Wagnerian orientation in film music, which she traces back to discussions in industry trade journals in the early 20th Century. She highlights a number of passages from early issues of *The Moving Picture World*, which claim that: "just as Wagner fitted his music to the emotions, expressed by words in his operas, so in the course of time, no doubt, the same thing will be done with regard to the moving picture" (1910); and "every man or woman in charge of motion picture theatre … is a disciple of Richard Wagner" (1911) (quoted in Flinn, 1992: 15). Flinn illustrates how, by the mid-1930s, a set of conventions had been established within Hollywood which employed the Wagnerian *Gesamtkunstwerk* as a model, both stylistically and theoretically (ibid: 17).

Considered against the backdrop of this neo-Romantic tradition, Herrmann's music of the early 1950s stands out sharply for his much more sparing use of music throughout the film, his brief, tonally ambiguous cues, his Ivesian harmonic language, and, above all, his unconventional orchestration. Even Herrmann's practice of orchestrating his own music was at odds with the prevailing customs of the Hollywood studio system. Lacking the 'warmth' of a large string section, Herrmann's score for *The Day the Earth stood still* both accentuates the astonishing alienness of the world it depicts and exposes the classical Hollywood score as a nostalgic construction of false unity.

Notes

1. The theremin's use as a signifier for the destructive and redemptive potential of modern science is curiously paralleled by the career of its inventor: as Steven Martin reveals in his

1991 documentary *Theremin: Electronic Odyssey*, Termen himself was eventually forced to work on Soviet military projects, where his duties included cleaning up audio-tape of conversations covertly recorded by the KGB.

2. The frequency series for orchestral chimes is not based on whole-number ratios, but irrational relationships: the partials sound at 1, 2.76, 5.4, 8.93, 13.34, 18.64, 24.81, etc., times the fundamental frequency.

3. The manuscript score in fact calls for *both* instruments to play *senza vibrato*, but the soundtrack in the film retains vibrato for theremin I.

4. Interval *classes*(ics) are determined by measuring the distance between two pitch-classes, expressed in terms of semitones traversed. An interval class includes a particular interval, its inversion or 'octave complement,' and its octave compounds. For example interval class 1 includes the minor 2nd, major 7th, minor 9th, etc. Four-note sonorities can contain as few as 2 different ics, as in the case of the diminished 7th chord (ics 3 and 6 only), or as many as 6, as in the case of all-interval chords.

Chapter Two

ATOMIC OVERTONES AND PRIMITIVE UNDERTONES
Akira Ifukube's Sound Design for *Godzilla*

SHUHEI HOSOKAWA

Introduction: Primitivism and Auteurism

No other filmic creature seems to have enjoyed such a successful and busy life as Godzilla (*Gojira* in Japanese). In 2002 the twenty-sixth of the series, *Godzilla v Meca-Godzilla* was released and simultaneously an exhibition entitled 'In the Age of Godzilla' was held at the Tarô Okamoto Museum (exploring changes in film artwork in relation to narrative). The increasing number of critical and photographic books on the series attests to the continuing Japanese enthusiasm for him[1]. To commemorate his popularity, Tôhô built a small Godzilla statue at the location of its former headquarter in Tokyo (today's Chanter Plaza). Godzilla's impact is especially strong in the US. To quote a phrase from the obituary to the producer of the *Godzilla* films, Tomoyuki Tanaka, in the *New York Times*, Godzilla was "among the first images that struck Americans when they thought of Japan"[2] (WuDunn, 1997: A28). Blue Oyster Cult's pop tune, *Godzilla* (1977) and the (eponymous) Hollywood remake of the film (1998) were also eloquent signs of the monster's presence. The creature has also been an object of fascination for US Sci-Fi aficionados and 'Asiamaniacs' (see, for example, Mark Jacobson's parody novel of *Gojiro* [1991], and the special issue of the fanzine *Oriental Cinema* – v3/4 October 1994).

The Godzilla saga is often discussed with regard to the increasing technical sophistication of special effects and the changing attitude of the Japanese to the A-bomb, the USA and Japan itself. The obvious reference to nuclear disaster in the original *Gojira* (1954) – which will be henceforth referred to by its English language name *Godzilla* – has been obscured in the sequels, especially after the 1970s. Some Japanese take a national pride in the series (due to its overseas fame) whereas others prefer its camp aesthetics. What characterises the Godzilla series since the 1990s is the awareness of genre rules and self-mythologisation. The younger directors declare their zeal for re-creating the fantasy they had in their own viewing of earlier Godzilla and other monster films in their childhood.

Godzilla is also a hero in academia. Susan Napier explains the repeated catastrophe stories in Japanese films from *Godzilla* to *Akira* (1992) with reference to Japan's anti-utopia and nationalism. The "nuclear allergy" (ibid: 332) in postwar Japan is widely yet dubiously contextualised in traditional aesthetics (harmony with the Nature, sense of *aware* [pity] or *ma* [void-in-terval]), by writers such as Jerome Shapiro (2002: 272–88). Chon Noriega (1996), in turn, identifies Godzilla and his enemies as a metaphor of Japan-US relations and international military politics from the Cold War era to the dissolution of Soviet Union (and beyond). The North American reception and domestication of Japanese monsters has been the subject of analysis by Nancy Anisfield (1995), Joyce Boss (1999) and Anthony Enns (2001), all of whom are concerned with narrative implications.

One of the reasons for the longevity derives from the fact that Godzilla has a name. Whereas Hollywood's hideous creatures are usually called nothing other than the 'thing', 'creature' or 'them', Japanese cinema monsters (all of whom were invented after Godzilla) have names. Naming is taming and classifying the unknown in order. By calling the monsters by name, Japanese do not only "domesticate" them in the midst of the horror (Noriega, 1996: 60), this also allows the film industry to secure the continuity of the genre.

Other than a name, our hero has an evocative leitmotif that is one of the best known film themes in Japan. Akira Ifukube's music for twelve of the twenty-six Godzilla films offers the clearest aural insignia for the monster(s) (overshadowing the music provided by other composers employed on the series). In the ever-growing Godzilla industry, the title music and *Allegro Marciale* have a variety of arrangements and recordings including concert suites (*Symphonic Fantasias n1-3*, 1983), heavy metal and brass band versions. Likewise, the sound effects of Godzilla and his siblings have also been fetishised, as can be observed in various LP and CD re-releases with detailed sleevenotes[3]. Without the aural triptych (music, stomping and roaring sounds), Godzilla could not have become an outstanding icon in film history. It is my purpose here to explain how this sonic portrait of the creature was produced and composed within the framework of primitivism and auteurism. My argument will be exclusively addressed to the original *Godzilla* film, directed by Ishirô Honda, which set the creative template for the series.

Primitivism. Honda's *Godzilla* is distinct in the Japanese monster (*kaijû*) film genre because it has clear references to contemporary reality. The opening episode of a fishing boat destroyed by a strange white beam is an adaptation of the Daigo Fukuryûmaru accident, when a Japanese fishing boat was exposed to radioactivity emanating from a US hydrogen bomb test in the South Pacific (in February 1954). In March, the so-called 'atomic tuna' detected in port caused general panic in Japan. In September, one of the crew died and anti-nuclear (and thereby anti-US) demonstrations and teach-ins were organised in many cities. The scene of political dispute in the film seemed to reproduce the real one concerning the importation of American nuclear weapons that occurred in the Diet Building. In the midst of Godzilla's raid, Tokyo citizenry recalled the wartime bombardment, evacuation of the country, the Nagasaki bomb and the dead. When *Godzilla* premiered on November 3rd, some newspaper reviews dismissed the political 'messages' of the film as minor aspects of what they regarded as a childish story. Honda has subsequently stated that it was his clear intention to make an anti-war allegory with a science-fiction storyline (1994: 86ff, 134)[4] and, appropriately, the film's narrative (and visuals) are notably darker than the light-spirited and battle-oriented sequels.

In *Godzilla*, the protagonist is a link between archaic past and emergent present, between nature and civilisation, myth and science, fantasy and reality. It is of considerable significance that the Godzilla's name stems from a local legend of the monster in the deep sea, orally transmitted in the Odoshima Island, Godzilla's first landing spot. The film critic Saburô Kawamoto rightly associates Godzilla more closely with the Golem, a giant in German/Jewish folk tale, than with other eerie creatures (1994: 84). Godzilla's trajectory from an abyss at the edge of Japanese territory to the metropolis symbolises the path from nature to civilisation, from the peaceful world to the tainted one.

The monster's interlinked aspects of primitivism and folklorism have been overlooked by critics more concerned with the nuclear overtones of the scenario (Shapiro, 2001: 272–88; Napier, 1993; Noriega, 1996; Musolf, 1998). Primitivism, originally denoting a trend in European art in the early 20th Century, represents a quest for the primal/primordial life-force attributed to the 'other' that is desired and feared by artists and their public (Torgovnick, 1990; Miller, 1991; Clifford, 1988). The primitivist idea operates on the dichotomies of civilised/uncivilised, white/other, West/East, master/slave and so on. It is more than a curious appendix to 20th Century art, it makes modernity modern because to be modern is defined by its opposite. The primitive is a necessary marker for modernity to claim itself as such.

In the first pages of his first book *Introduction to Music*, Akira Ifukube (1914–) insists that the "auditory sense is probably the most *primitive* among the senses serving the arts" (my emphasis) and asserts that music is the most intuitive, immediate and "primitive" expression of human senses (1951: 7). Ikufube's claim for the priority of rhythm over melody and harmony (ibid) and the pursuit of the primordial, the intuitive and the instinctive in music, provides a statement of his primitivist aesthetic. Primitivism exploits 'raw' materials from other worlds to 'cook' for its refined audience, shocking the gentle order of art. What matters to Ifukube is the deviation from German canon that comprises the dominant strand in Japan's western-music world.

It is obvious that primitivism easily slips to folklorism, particularly when applied to the rural 'Other'. When applied at the periphery of cultural empire, primitivist-folklorism often manifests itself as an expression of distinctively national values. Vanishing (or vanished) indigenous groups are usually the paramount candidates for such expressions. The relationship of the minority to the nation is metonymical. Villa-Lobos's *indios*, Albeniz's gypsies, Rimsky-Korsakov's tartars are all exemplify this. The Ainu, the indigenous people of Hokkaido, Ifukube's birthplace in northern Japan, serve as his intellectual totem. It is, however, difficult to establish any precise links between Ifukube's work and Ainu musical heritage. Although Ifukube had contact with Ainu culture in his home village while growing up, the composer did not go on to mimic or incorporate this music in his oeuvre. Instead, Ifukube drew on this source for local colour and exoticism (following the western/European Model) and also invented new musical languages to evoke the national. Here, the particular-national and the universal-European coexist in both harmony and conflict.

Comparisons with Bartók are compelling. Bartók was a western-orientated modernist who discovered Hungarian peasant music as a genuinely Hungarian (yet universal) heritage. For him, as the musicologist Julie Brown notes, "the Orient was not an exotic other, a realm of sensuality and mystery to be mastered and represented" but rather "the most powerful force in Hungarian musical culture, as conceived not only inside but also outside Hungary" (2000: 125). Bartók's "Orient" corresponds to Ifukube's Ainu. Both composers, knowing the peripheral position of their countries in the concert music world, rejected exoticisation (or 'recentralisation') *by* the metropolis. As an alternative, they proposed the cultural relocation of the periphery to a position inside the nation. This approach considered the peripheral (ie the peasant or the Ainu) as culturally authentic because the metropolis (eg Vienna and Tokyo) had not discovered and spoilt it (yet). Just as Bartók refused the 'Gypsy fantasy', promulgated, especially, by Brahms and Liszt; Ifukube rebuffed the *japonisme* (principally based on certain pentatonicisms) distilled, for example, by Puccini and Massenet, and adopted by Japanese concert composers in the 1930s. The Ainu may represent, so to speak, the Ur-Japanese – an internal other who possesses a cultural legacy more ancient than Japanese. The difference between Bartók and Ifukube is that the latter had no obsession to transcribe and classify the folk music he encountered. The principal reason, as Ifukube expressed it, is that the western notational system is insufficient to store the beauty that can only be experienced in live performance (1959: 21). For him, notation, in this instance, can be likened to a dried flower. His relationship with the Ainu is more concerned with his childhood memory than with the fieldwork, more with spiritual aspects than material.

What characterises his composition is the complexity of his modal melodies; his asymmetric rhythms and ostinati; unconventional instrumentation and performing technique, and dynamic orchestration. These compositional techniques constitute his primitivism/nationalism. Ifukube's adoption of modality evidences his desire to go beyond the simple *japonisme* derived from western Orientalism. It is significant that his search for modal music became focused through *Dozokuteki Sanrenga* (subtitled *Triptyque aborigène*) (1937), his second orchestral work. The use of the Phrygian mode makes it distinct from his first orchestral work, *Nihon Kyôshikyoku* ('Japanese Rhapsody') (1936), a composition mostly based on folk pentatonic scales. For the composer, Ur-Japanese ("Eurasian") music is structured on the tonic with a semi-tone upper tone and a whole-tone lower tone. The note progressions used – III, IV, VI, VII, [VIII], I, II and VII, I, III, IV, [V], VI, VIII – are both variants on minor modal structures and are most closely related to the Phrygian mode (III, IV, V, VI, VII, I, II, III). The use of these modes is fundamental to his later compositional work. Since three movements of *Triptyque aborigène* are subtitled in Ainu language, the "aborigène" in the title obviously refers to them. The subtitles appear to function as an autobiographical record and poetic stimuli for the composer.

Auteurism. Similarly to the West, Japanese film music has been more or less dependent on concert music. The filmography of many notable Japanese 'concert composers' is impressively long: Tôru Takemitsu scored 105 works; Fumio Hayasaka, 95; Toshirô Mayuzumi, 192; Yasushi Akutagawa, 112; Akira Ifukube, about 300 (Kobayashi, 2001a and 2001b). Film was both a staple means of living and an artistic interest for these auteurs, providing opportunities to experiment what they rarely wrote for concert music. For all his prolific and creative work in film scoring, Ifukube identifies himself as concert composer: 'autonomous music' is his artistic ideal. Although he dislikes the label of 'Godzilla composer' that tends to overwhelm the vast body of his lesser-known concert works, his *Godzilla* score clearly embodies the stylistic characteristics in concert music mentioned above[5].

For a composer who sometimes scored more than ten films a year, borrowing from one film to another and recycling concert materials for film scores (although not the reverse) was inevitable. However, Ifukube always transformed his re-used materials in new fashions by way of special instrumentation and thematic developments, making surprising co-ordinations between image and narrative. Reusing the same material has been an unhappy compromise for him but can be seen as a practice that fragmentalises the totality of music work for the purpose of creating an alternative sound-vision-narrative totality of filmic work. The same motif, when extracted from a coherent continuity of concert work, conveys a totally different meaning to film audiences. Any filmic sound, consciously or not, is perceived and interpreted in association with synchronised image and narrative flow. For instance, the famous title music of *Godzilla* comes from the first movement of his *Rapsodia Concertante per Violino ed Orchestra* (1948), which, in turn, may be inspired by the third movement of Ravel's

Violin Concerto. However, these 'sources' do not communicate the awe that the *Godzilla* theme does. The difference is astonishing. The metamorphosis is complete[6].

Unlike Takemitsu, who sometimes flirted with popular song, jazz and tonal tunes he rarely deployed in concert pieces, or Masaru Satô, who was dexterous in adapting a variety of styles, Ifukube has been stubborn and consistent, whether in concert work or film work, entertainment or art film scoring. Although Ifukube's film scores are closely linked with his concert music, it is difficult to regard his work as 'classical Japanese film music' in a similar manner to examples of 'classical Hollywood music'. In the 1930s the Japanese film industry established a similar production line to Hollywood but there were no canonical composers such as Steiner and Waxman or dominant techniques such as late Romanticism. Even in the 1940s and 1950s, it is difficult to point out dominant compositional models. Ifukube, along with select few, provided quality scores but his style did not become a standard. This is also the case of Hayasaka, Satô, Takemitsu, Mayuzumi and other auteurs[7].

As has been often argued, there are no actual 'film music' styles but rather, a melange of extant concert and popular styles and ways of editing and mixing them. Much has been written about the adaptation of the compositional technique of concert music -especially that of 19th Century tonal and atonal music – to classical Hollywood soundtrack. Auteurism has become a standard paradigm of film music study and there are several books on the history of film music devoted to 'great masters' and their masterpieces. Additionally though, instead of focused formal score reading, several informed scholars have analysed harmony and orchestration in order to discover the narrative economy, psychoanalytic effect, visual association, spectator's perception and other specificities of audio-visual cinema.

As much as musicology has conventionally privileged western/European art music, film music studies, especially in English, have been centered on prominent North American (and a few French and Soviet) composers. Although I acknowledge recent critiques of auteurism[8], this chapter attempts to expand the national focus of emergent research on film music with reference to Ifukube as an auteur. This chapter will follow the auteurist trail in part because Ifukube has had little recognition in anglophone academia. By examining a single composer's film work in the (dim) light of his concert corpus, I attempt to underline the importance of stylistic analysis in combination with filmic-narrative interpretation.

The Magnetic Tape Revolution: *Godzilla's* sound effects and high-tech Primitivism

Ifukube recalls his reaction to his first reading of *Godzilla's* scenario in the following terms:

When I read the scenario, I intuitively felt the philosophy of anti-tech-

47

*nology... After we lost the war, I was more shocked by the technology
and science imported from America, one after another than I was
dissatisfied with the shortage of food. I had a strong impression that we
had been defeated by them [ie science and technology]... I had an
inferiority complex about the highly advanced scientific weapons over
there [in the USA] but the airplane, the jet plane, the electricity were all
no use for Godzilla. He pulled down the high voltage poles. Nothing can
beat him. I felt so good. I felt the film suggested anti-civilisation and the
limit of today's technology.* (quoted in Kobayashi, 1998: 84 – my
translation)[9]

Just after the US occupation, as this quote shows, anti-War attitudes often
coated anti-Americanism. For Ifukube, Godzilla symbolically opposed science
and technology. The monster was mutated by nuclear power and overcame
US military technology but succumbed to a (fictional) Japanese invention,
the 'oxygen destroyer'. The ambivalence of science and technology is consti-
tutive of the life and death of Godzilla.

Godzilla did not only narrate scientific experiments but also experimented
itself with the new sound technology of the magnetic recording system. Tôhô
Studio purchased the Westrex Cinecorder in 1954 and *Godzilla* was among
the first works (along with Kurosawa's *Seven Samurai*) to use it. The first
sound – before the title credit 'Godzilla' appears – is the strange noise of
something stomping and roaring. The sound engineer Ichirô Minawa[10]
remembers that *Godzilla* was the "most difficult" work for him because he
had to invent the sound of an imaginary and gigantic creature from scratch:

*First, I'm going to talk about the roaring sound. After a conversation
with the recording assistant, Hisashi Shimonaga, we decided to use
musical instruments and we played the bass. But in order to efface the
instrument-like sound, we loosened all the strings and played various
parts of them. So the original sounds were very ugly. We tried to record
hundreds of such sounds and selected the usable ones. Then we changed
the speed of tape and added echo, and synthesised and processed them.
Thus Godzilla's voice came out. The original sound was used only in the
first* Godzilla. *Because Mr. Ifukube's music was based on the low sound,
we adjusted Godzilla's voice a little higher by the tape manipulation
from the second of the series. Otherwise, the fine grain of Godzilla's bass
voice would be cancelled by the music* (1995: 29–31 – my translation).

This quote gives a good explanation of how a musical instrument can become
an imaginative and creative sound maker if it is used in a non-conventional
way in cooperation with magnetic recording technology. It also shows how
Minawa and his staff, in collaboration with Ifukube, patiently and persistently experimented with reel-to-reel tape recorders in order to obtain an
appropriate sound to represent a fantastic reptile[11].

The idea for Godzilla's stomping sound occurred to Ifukube when he stumbled over a wooden box in the studio and heard a strange sound from the speaker – an over-echoed crashing noise (Kobayashi, 1998: 89). This was a *eureka* moment for him in understanding the creative potential of the microphone and noise. The stomping sound was then synthesised from sound samples of Japanese fighters, firearms, bombs etc. archived in the Tôhô sound library on magnetic tapes (transferred from wartime optical soundtracks). Similarly synthesised sounds were used for the sound effects of the demolition of buildings in the film. *Godzilla's* material debt to the War is evident here, since the Tôhô sound archive results from the company's close connection with the military during wartime[12].

Godzilla's sound effects were a pioneering experiment in the history of tape recording in Japan. The first tape recorder known in Japan was installed around 1948 in the headquarters of the NHK (Japan Broadcasting Association). In 1949 a small electric goods company experimented with the first domestic tape recorder and the following year saw the release of the first recorder. The company, later renamed Sony, invented a portable model in 1951 that was purchased by many primary schools for educational purposes. Sony's tape recorders entered in film studios in 1953. It was Tôhô that got most interested in new recording technology partly because Sony's co-founder, Dai Ibuka, had once worked as a sound engineer in the PCL Studio (which merged with Tôhô in the 1940s) before the war (Tanaka, 1998: 60).

Magnetic tape soon became indispensable both for avant-garde concert music and film soundtrack. In the former context, the first known Japanese electronic piece is Yasushi Akutagawa's *Music for Microphone* (1952), a piece with live orchestra and pre-recorded and modulated orchestral sound. In 1953 Toshirô Mayuzumi made *X.Y.Z. A Work of Musique Concrète*, a three-part composition. Since these two composers had studied with Ifukube in the late 1940s, he may have been aware of the new trends in electric music.

In film studios, in turn, magnetic recording technology brought about a series of radical changes in sound production and reproduction[13]. Unlike the previous optical recording system, in which music and sound effects had to be recorded simultaneously, the magnetic recording system enabled post-performance tape editing to make real and surreal sounds. For example, Hayasaka, Ifukube's high schoolmate, used reverse tape operation in the nightmare sequence in Akira Kurosawa's *Drunken Angel* (1948), inspired in part by Maurice Jaubert's famous 'reverse waltz' in Julien Duvivier's *Un Carnet de Ball* (1937). In Kurosawa's *Rashomon* (1950), Hayasaka also used the modulated music of oboe and strings in the scene of the shaman's supernatural narration. In the same scene, the voice of the dead samurai resurrected by the shaman was processed through narrowing frequency and adding noise probably generated in the sound editing (Akiyama, 1974: 404). Another contemporaneous example of tape manipulation is found in Tomu Uchida's *Kiga Kaikyô* (1954), whose climax, the killing of two deserters by their peer, develops with the horrifying sound of reverse tape music designed by Isao Tomita. *Godzilla*'s sound effects were thus among the vanguard of experiments in tape music/sound in the mid-1950s.

While Ifukube has rejected electric/electronic apparatus in his concert music, his work as a film composer shows that he is conscious of the effect of technological mediation on audience perception. In 1948, one year after he scored his first film, he complained about the sound deterioration resulting from a recording system (Kobayashi 2001a: 42–43). His familiarisation with technology soon grew however, and he came to understand the "magic" of recording processes (1953: 261) and experimented with a variety of instrumentation, volume, microphone positions etc. The sound effects of *Godzilla* draw on his knowledge of film sound technology and Minawa's craftsmanship.

The Road from *The Rite of Spring* to *Godzilla*

After the strange stomping and roaring sounds, the audience of *Godzilla* hears the music starting as the composer's credit appears. This music has unmistakable rhythmic and melodic patterns (M-1)[14] and consists of the two contrasting cells: the melody-centered A and the chord-centered B (Example 1)[15]. The overall structure is A-A'-A-A'-halfA-B. The A has a sequential and repetitive melody of do-si-la, while its variation A' moves to an upper tone: re-do-si. Both melodic lines are analogous – simple ups and downs of sequential four notes – and are so simple as to be easily memorised. There are no counter-lines against the ostinato. However, the piece is far from being monotonous. The trick is in its metric complexity. The A is based on the alternation of 4/4 and 5/4 (2+2+2+1+2), while the A' develops a similar yet not the same pattern: 4/4, 5/4, 4/4 and 4/4. Here the first two bars replicate the accent pattern of A, which is followed by the variant (2+2+2+2). The piece is neither 4/4, as the first bar makes the audience expect, nor 9/4, as the reiterated A cells would suggest. Furthermore, after the second A', the subunit of A is not repeated twice as is in the previous times (hence "halfA"). Therefore this part is not a symmetric A-B-A form but irregular in the sense that there are moments in which an odd meter is added or cancelled, or a stretch of bars is lacking. The B cell that follows (five 4/4 bars) sounds metrically more stable yet the asymmetrical accents (6+2+4+8) prevent the smooth flow. To sum up, the intermittent 5/4 bars and asymmetrical accents break the metric regularity. The piece goes far beyond the regular duple or triple time. The audience does not feel a stable beat progressing.

The metric complexity is compensated by the harmonic simplicity (see

Example 1.

Example 2.

below). The A is put to F major tonic, whereas the A' to G major tonic. The B is structured on the throbbing succession of the E major tonic. This harmonic succession is of course non-functional. The phrase ending with I–VII produces a Phrygian feel (the "si mode" in Ifukube's term) as mentioned above. In terms of orchestration, the first A and A' are played by the strings and clarinets, the second A and A' add to them flutes, oboes, and trumpets. The accents of B are *tutti* of strings, clarinets, bassoons, horns, trumpets, trombones, timpani and tone clusters of piano (by elbow). In the reprise one hears the cymbal 'thundering' (struck by mallets). These intense accents are redolent of Stravinsky's *The Rite of Spring* (eg 'Dance of the Youths and Maidens'). The Stravinsky-like rhythmic and timbral treatment is clearer in the famous scene of the self-sacrificing broadcasters (MB), probably the only tragicomical moment in the raid scene. The *tutti* strings playing the bitonal chords (Example 2) are sharply contrasted by the irregular accents by the atonal brass cluster and timpani.

The musicologist Glenn Watkins has summarised Stravinsky's "Russian style" as one where the "bitonal clashes and the cellular rhythmic structures … prosper alongside a folk melos" (1988: 216) and this characterisation is equally applicable to Ifukube's work. Ifukube's debt to and enthusiasm for Stravinsky arose in his adolescence:

> *I got an electric shock when I listened to* The Rite of Spring *and* Petrushka [in his high school period]. *Instinctively I felt that Stravinsky's musical vision was not European but close to ours. My afterthought was that this was because of the aesthetic sympathy coming from the* [shared] *blood … Before then, I performed and studied European music and found it very interesting but it was still not mine but someone else's. Stravinsky appealed to me directly. I felt sympathy because I already had it. Rather than receiving inspiration from him, I found him doing what I wanted. Stravinsky let me know an alternative form of European music. He encouraged me to think of writing music.* (quoted in Sagara 1992: 154f – my translation)[16]

His encounter with Stravinsky and the shock of identification he felt for Russia were so deep that he wrote the title of original score of *Godzilla* in Russian letters (reproduced in Tanaka 1983:481). The above quote shows his clear sense of affinity for Russian music. He justifies this by a bluntly racialised – and dubious – theory, namely that Russians, raped and ruled by the Mongolians from the 13th to the 16th Century, were infused by Asian genes. Since the Mongolians are often considered as the racial origin of Japanese, Ifukube considered that Japanese and Russians are biologically related via the Mongolian connection. He even finds a Mongolian sensibility underlying *The Rite of Spring*. In his understanding, Russians are the miscegeneous offspring of Occidental and Oriental races, so their aesthetic is located virtually in the middle of western/European and Japanese aesthetics.

Russians were, as is well known, often depicted as Oriental in Germany, France and Italy, the axes of 19th Century music (and Russian artists, in turn, exploited this view to gain a cultural status in Paris). Ifukube looked at the periphery of Europe from the other side of the Eurasian continent. An Oriental 'other' for Parisians was an Oriental self for him. He inverts western Orientalism to produce an eastern self-Orientalism. His fondness for de Falla can be accounted for in a similar way (ie Spain was invaded by the Arab empire and consequently Spanish have Asian blood and sensibilities). What is at stake is not the geographical distance from Japan but the epistemological distance from metropolis, the peripheral position in the musical empire of Europe. He calls the periphery of Europe "Eurasian" rather than "European"[17] and expresses his self "projected onto a people remote in time, place or character" (Lemke, 1998: 29)[18]. In 1942, however, when he premiered *Sinfonia Concertante per pianoforte ed orchestra*, a German-oriented music critic harshly caricatured it as follows:

> *his face is Stravinsky, his hands Falla, his legs Rimsky-Korsakov, his body Ravel. And he is marching with the Buddhist taiko drums.* (quoted in Kibe, 1997: 330).

If one conceives music according to (preconceived) national elements, Ifukube's style sounds like a pastiche of these different composers. But from his "Eurasian" aesthetic viewpoint, they are compatible with Japaneseness, a quality that all the composers were then searching for in one way or other.

Allegro Marciale

The popularity of the title music analysed above may in part derive from the harmonic simplicity that counterbalances its rhythmic complexity (one of the distinctive traits of Ifukube's film music). He prefers basic major and minor chords to, for example, the thick harmonisation of classical Hollywood score or the Debussy-like subtlety of Tôru Takemitsu. This characteristic can be best perceived in *Allegro Marciale*, which accompanies the frigates in *Godzilla* (M11, M21). It has been repeatedly used to accompany and enhance the march of positive forces (ie good monsters and/or armies) in about ten other Tôhô *kaijû* films and has become a musical symbol for the genre. This melody, also nicknamed the 'Monsters March' or 'Self-Defense Force March' by filmgoers, originated from *Heishi no Jogaku*, a brass band piece probably commissioned by the Imperial Armies in 1943. *Heishi no Jogaku* was reportedly used in the welcome ceremony for the arrival of

Example 3.

General Douglas McArthur at Atsugi Airport on 30 August 1945. Again, we find the relationship to war underlying *Godzilla*[19].

The popularity of *Marciale* may result from the simple but powerful melody that consists of a sequential progression (Example 3). Though the principal part is harmonised by the C major tonic, the whole motif lacks in functional harmony. *Marciale* uses the duple time and sounds essentially cheerful but it does not evoke the patriotic excitement typical of pre-War Japanese marches. To avoid the militaristic formula, Ifukube uses irregular meter at the each end of strophe, the alternation of major and minor keys and the use of strings and wind instruments beside the brass ensemble. He did not intend to compose a straightforward military march but a "march for ears" (Kobayashi, 1998: 212–3), or a concert piece. It was a personal resistance to military oppression.

The Folkloric

Godzilla includes a sequence in which the Odoshima Islanders perform a masked dance to music in order to calm the spirit of a supernatural being (M6). Although the scene only lasts one minute, it anchors the folk-mythical subtext of the monster that has been downplayed in the sequels. The sense of awe and reverence (as opposed to horror and terror) that is specific to this original characterisation of Godzilla stems, in part, from his linkage with folk legend. *Godzilla*'s ritual scene, from a narrative point of view, resembles the *Aboriginal Sacrifice Dance* scene in *King Kong* (1933). While *Godzilla* depicts Japanese reporters believing that the Odoshima ritual is absurd in the age of science, the US entrepreneur and his crew in *King Kong* regard the 'savage' dance as attractive for their exotic film and consider the monster worthy of exhibiting. Godzilla, as it were, punishes impiety, reminds the Tokyo citizen of the fear of war, and dies quietly at home. By contrast, King Kong falls into the human (American) trap and military technology. Despite the tenderness he exhibits towards his blonde female captive, he is a total enemy of New York citizenry, whose fate is to be killed far from home, falling piteously from that symbol of western civilisation, the Empire State Building. The victory of human over nature, the civilised over the primitive, is obvious. In *King Kong*, Max Steiner adopted those musical motifs of 19th Century exoticism (popular in the silent era) that became associated with the portrayal of 'Red Indians' in classic Westerns (Brown, 1994: 41; Gorbman,

Example 4.

2000). The Skull Islanders and their totem are depicted as cultural objects Americans can film, collect, display in public, and destroy. There is scarcely a moment to be sympathetic with the homeless, wounded and finally, dead gorilla.

Godzilla has a different aspect. The Odoshima ritual, although regarded as nonsense by the reporters from Tokyo, signifies 'our' ancestral legacy to a Japanese audience. Instead of arranging or using authentic *kagura* (Shintoist [Japanese vernacular religion] music), Ifukube recycles a motif from the second movement (subtitled 'Matsuri' or 'Folk Festival') of *Japanese Rhapsody*. The phrase consists in the simple repetition of two different motifs in a whole-tone scale (si-re-mi-fa♯) – the first is oriented to a folk tetrachord while the second has a *kagura* tone structure – so that the Japanese audience can sense familiarity or even nostalgia (Example 4). This is the only track with immediate reference to Japanese folk music. This diegetic music is played by the piccolo in the guise of a *shinobue* (folk flute) and harmonised by the oboes emulating a *hichiriki* (a double-reed instrument). The percussion plays a fixed pattern and the harp imitates the sound of an ancient string instrument, generating an archaic atmosphere.

In contrast to those Hollywood monsters expelled from human society as a "complete Other" (Noriega, ibid: 59), the original Godzilla is, for many Japanese viewers, an internal alien, a reminder of the far and near past of 'our' history. He is figuratively a noble savage, a compound trope of irrational barbarianism and sublime innocence, violence and vitality, the pristine and the pure, the pagan and the passionate.

The Voluminous

Ifukube believes that scoring monster films is worth doing because the plot is simple enough to maintain the autonomy of music (quoted in Tanaka, 1983: 65). In other words, music can lead the image and express itself without depending too much on the narrative. He expects that the audience can clearly understand the relationship the music has with characters and story. The music magnifies the unbeatable vital force and massive volume of Godzilla more with the low register and 'heavy' timbre than with the physical tone volume (*fortissimo*). In many cultures, slow tempo is synaesthesically associated with the grave, the solemn, and the heavy. The raid music, portraying the slow stomping of the monster, is understandably much slower than *Allegro Marciale* and the title music[20].

Sound perception depends not only on loudness but also on register, tempo, and timbre, as Ifukube examines in his textbook on orchestration (1953:

Example 5.

10ff). The film's raid music is illustrative of this theory. The theme of the first landing (M14) has an introduction of half-tone descendent motif performed by a double bass. Its extremely low range gives an ominous effect. With Godzilla invading the city, the music goes to the second part, an ascendant figure (Example 5). To represent the volume and weight of the monster, it features brass instruments and emphasises the bass sound (trombones, tubas). A piano tone cluster amplifies the shock effect[21]. In a subsequent scene, the monster is accompanied by a dodecaphonic motif with many semitone intervals (*Adagio grottesco* – Example 6). While Ifukube rejects Schönbergian technique in his concert music he uses it to represent the otherworldly creature (and this motif is so evocative that has been reused in several sequels and *Symphonic Fantasias No.1* and *No. 2*). To amplify the emotive quality, this angular motif is performed by the brass section and timpani in unison.

Example 6.

Music for Godzilla's withdrawal (MC) is characterised by a counterpoint of two voices, one in 4/4 (bass), the other in 7/4 (melody) (Example 7). Both are structured by semitones, diminished fourth and augmented fifth and their combination suggests a fugue. The cell of bass voices consists in two open fifths with a semitone difference (II-V, VIII-IV) and evokes both anxiety and stability, a mixed emotion fitting for the scene. This emotion is reinforced by the slow tempo, the bassoons (no brass instruments), and the descendent

Example 7.

55

figure, in contrast to the ascendant one used in the music for Godzilla's slow walk (MA'). In this way the overwhelming, unhurried and heavy presence of Godzilla in Tokyo is choreographed with a variety of vibrant low range and variegated sounds.

Requiem for Godzilla

While the raid music underlines the aggressive aspect of *Godzilla*, the music for the ruins and hospital (M17) evokes a state of stupor and sadness by means of extremely slow tempo, strings-centered instrumentation and the modest melody based on the simple alteration of C minor and B♭ major (with additional move to E♭ major). This harmonic simplicity makes the piece lucid. The principal melodic tones are put on the third of these three chords (E♭ to C minor, D to B♭ major, G to E♭ major) and move almost in a parallel way. Such a simple – almost artless – structure effectively conjures up sorrow. The contrast to the dynamic raid music is almost too obvious. Much as the images predictably draw on footage of Hiroshima and Nagasaki, the music comes from Hideo Sekikawa's *Hiroshima* (1953), one of the most realistic and straightforward anti-nuclear films, famous for its lengthy reproduction of the inferno by the citizens of Hiroshima themselves.

Interestingly, the same score (which is sometimes referred to as a 'requiem') is repeated in the scene of Godzilla's last moment (M22). It begins when Ogata and Serizawa start descending under the sea to search for Godzilla. It looks like the mythical descent to 'another world'. The scene has no dialogue and its audio track comprises bubbling sound effects and solemn music. The music subtly associates Godzilla's atrocity on land with his being victim of human aggression to marine ecology. This double aspect is crucial to the story and the music functions as a hinge to connect one with the other.

When the oxygen destroyer starts operating, the music changes key. When he is awakened and doomed to decomposition, the piano plays Spanish-like tonic chords in fortissimo (E major– F major) to dramatise the monster's final agonies. Its last chord (E major) is a strong expression, dedicated to the sublime death of the transcendental creature. Such a sublime moment is unusual and hard to find elsewhere in the monster film genre. What follows it is a mournful choir. Again, this music is used twice to aurally illustrate the double face – the violence and vulnerability – of Godzilla. The music first appears in the scene in which Serizawa, Emiko and Ogata quarrel over the use of the oxygen destroyer. The music emanates from a TV that is screening a special, nationwide program grieving the victims of Godzilla's raid. Accompanied by images of ruins, victims and a schoolgirls' 'celestial' choir, the grave male narration reads the lyrics: "Oh peace, oh light!/Ye shall return/We pray for you from the heart/Ye shall return for the sake of our pitiful song" (lyrics by Shigeru Kayama, the original story writer of *Godzilla*)[22]. Seriwaza is so profoundly touched that he makes up his mind to use his invention (for once in his life). Emiko realises that Serizawa's stiff egotism will be dismantled by the power of the choir[23]. The program's music resolves his ethical conflicts, sentimental crisis and regret as a scientist. The extremely slow tempo and a melodic line that moves within a narrow range without characteristic phrases makes the piece seem static (and almost monotonous to some ears). The melody is based on E Phrygian and has rudimentary harmonisation (all the long tones – the end of the phrases – fall on the tonic, third or fifth of the chords). The requiem lacks the teleological structure characteristic to western (and Hollywood) classical music.

By repeating the sombre piece, the film clearly associates the human victims with the monster that attacked them. Godzilla is as much a victim of the nuclear experiment as an aggressive entity. The reprise may refer to the inseparability of the doomed couple of Serizawa and Godzilla. Since the scientist was injured (implicitly during the War), he has become misanthropic and has given up hope of marrying Emiko. The war damaged his face to the extent that he lost his faith in his future spouse as well as in human beings in general. It is as if he has committed a sort of double suicide with the other ill-fated victim of the nuclear 'experiment'. If Godzilla is Moby Dick, with respect for the sublime and transcendent, the destructive and gigantic, then the one-eyed Serizawa obviously incarnates the one-legged Ahab. In the same way as the white whale and the captain are tied, Serizawa and Godzilla are bound to each other and make a fatal couple. If the nuclear experiment is an extension of the Pacific War, the scientist and the reptile are stigmatised by the common cause. After his last roar, we only see his skeleton in deep water. Godzilla dies solemnly. Unlike the battle-oriented sequels, the death of Godzilla here does not automatically mean the triumph of human being and the end of tragedy. There is no happy ending (ie 'the evil is gone'). Such an ambiguous ending makes *Godzilla* unique in the series and the monster genre at large. Ifukube's score is principally responsible for this empathetic characterisation of the monster and the psychological complexity of Serizawa.

Conclusion

This chapter has addressed Ifukube's sound design of *Godzilla* and has demonstrated the manner in which he was responsible for the sound effects in addition to the music. In the process of producing the soundtrack, he extended his primitivist techniques and ideas through tape recording technology. This attitude was paralleled by the characterisation of Godzilla, an archaic creature awakened by the latest science.

Film composers and, indeed, film music scholars, have tended to be preoccupied with musical unity. In *Godzilla*'s case, a limited number of themes (title music, shipwrecking-storming, the *Allegro Marciale*, Odoshima theme, oxygen destroyer passage, requiem) are repeated twice to make the storyline clearer. They are not leitmotifs in the strict sense but contribute to create a consistent mood throughout the film. Another technique that ensures unity is the general use of Phrygian mode, Ifukube's favoured mode for articulating a "Eurasian" primitivism drawing on Russian music and his imagination of Ainu identity.

As the original *Godzilla* film has been serialised, the focus has shifted from atomic force and primitivism to spectacular battles, ultra-powerful beams, and the destruction of miniature sets, special effects and extravagant creatures. Probably the group of the primitivist Godzilla films closed with *Godzilla v Destroyer* (1995), Ifukube's last film score. The change is audible especially when we hear the tonal, John Williams-like, music by Kôichi Sugiyama (*Godzilla v Biollante*, 1989) and Takayuki Hattori (*Godzilla v Space Godzilla*, 1994) – music that sounds closer to David Arnold's score for TriStar's US-remake of *Godzilla* (1998) than Ifukube's. To my ears, at least, the tonal scoring lacks the voluminous and the sublime connotations the original *Godzilla* conveyed. The tonally depicted monsters, no matter how they may be ultra-magnified and infuriated, look and sound like beasts tamed by Hollywood's language.

Thanks for the valuable suggestions and generosity of Mark Abe-Nornes, Yohani Kibe, Jun Kouda, Akira Mizuta-Lippit and Kôji Ueno.

Notes

1. The gender of Godzilla is unspecified. I treat Godzilla as male following the tacit agreement of many previous publications.

2. It is notable that reference to Godzilla overshadowed Tanaka's work with Akira Kurosawa in this obituary.

3. A curious remark is found in the sleevenotes for the CD of brass band arrangements of *Godzilla* music: "the use of these effects [included in this CD] in the concert hall will produce a dynamic performance as if the audience was viewing the film *Godzilla*" (VICG-60200).

4. On the production process, see Inoue (1994) and Takeuchi and Yamamoto (2001).

5. Prewar 'nationalist' composers became considered passé in the 1950s and 1960s when successive waves of avant-gardism – including dodecaphonism, serialism, electronica, aleatory, graphic score, minimalism and others – entered from abroad. It was not until 1977 that Ifukube was 'revived', when an album-length LP anthology of his film music was released (despite his initial unwillingness to make his film music available separate from the image). The 'discovery' of monster film music was more or less synchronous with the emergence of a monster film fan community in Japan. Several sequels, the postwar premieres of his old works and the commission of new works followed the first LP. The Ifukube revival, I believe, coincided on one hand with the return of tonal/modal music and national/ethnic elements in concert hall ('New tonality') and on the other with the blurring of boundaries between concert music and popular music. As Philip Hayward's Introduction to this volume notes, 1977 also marks the year zero of *Star Wars*, a milestone for the return to Korngold-like classicism in Hollywood.

6. The melodic variations are used in the scenes in which a yet-unknown power overwhelms human life (Eikômaru's shipwreck and storm at the Odoshima). In these scenes (M3 and M7) we sense something menacing before we recognise the monster. Since the four-note motif is thus strongly connected with the transcendental power of Godzilla, it is hard to agree with Ifukube's words that the title music does not represent Godzilla but the human power to face him. (See footnote 14 for specifications of track referencing.)

7. The relative absence of the 'classical score' in Japanese film history – an issue concerning

not only the talent of composers but also the dominant genres, production budget, advertising strategies, expectation of audiences (and others) – merits discussion elsewhere.

8. Such as those that have addressed the 'art' paradigm, acknowledging aspects such as the dichotomy between art and commerce, and the person v name debate (see Yoshimoto, 2000: 54–8).

9. An important subtext of *Godzilla* is that the composer himself fell sick in August 1945, probably because of radioactivity he had been exposed to during forestry experiments. (He had obtained a degree in forestry science in 1935 and worked for the Imperial Wartime Scientific Research Centre in the 1940s.) In 1942, his elder brother, an engineer and amateur guitarist, died, presumably from a similar cause.

10. Ichirô Minawa (1918–) studied western singing at the Tôyô Music School and worked in wireless communication during his military service. In 1942 he joined in the Sound Effects Section of Tôhô after brief experience as sound assistant with a performing troupe that his elder sister worked with. He restarted his postwar career with Kurosawa's *No Regrets for Our Youth* (1946). His name is credited in major works from Tôhô Studios in the occupation period such as *Drunken Angel* (Kurosawa, 1948). Before *Godzilla*, Minawa was already known for his expertise in creating sound tracks.

11. It is also known that the loosened strings of double bass were pulled with a resin-coated leather glove (Akiyama 1974: 331).

12. Both Ishirô Honda and Eiji Tsuburaya (the special effects director) started their career with Tôhô during the wartime (Takeuchi, 2000; Takeuchi and Yamamoto, 2001). For them, *Godzilla* was a clear war allegory, looked back on after the occupation.

13. Timothy Taylor's analysis of the primitive undertones of musique concrète (2001:55–60) offers an intriguing hint to grasp *Godzilla*'s sound effects in the wider context of sound technology. On the magnetic recording system in the US, see Belton (1992).

14. The designations M1, M2, MA, MB etc. indicate the track numbers of the original tape – as released on *Godzilla, Rodan* (TYCY-10047).

15. All the music examples are transcribed from the above-mentioned CD by the author.

16. Also see also Ifukube's obituary to Stravinsky (1971).

17. Ifukube's "Eurasianism" was probably stimulated by his mentor, Alexandr Tcherepnin, a Russian composer (1899–1977) who visited Japan in 1934, 1935 and 1936 for substantial periods. Ifukube's *Japanese Rhapsody* won the Tcherepnin Prize, a prize he founded to promote East Asian composers in Europe. James Lincoln Collier's entry in *The New Grove Dictionary of Music and Musicians* remarks that Tcherepnin "considered himself a 'Eurasian' composer. Conciseness, contrapuntal textures and strongly articulate structures are typical of his works" (2001: 186). Ifukube's affinity with Russian music can be also explained by the cultural milieu of Sapporo, Hokkaido's capital, where he spent his school and college years and met many Russian (Jewish) émigrés after 1918.

18. On the concept of projection and belonging, see Middleton (2000: 62).

19. In July 1954, Japan's Self-Defense Force (*jieitai*) was established as a result of reformation and reinforcement of military force after the end of occupation (1952) and the Korean War (1950–53). It meant military 'independence' from the US but opposing parties insisted that the force violated the postwar Constitution that stipulated the non-possession of military forces. The very first title of *Godzilla* reads (in English translation) "Acknowledgments to the Maritime Safety Agency". *Godzilla* is indeed the first film the newly sanctioned Force collaborated with, as is shown in the sequence of (real) frigates at sea. One wonders whether the depiction of "Defense Force" (*bôeitai*) in *Godzilla* (curiously, the prefix of "self-" is elliptic in order to fictionalise the military forces) is positive (brave and powerful) or negative (impotent).

20. See Hollywood's galloping Godzilla for a different approach.

21.   Ifukube's percussive use of piano (tone cluster by elbow, four-octave unisons in mechanical beat, for example) became prominent in his *Sinfonia Concertante per pianoforte ed orchestra* (1941). In *Godzilla*, tone clusters and string strumming are used in the tracks for Eikômaru's shipwrecking and accompanying the oxygen destroyer. Both suggest the worst outcome. The motif of the oxygen destroyer is especially intense. The jarring sound of the violins (trills using the part below bridge) is followed by the piano tone cluster. It is only with the second appearance of the oxygen destroyer that we witness its horrible power. Accompanying the image of discomposed fish and the three characters in conflict, the cello plays a solemn (almost funeral) melody in Phrygian mode on the pedal point of F performed by piano.

22.   Ifukube reused this melody for *Biruma no Tategoto* ['The Burmese Lute'], directed by Kon Ichikawa, 1956, a story of a Japanese soldier converting to a Buddhist monk who makes a pilgrimage to his last battlefield in order to pray for his dead companions. The narrative resemblance is obvious. Saburô Kawamoto regards Godzilla as a phantom of Japanese soldiers killed in the Pacific (1994:85).

23.   A passing yet important scene that drops a hint as to Serizawa's final conversion through music is that of the first appearance of Serizawa in film, where he is visited by Emiko while listening to Haydn-like piece for string quartet on radio. Ogata, in turn, is forced to cancel his date with Emiko to attend the concert of Budapest String Quartet (which actually performed concerts in Tokyo in February 1954) because he receives an emergency mission to investigate the mysterious shipwreck. The trio is, I presume, bonded both by science and classical music.

Chapter Three

FORBIDDEN PLANET
Effects and Affects in the
Electro Avant-garde

REBECCA LEYDON

The electronic music soundtrack for the 1956 film *Forbidden Planet* represents an important milestone both in film-music practice and in the field of electronic music. *Forbidden Planet* is regarded as the first feature-length film to employ electronic scoring throughout; moreover, the music was produced in one of the very first studios to combine electronic sound generation with the technologies of magnetic tape. At a time when electro-acoustic music and *musique concrète* were the esoterica of ivory-tower pursuits, *Forbidden Planet* disseminated a new sound palette to a popular audience. It thus played an important role in anchoring the signifying relationships between a new category of musical sounds and their narrative connotations.

This chapter explores the circumstances that led to the creation of the *Forbidden Planet* soundtrack and some of the features of the music itself. To begin, I stress the essential weirdness of electronic music within the context of Hollywood film-scoring norms, and I highlight the peculiar status of these now-antiquated sounds today. I then consider a rationale for why electronic sound in general emerged as an index for both Outer Space and intra-psychic space. In the second part of the chapter, I focus more specifically on *Forbidden Planet* and on its soundtrack. I describe how the pioneering work of the composers Bebe and Louis Barron coincided with a period of international experimentation in electronic music that led to the founding of electro-acoustic studios throughout North America, Europe, and Japan. I then discuss how the Barrons' approach differed in fundamental ways from that of the 'classic studio' movement. Referring to specific segments of the soundtrack (CD track numbers are provided for the 1989 GNP Crescendo release), I illustrate how the Barrons' idiosyncratic compositional methods play out in the musical and narrative details of the film.

Electronic Tonalities

Forbidden Planet represents a radical departure from the 'classical Hollywood score', a genre steeped in the late 19th-century Teutonic sensibility. Since the 1930s, this compositional model had been strenuously maintained by the Hollywood studio system, especially in the hands of Franz Waxman, Max Steiner, Erich Korngold, and Dmitri Tiomkin[1]. Against the conventions of orchestral scoring and Wagnerian chromaticism, *Forbidden Planet* fabricates a non-tempered pitch universe and a set of bizarre timbres, replacing the classic Hollywood score's associative use of key-centers and themes with an idiosyncratic leitmotif technique based on the behaviour and 'life cycle' of sound-generating circuits. Pre-dating the development of transistors and integrated circuits, the Barrons homemade sound generators were constructed using vacuum-tube oscillators – similar to those used in the theremin and ondes martenot, but with elaborate feedback paths incorporated into their design. Photos of the Barrons' studio show masses of wires and parts and potentiometer knobs chaotically assembled on wooden boards[2]. Louis Barron, a self-taught electrical engineer, designed many of these components himself. The sounds emitted by these complex circuits were recorded on magnetic tape and subsequently subjected to a variety of studio techniques – changes of tape speed and direction, tape echo and reverb, montage, and other types of analog processing. The assortment of strange and wonderful sounds that we hear in *Forbidden Planet* is the result of these arduous experimental methods.

For all its novelty, however, the Barrons' soundtrack failed to establish any sort of trend or 'school' of film-music practice. The promise that the electronic sound-world of the 1950s represented was only partially realised much later in scores like Giorgio Moroder's for *Midnight Express* (1978) and Vangelis Papathanassiou's *Chariots Of Fire* (1981). In these scores their exclusive reliance on keyboard synthesisers precluded anything like the kind of microtonal pitch-space that unfolds in *Forbidden Planet*. Today, the film's music seems dazzlingly inventive and at the same time pervaded by an archaic monaural melancholy. It speaks of obsolete music-making skills.

Part of the fascination of this music has to do with the sheer labour involved in the hit-and-miss experimentation and the painstaking work of recording and splicing that was required to obtain these results in the mid-1950s. On one hand, the sound generating techniques that created this music are at a primitive enough level that most listeners today can at least comprehend how the effects were produced: manipulation of tape speed and direction, for example, are easily grasped concepts, and the sound-generators themselves were constructed of quotidian materials. On the other hand, practical knowledge of this kind of music-making has almost entirely vanished, as a result of the efficiency of digital audio. The Barrons' music became largely non-reproducible within the sound-worlds of keyboard-driven synthesisers that emerged in the ensuing decades. In fact, much of the music could not have been duplicated even within the contemporaneous 'classic studios' that were created in the 1950s through the institutional support of universities and radio stations. Pursuing a very different sound ideal in their self-built workshop, the Barrons developed a unique vision of the music of the future, which quickly became part of Hollywood's past.

Sounds and Symbols

In retrospect, the pairing of the film's futuristic images with electronic music seems entirely suitable but amid the dominant musical practices of Hollywood in the 1950s, the Barrons' music is singularly anomalous. Why did such experimental music strike MGM producers as appropriate for this picture? The reason has to do with electronic sound's indexical relationship to intangible spaces, both cosmic and psychological.

The relationship of sound to cinematic image speaks to broader issues of music's signifying potential and raises questions about how specific signifying relationships arise in the first place. Some recent approaches to musical semiotics have considered sound-perception in terms of vicarious sound-projection: sounds that signify – sounds that are worth attending to – are sounds that listeners can imagine making themselves. Arnie Cox's "mimetic hypothesis" (2001) for instance, posits that the foundation for all processes of musical signification is unconscious imitation of observed action. Cox asserts that, "(1) we understand sounds in comparison to sounds we have made ourselves, and that (2) this process of comparison involves tacit imitation, or mimetic participation, which in turn draws upon the prior embodied experience of sound production" (ibid: 195). Naomi Cumming's "musical subject" (1997) involves an analogous model of the signifying process: musical sounds act as "affordances" for emotionality and intentionality in listeners who identify with particular attributes of timbre, gesture, and syntax. For both Cumming and Cox, sounds function as evidence of particular actions that produced them, and are apprehended as "meaningful" when there is a readily imagined sound source. A similar approach is Denis Smalley's "spectromorphological referral process" (1997) where perceived sounds are related back through a series of cognitive levels, from imagined sources to inferred gestures and motor activity to remembered proprioception and psychological states. Electronic music, Smalley emphasises, represents a special case of this "referral process", because the sources of electronic sounds are necessarily concealed, remote, detached. Envisioning a cause for such sounds induces what Smalley terms "gestural surrogacy," an additional step in the deduction process that links a sound with a meaning (ibid). For listeners, then, electronic sounds represent a distinct challenge. This seems particularly true of the sounds generated by the electro-acoustic technologies of the 1950s, which, from an embodied perspective at least, are exceptionally strange and seldom 'life-like' in any tangible way. Such sounds do not suggest readily attributable sources, yet they are salient precisely because of their enigmatic status.

Accordingly, the earliest couplings of electronic sounds and cinematic images consistently involved the uncanny and the alien. When electronic sound resources first begin to appear in movie scores, the initial audio-visual linkages have to do with representations of aberrant states and objects. Miklos Rozsa's score for *The Lost Weekend* (1945), for example, employs a theremin is to signify the psychological torment of an alcoholic[3]. In *Laura* (1944), David Raksin's 'len-a-toned' piano chords, in which the initial attack is cut off and the decaying after-sound subjected to a variable-speed loop, anticipate the hallucinatory moment of the title character's first appearance on the screen[4]. Bernard Herrmann employs the recorded sound of vibrating telegraph lines to represent Mr. Scratch's violin in *The Devil and Daniel Webster* (1941), and his score for *The Day the Earth stood still* (1951) incorporates an array of electronic instruments to characterise the extra-terrestrial Gort[5]. These examples illustrate how electronically generated and processed sounds initially played a role comparable to the use of atonality within the tonal norms of the classical Hollywood score. As Philip Brophy notes:

> In short, atonality in the film score signifies the Other: the monstrous, the grotesque, the aberrant. Its deviation from diatonic scripture is never slight, always excessive. Like the ultimate death which must befall the movie monster, the presence of atonality must be hysterically marked as transgressive and unforgiving. Far from being emancipated, dissonance is condemned; ritualistically sacrificed at the grand altar of tonal resolve as "The End" uncannily appears on the screen like an epitaph for the avant garde. (1998 [2002]: np)

Like dodecaphony, electronic timbres emerged as a monolithic class of sound objects anchored to images of the aberrant[6]. Later, as electronic sound media became more widespread, as listeners correspondingly developed a greater 'spectro-morphological competence', certain electro-acoustic elements could be mapped on to more finely differentiated visual and narrative associations, as in Jerry Goldsmith's moog-inflected score for *The Illustrated Man* (1969) or in the 'retro' applications of the moog and theremin in recent years. But the sounds of the earliest electronic studios of the 1950s were doomed to a semiotic limbo of sorts. Unlike the sonic palette constituted by the keyboard-driven synthesisers of the 1960s and 1970s, the sounds of the first electronic music studios were never fully absorbed into a mainstream sonic language. They remain enigmatic and their sources remain mysterious. Paradoxically, these discarded, residual sonic signifiers seem even more appropriate today for a story that deals with the theme of intangible spaces, both extraterrestrial and psychological.

MGM's Pet Project

As *Forbidden Planet* begins, Commander J.J. Adams (Leslie Nielsen) is leading a rescue mission to a distant planet, Altair IV, where Doctor Morbius (Walter Pidgeon) and his daughter Alta (Anne Francis) are the sole survivors of a colonising expedition that began twenty years before. The space cruiser lands on the desert-like planet, despite Morbius' warning to turn back and avoid the mysterious fate that befell the original colonists. The crew is greeted by Robby, the robot constructed by Morbius during his years of solitude on Altair. The crew is taken to Morbius's home, a sort of Malibu Beach dream house, flanked by gardens and wildlife. Before long, a romance develops between Commander Adams and Alta, who has never seen a human male other than her father. Meanwhile an invisible monster begins to menace the crew, leaving a trail of enormous footprints behind after each gruesome attack. The reluctant Morbius introduces the crew to his discoveries of an advanced technology, created by the former inhabitants of Altair IV, the Krel, who apparently vanished thousands of years earlier. Morbius's careful study of the ancient Krel documents has empowered him with the knowledge to create Robby the robot as well as the amazing house in which he and Alta live. It is gradually revealed that the Krel technology had at some point advanced to a stage where matter could be created from thought alone – "a world without instrumentalities". This seems to have had something to do with the energy harnessed by a massive underground power grid, which Morbius shows the others. It turns out that Morbius, as a result of his tinkering with some Krel mind-expanding technology, has unwittingly generated the monster with his own mind: it is a product of his subconscious, a projection of Morbius's repressed incestuous love for Alta and his aggression toward her suitors, as well as his desire to protect his claim to the discoveries of the Krel civilisation. Apparently, the Krel's failure to foresee their own 'monsters from the Id' is what led to the destruction of their civilisation long ago. At the climax of the story, Adams' pleads with Morbius that "we're all part monster in our subconscious – and so we have laws and religion!" Morbius thus comes to the realisation that he is 'guilty', and that the monster is an incarnation of his own evil self. The crew escape, Alta and Robbie in tow; poor Morbius is left behind and the planet self-destructs[7].

Forbidden Planet's unusual screenplay was meant to stand out amidst the era's more typical Sci-Fi 'dreck'. Cyril Hume's adaptation of a story by Irving Block and Allen Adler draws upon elements of Shakespeare's *The Tempest*, with Prospero and Miranda re-imagined as the futuristic philologist Morbius and his innocent daughter Alta, and Prospero's books transformed into the Krel brain enhancer. Readers of classic science fiction would appreciate references to Isaac Asimov's 'laws of robotics', and to Robert Louis Stevenson's 'Dr. Jekyll and Mr. Hyde'. Many of the story's hi-brow themes would appeal to sophisticated movie-goers, including notions of the measurability of intelligence and, above all, Freudian theories of the unconscious[8]. The plot calls for a range of special effects, not only for the representations of space travel, an extra-solar planet, the robot, and the remains of an advanced alien civilisation, but also for the monstrous phantasmagoria generated by the mind of Morbius. The special-effects team, which included a Disney animator, produced some truly impressive results. For the first time, the special effects of a science-fiction film were on par with those of big-budget fantasy pictures, musicals, and even Bible flicks[9].

Today *Forbidden Planet* is often celebrated as vintage camp, a classic B-flick, but in fact the film's production costs were as high as those of MGM's A-list pictures. The studio had originally committed to a 'below the line' project, with expenses close to $500,000. Over its fifteen months of production (December 1954 to February 1956), however, budget over-runs in set construction and special effects escalated production costs to nearly two million dollars[10]. After MGM production-chief Dore Schary paid a visit to the set-construction sites at the MGM sound stages, he began envisioning the project as a kind of prestige venture and he enthusiastically approved each new request for additional funds. A substantial chunk of the budget was devoted to sets and props – $125,000 and two months of labour for Robby the Robot alone. At one point, sets and painted backdrops occupied 98,000 square feet of space on MGM sound stages[11].

The lavish expenditure did not pay off in correspondingly high box-office receipts. Many critics, however, appreciated the film for its sumptuous visual and sonic effects as well as for its intriguing script. A *Time* magazine critic compared the film favourably with the more vapid Sci-Fi fare of the era:

> In recent years, though many a Thing has landed on the movie screen, the Space it came from has always, all too obviously been located between the scriptwriter's ears; and the science in the fiction has generally been of a sophomore sort that gives a loud wolf-whistle at the curvature of the universe. In this nifty interstellar meller, however, the gadgets are so much more glamorous than any girl could be that in many scenes the heroine is technologically unemployed. (unattributed, 1956: 112)

The film's special effects were found to be particularly impressive, and, despite some patently absurd dialogue ("the number 10 raised almost literally to the power of infinity!" quips Morbius in one scene), even the science was deemed plausible: "It makes King Kong look like an organ grinder's monkey", the *Time* critic remarks, "and will probably have the most skeptical scientist in the audience clutching wildly for his atomic pistol" (ibid). An Oscar nomination for 'Best Effects, Special Effects' corroborated the favourable critical reception.

Whether to consider the Barrons' score for the film within the category of 'special effects' was a problem confronting MGM's contract lawyer, Rudy Monte, who foresaw potential conflicts with the musicians union should the term 'electronic *music*' appear in the credits. Because the Barrons' music performs double duty as both sound effects and underscoring, there was some latitude regarding exactly how to characterise the composers' contributions. Dore Schary coined the infamous designation 'Electronic Tonalities' that appears in the opening credits, thus circumventing the musicians union's jurisdiction but also calling attention to rather odd permeability of the various sonic functions in the film.

Bebe and Louis Barron had initially sought out Dore Schary at an art gallery reception in Manhattan. Eager for a paying gig, they introduced themselves and attempted to interest Schary in their work. Fortuitously, Schary engaged their services after hearing some of the music the Barrons had produced for Ian Hugo's *The Bells of Atlantis* (1952). He even offered to relocate the couple's studio from New York to Los Angeles. The Barrons persuaded Schary to allow them to work on the project in New York and, in unusual departure from studio policy, the Barrons were provided with their own 16mm work-print and scratch mix. *Forbidden Planet* was the first MGM film score to be produced off the studio lot. The contract promised a minimum fee of $5000, with additional earnings to be determined by the number of screen-minutes of music. The project eventually netted the composers $25,000 – a significant windfall for the insolvent couple.

Greenwich Village v the 'Classic' Studio

The impracticability of transporting the Barrons' gear across the country is evident from the extant photographs of their 8th Street studio, which had been fully operational since 1948, shortly after their marriage in 1947. Their studio, together with Raymond Scott's Manhattan Research, Inc. in nearby Farmingdale, New York (established in 1946) are in all likelihood the first places anywhere where electronically generated sounds were combined with the sound-manipulation capabilities of magnetic tape. The Barrons' first substantial composition, *Heavenly Menagerie* (1951), thus antedates by several months the founding of the Studio für electronische Musik at the Nordwestdeutscher Rundfunk in Köln (October, 1951), an event usually considered foundational in histories of electronic music.

The Köln composers – Stockhausen and Herbert Eimert among them – had allied themselves with the new principles of integral serialism, recently introduced by Pierre Boulez and his circle. Consequently the types of sound equipment they developed tended to reflect their preoccupations with maintaining control over as many musical parameters as possible. Ollie Powers has noted among the Köln composers "a kind of ideological identification with the purity of the sine wave", an ideology that ultimately determined the kinds of equipment deemed essential to a well-stocked studio: sine-wave oscillators, wave-shaping circuits, a white-noise generator for subtractive synthesis (1997: 132). Oscillators that produced very stable pure sine waves were highly prized, and additive synthesis emerged as the predominant model of the compositional process. Subsuming timbre into the serialised design of a composition became a chief concern for the Köln group, as Stockhausen's *Gesang der Junglinge* (1955–6) illustrates. Köln's techniques and gear served as a template for institutionally supported studios that sprang up under the auspices of state radio stations and universities around the world, including the Columbia-Princeton Electronic Music Center, the *Groupe de Recherches Musicales* in France, the *Studio di Fonologia Musicale* in Milan, the University of Toronto Studio, NHK in Tokyo, NRU Studio in the Netherlands and many others. Specific types of components were common to all of these studios and the components themselves became relatively standardised.

In contrast to their institutionally sponsored counterparts, the Barrons' idiosyncratic approach eschewed entirely the predictable results afforded by stable-tone signal generators. That the pure sine wave was somewhat foreign to the Barrons' sound ideal is emphasised in a 1997 interview, where Bebe Barron remarks upon the difficulty of obtaining sinusoidal timbres. Recalling the film-maker's request for some "love music" in *Forbidden Planet* Bebe notes:

> *That kind of sine wave was virtually impossible at that stage of the technology. Because there were no sine wave generators, we went through absolute hell to get something that didn't sound awful, like monsters or war.* (quoted in Burnam, 1997: 260)

Instead the Barrons cultivated the kinds of complex sonic properties that emerged spontaneously from their own home-made instruments: the feed-back paths integrated into their design resulted in erratic sound patterns, as escalating feedback altered the spectro-morphology in unpredictable ways. The circuits were capricious to the extent that they would frequently self-destruct in performance: some of the circuits would perform only once, and had to be captured on tape in a single 'take'. The inexpensive tubes could be easily replaced, although preferably the equipment would survive the ordeal, and could be re-activated later. As Louis expressed in a 1986 inter-view:

> *Tubes are forgiving. The grid of a power tube may be expected to take one or two volts, let's say.If you accidentally touch it with 300 volts, it'll heat up, it'll get red in the face. Take the voltage away and it'll cool down, ready to do its normal thing. A transistor would blow in a fraction of a millisecond. And even if they don't cost much, they're a damn nuisance to keep changing... You have to be free to abuse the circuit.* (quoted in Greenwald, 1986: 60)

The Barrons' habit of deliberately burning out circuits would certainly not have been practicable in the institutionally funded studios of the period, where the cost of an individual oscillator was about $300. Constructing their own circuits from 79-cent tubes, the Barrons had the freedom to explore the limits of the equipment. "The thing would just be tortured to death. You could really hear it", Bebe says of a typical homemade circuit (quoted in Burnham, 1997: 260). For her the sounds recalled "the last paroxysms of a living creature" (quoted in Clarke and Rubin, 1979: 44).

The sadistic torturing of circuits was one of several factors that contributed to the distinctive sonic repertoire that emerged from the Barrons' studio. A singular aspect of the homemade circuits was that they provided comparatively long, drawn-out segments of sounds; tape recordings would capture the circuit's entire frenetic performance, which might result in a brief musical piece in itself. A consequence of these long-winded performances was that fewer tape-splices were involved when it came to assembling the sounds into extended musical sequences. Ollie Powers suggests that this is what imparts a strong sense of linearity to the Barrons' music, quite different from the kind of atomistic or constructivist quality heard in contemporaneous work of the institutional studios. Furthermore, as Powers points out, the Barrons' circuits were unhampered by the limited options for range-switching in standard oscillators like those used in the institutional studios. They exhibit a remarkable degree of pitch flexibility: their capacities for glissandi and microtonal intervals, again, impart a markedly melodic and fluid aspect to the sounds.

Ultimately, it is the Barrons' fundamental aesthetic stance which distinguishes their work from that of the prestigious institutional studios of the day: the couple were disinclined to work out detailed compositional plans in advance – serialist or otherwise. Rather they adopted an improvisatory approach that embraced the arbitrary results of their unique sound-generating processes. In this respect the Barrons were doubtless encouraged by their interactions with John Cage. Both Bebe Barron and Cage had been students of Henry Cowell at New York's New School for Social Research. Cage utilised the Barrons' studio and expertise for his own initial foray into tape music, *Williams Mix* (1951–2). The studio subsequently became a base for the *Project of Music for Magnetic Tape*, undertaken by Cage, along with Morton Feldman, Earle Brown, Christian Wolf, and David Tudor. Bebe and Louis served as sound engineers for the project. Bebe recalls the enthusiasm Cage imparted to the team:

> He paid our rent—it was wonderful. Working with John was incredible because he gave you the feeling that anything goes. There are no rules; you can do what you like. So we did. (quoted in Burnam, 1997: 255)

Cage's interest in chance methods and his attention to incidental noise as musical sound reinforced the Barrons' own 'noninterventionist' approach to electronics. Instead of executing previously developed compositional plans, they simply observed the behaviour of the electronic processes they had set in motion.

Circuit design itself was influenced by Louis Barron's encounters with information theory through the writings of Norbert Wiener. Bebe and Louis's claim that their circuits "function electronically in a manner remarkably similar to the way that lower life-forms function psychologically" (1989: np) was inspired by passages from Wiener's *The Human Use of Human Beings* (1950). The following, for example, must have struck a chord:

It is my thesis that the physical functioning of the living individual and the operation of some of the newer communication machines are precisely parallel in their analogous attempts to control entropy through feedback. Both of them have sensory receptors as one stage in their cycle of operation: that is, in both of them there exists a special apparatus for collecting information from the outer world at low energy levels, and for making it available in the operation of the individual or of the machine. In both cases these external messages are not taken neat, but through the internal transforming powers of the apparatus, whether it be alive or dead. The information is then turned into a new form available for the further stages of performance. In both the animal and the machine this performance is made to be effective on the outer world. In both of them, their performed action on the outer world, and not merely their intended action, is reported back to the central regulatory apparatus. (1950: 26–27)

Bebe recalls some of the practical applications that Louis found for Wiener's *Cybernetics* (1948):

Louis took some of the circuits that were in the book and adapted them for sound … We would do the craziest things. Those circuits were really alive: they would shriek and coo and have little life spans of their own. It was just amazing. They would start out and reach a kind of climax and then they would die and you could never resurrect them. (quoted in Burnam, 1997: 256)

For the composers, Wiener's cybernetics must have resonated with the Freudian themes of the film – Freud, that is, as filtered through the mechanistic drive theories of Clark Hull[12].

Listening to Monsters from the Id

The notion of the sound-generating circuit as an electronic 'organism' suggested an approach to the scoring of *Forbidden Planet* in which individual circuits might be designed to correspond to each of the characters in the film. Accordingly, the Barrons constructed a special 'monster' circuit, a 'Robby' circuit, and so on. Bebe was particularly proud of the monster circuit:

This was an amazing circuit: the sounds which came out were tinkly and bubbly – very high-pitched with lots of complex activity. I was sure that, if we slowed it down, lots of activity we weren't able to hear would come to the foreground. So we slowed it down fifty or sixty times, which was a very laborious process because the only thing we could do at that time was to record it at 15 ips and then play it back at 7. Of course you build up staggering amounts of tape noise. It was just amazing what came out of it. A whole rhythm emerged, because obviously when you slow down reverberation enough times, you get rhythm – that was the only way we had to get rhythm. (quoted in Burnam, 1997: 259)

So the initial output of the monster circuit was scrutinised and its concealed rhythmic and motific attributes were revealed under the magnifying lens of variable tape speed. The result is a multi-layered sonic texture, the most salient features of which are a regular deep-pitched boom (occurring roughly every 3 to 5 seconds), a faster-moving, more irregular knocking noise in the middle register, and a high-pitched sinewave-like whine that traces out long slow semi-tone glissandi (CD track 9). Bebe describes how the latent details of the monster-circuit's sound were made increasingly manifest as the theme recurs in the film. Finally an explicit sonic link is made between the monster music and Morbius himself:

> when Moebius [sic] dies, we used the actual dying of that circuit; you can hear it going through agonies of death and winding down. It was really sad, very pathetic. We could never get that circuit to do anything afterwards. (quoted in Burnam, 1997: 260)

While individual circuits could be used to represent characters, the story also suggested a web of interactions among the leitmotifs: the ancient Krel and their technology are reactivated through Morbius; Morbius *is* the monster; the monster is conjured up by Alta's emerging desire for Adams. None of these connections is made explicit in the narrative until near the end of the film, but hints and clues are worked into the soundtrack throughout. To begin with, the use of the same music both for effects and for underscoring creates a sense of confusion about what exactly is inside and outside the diegetic space. This blurring occurs from the very beginning of the film as the 'Overture' accompanies the opening titles: as credits appear for 'Robby the Robot', we hear the Robby-circuit's characteristic plinks and plops; in the same sequence a kind of 'mickey-mousing' effect takes place as the music's sweeping glissando gestures track the motion of the flying saucer across the screen. During the film's early scenes where the shots alternate between the exterior and the interior of the space ship, the sound edits are not consistently synched up with the visual cuts, so that it is unclear whether the strange sounds are emanating from the spaceship, from space itself, or from outside the diegetic world altogether. This permeability of the diegetic/non-diegetic sound boundary acts as a kind of metaphor for the monster/Morbius situation, where the boundary between mind and matter is similarly porous.

Later in the film, the direct link between Morbius and the monster is made musically evident when the 'monster music' ceases at the very moment that Morbius wakes up in his study (end of CD track 19) – that is, with Morbius's 'return to consciousness'. Other musical connections are more subtle. For example, several passages in the soundtrack feature a 'planing' process, in which an entire sustained sound mass is pitch-shifted up through a glissando spanning roughly six semitones. The process occurs first during the grave-yard scene (CD track 7) when Morbius shows the crew where the original colonists are buried. The same device appears in the music during the scene in which Adams and the ship's doctor are prying about in Morbius' study (CD track 12). Finally, the pitch-shift is applied to the eerie 'monster theme': its first two manifestations (CD tracks 9 and 16), are identical, whereas the next two appearances (CD tracks 17 and 19) are transposed up a tritone compared with the earlier tracks (this is most obvious in the high warbling sinewave sound which shifts from approximately Bb to E natural).

Because the Barrons allowed their circuits' sound patterns to unfold more or less spontaneously, much of their creative energy went into the manipulation of magnetic tape onto which the circuits' performances had been recorded. Bebe reports experimenting with the German tape recorder that was given to the couple as a wedding present in 1947: "the techniques were so utterly simplistic that I hate to even mention them, but we did dumb things like playing tapes backwards and slowing down the speed" (quoted in Burnam, 1997: 260). Eventually, their efforts to stretch the capabilities of the technology led them to make extensive use of tape echo. The echo is produced in the time it takes for a bit of tape to move from the record head to the playback head, using the tape itself as 'memory'. Multiple echo is produced when the output of the playback head is connected in the same circuit as the input to the recording head. The capabilities of the German Magnetophone machines were somewhat limited by the fixed tape-head positions and only two running speeds; the same is true of the first American Ampex machines (one of which can be seen in extant photos of the Barrons' studio) that were modeled on the original German product. With tape heads fixed at 2.1 inches apart, moving the tape along at the standard speed of 15 inches-per-second produced a delay of 0.14 seconds; running the tape at half speed, or 7.5 ips, lengthened the delay to 0.28 seconds, and slower multiples of these echo-rates could be obtained by re-playing and re-recording at the two available speeds. Without adjustable tape heads, the Barrons' tape-echo was thus restricted by the fixed gap between the heads, and one consequence is that the entire *Forbidden Planet* soundtrack is dominated by particular 'echo rhythms': 108 bpm, 216 bpm, and even-numbered subdivisions of these pulsation-rates characterise almost all of the music in the Barrons' score. Within these restricted parameters, however, a great variety of effects are achieved, including retrograde echoes, echoes combined at the various available speeds and layered in complex alignment patterns. These effects are most pronounced in Alta's music, the rippling 'love theme' which accompanies each of Alta's encounters with Adams (CD tracks 6, 11, 20, and 22).

The consistent echo periodicities provide a kind of continuity throughout the film, a basic fabric of rhythmic uniformity against which extraordinary rhythmic patterns seem to stand out. Ollie Powers has identified deviations from the regular echo rhythms at several points (1997: 104ff). A notable passage is the 'Ancient Krell Music' section, where a long delay of 1.7 seconds can be heard, first on the high B-G♯ descending glissando motif at the beginning of the track, and then on other glissandi throughout the segment. Powers speculates that this effect could have been generated by threading the tape between two separate recorders, so that the tape heads would lie about 26 inches apart. Certainly this portion of the soundtrack required some sort of special treatment, since it is the one moment in the narrative featuring diegetic music: the alien recording, as Morbius explains, was actually "made by Krel musicians half a million years ago". MGM's Dore Schary had at first considered hiring a different composer to provide this segment so as to create the necessary contrast with the film's underscoring: Schary's choice for this was to have been the microtonal composer and instrument builder Harry Partch.

In the end, the task fell to the Barrons. Their Krel music is appropriately set off from rest of the soundtrack not only by the long delay loops, but also by its intricate contrapuntal texture (CD track 13). Along with the leisurely-looping glissandi in the high register, the texture consists of at least five other melodic layers of wooly drones and thrums. (The wooliness here is likely a consequence of Bebe having rolled off the high frequencies to eliminate tape noise, which suggests that these sounds were obtained through recursive transpositions of higher-pitched sources). The most distinctive element of the texture is a recurring fragment of short bursts – a muffled tune that sounds as though it is being played under water on a plucked string. The tune is first heard, very faintly, at 8 seconds into the track, and then much louder at 17 seconds. An octave transposition of the motif enters 7 seconds later, almost like an imitative fugal answer. The motif then trails off into a kind of random developmental episode. Both the 'subject' and transposed 'answer' recur periodically throughout the passage over the constantly varying wooly background. The music evokes the feeling of an archaic *ricercare*, perfectly fitting for this representation of alien antiquity.

In order to draw the Krel technology into the web of associations that links Morbius with the monster, the Krel music's 'fugue subject' is later inter-woven into the fabric of other leitmotifs. The fugue subject recurs, subtly, as the ship's doctor unveils a plaster cast made of the monster's footprints. "There's nothing like this claw found in nature", the doctor observes, and the music shifts directly from the Krel fugue subject to the monster motif (CD track 17). During the final encounter with the monster, the Krel fragment reappears once more, but now at half-speed: the melodic bursts are drawn out into a sequence deep lumbering thumps (CD track 21)[13].

Sentiment, Simple Blasters and the Secrets of the Krel

Despite its unorthodox sonic palette, the Barrons' music sometimes works in a way comparable to traditional Hollywood underscoring. An overview of the *Forbidden Planet* soundtrack reveals several broad leitmotific catego-ries, one being the set of affective signifiers comprising the monster theme and Alta's theme. These themes are presented and developed in a manner not unlike the leitmotifs of a Steiner or Friedhofer score. The monster music, of course, represents the darkest recesses of the human heart – Morbius's jealousy and covetousness. Accordingly, it retains and augments its most frightful musical qualities throughout the film. Alta's music, on the other hand, undergoes a process of 'sweetening' as the film progresses. As Bebe recalls:

> *We brought Johnny Green* [head of MGM's music department] *this music which was supposed to be* Love in the Garden. *I thought it was so beautifully romantic, but Johnny shrieked, 'Oh my God, I didn't want the end of the Earth, I want love music!' Well, love music was the hardest for us to make. So he asked us to go and add sweeteners to it... it was a tough assignment. I found some stuff that was legato notes, almost like a viola sounds, although we would usually dump things if they resembled existing instruments. I added these sounds at random, and amazingly they formed a harmonic relationship with what was there. I think luck and timing were on our side.* (quoted in Burnam, 1997: 260)

Alta's 'love theme' thus becomes the most 'normalised' music in the film, inasmuch as it is the only music that approximates identifiable harmonic relationships among relatively pure, stable pitches. The music tends to occur precisely at moments of 'ego-syntonicism', the moments depicting Alta's transference of libido from her father (and her pets) to Captain Adams. Its most lush and sweet presentation is reserved for the 'Homecoming' scene, after the monster/Morbius is vanquished (CD track 22).

In addition to this 'irrational' affective music representing *Eros* and *Thanatos*, the soundtrack includes a second broad category of leitmotifs representing rational technology. Three different kinds of technology are presented in the film. The first is the 'mundane' technology of the fictional world, the quotidian machinery under the control of Adams and the ship's crew, including the space cruiser, its navigation equipment and the blasters used by the crew as tools and weapons. The second is the unfathomable, extraordinary technology of the Krel: the mind-expanding machine, the underground shuttle and power station, and the recording of the ancient Krel music. The third category is represented by Robby the robot: Robby illustrates aspects of Krel technology put to benign purposes: his compliant fetching and carrying, flower arranging, dressmaking, and industrial tasks. Musically, these three kinds of technology are differentiated through different types of sonic textures and processes. For example, the sounds representing mundane technology are those that can most consistently be identified by the viewer as straightforward diegetic noise. Music representing the abstruse technology of the Krel, on the other hand, is more apt to blur the lines of demarcation between source-sound and underscoring. It is also the most contrapuntally dense music in the film: the Krel power station is represented by dense clusters of glissandi, roaring, humming and grinding; likewise, the ancient Krel *ricercare* features an intricate and multi-layered texture. Finally, Robby's benign robotics are accompanied by discrete plinks and plops, short reverberated impulses, with uniform echo rhythms. Robby's music also regularly features monaural panning (the sound drops out entirely from one speaker as it pans from side to side). These are 'friendly' sounds. As J.P. Telotte has noted, Robbie is a new kind of cinematic robot, in contrast to menacing brutes like Gort in *The Day the Earth stood still*, and a precursor to the 'droids' of the *Star Wars* series (1995: 114–115).

The tension between benign and malignant technology is a theme revisited time and again in Science Fiction genres. Beating a retreat from the techno-logical is a common outcome in many a Sci-Fi plot, and *Forbidden Planet* embraces this convention. As Telotte notes:

> [The film] *concludes with its characters abandoning the technologically advanced world of the Krel ... and with the destruction of this planet whose technology has provided so many of the movie's attractions...* Forbidden Planet *admits to the lure of the mechanisms it constructs and parades before us, only to pull back, like so many other science-fiction films, from that lure, as if it had reassessed the very images or signs with which it so powerfully speaks.* (ibid)

But Telotte overlooks the fact that there is no such retreat from the techno-logical in the *sonic* dimension. Granted, Alta's music prevails in the final scenes, and to the extent that the love music is the most normalised of the film, it does provide a sonic resolution of sorts. But while we may have overcome the Krel's legacy of dystopic cyborgism, the film's conclusion still feels unsettled. In terms of the broader context of film-music practices, the absence of soaring strings and tonal grounding renders the narrative closure here decidedly spurious.

The Barrons' soundtrack retains some of the conventions of Hollywood underscoring, particularly in its treatment of the affective leitmotifs. In the end, however, these conventions are overshadowed by the sheer weirdness of the sonic palette and the persistent ambiguity of the diegetic horizon. The ongoing interpenetration of source-sounds and underscoring turns out to be a perfect sonic counterpart to the narrative themes of the alien and the uncanny – the *unheimlich*, that which is at once terrifyingly mysterious and strangely familiar[14].

Forbidden Planet's premise of the Jekyll-and-Hyde 'fugue state' would be revisited in many films – most recently in David Fincher's *Fight Club* (1999) and Christopher Nolan's *Memento* (2000) It is a premise for which the cinematic medium is ideally suited. For all its campy short-comings, *Forbid-den Planet* was one of the first films to successfully explore cinema's unique ability to play off the ambiguity of 'voice' and point-of-view (who is seeing? who is *hearing?*). The film thus enjoins two of the cinema's indigenous genres: the Science Fiction spectacle and the narrative of self-mis-recogni-tion. It is the Barrons' extraordinary soundtrack that most vividly depicts and fuses these elements.

75

Notes

1. See Flinn (1992).

2. For photos of the Barrons' studio, see unattributed, 1959: 94–97; Clarke S and Rubin, S (1979: 62) and Vale, V and Juno, A (1994: 194).

3. For this and other early uses of the theremin see Hayward, P (1997).

4. See Kathryn Kalinak's discussion of Raksin in *Settling the Score* (Kalinak, 1992): 178.

5. Herrmann's telegraph-wire technique is described in Palmer, C (1990: 267).

6. This is not to say, however, that film-composers themselves have been insensitive to the subtleties of atonality and its potential for fine shading. The 12-tone techniques that colour Leonard Rosenman's scores for *East of Eden* and *The Cobweb* attest to the effectiveness of Schoenbergian methods in cinematic contexts. Sabine Feisst has enumerated a number of other examples, including Ernest Gold's score for *On the Beach*, which adopts a 12-tone set approach to illustrate the physics of a nuclear reaction. See Feisst, S (1999): 93–113.

7. So much for the 'talking cure'!

8. Eventual cuts in the dialogue rendered the film's 'incest taboo' theme much more muted in the final version. Such cuts were justified on the grounds that the film had to appeal to children; despite the studio's ambitions the kiddy-matinee crowd was still expected to make up the bulk of the audience, as it had for all Sci-Fi pictures to date. One of the cuts involved a bit of dialogue in which Adams and the ship's doctor discuss Alta's relationship to the wild animals that live in Morbius's garden: their conversation makes reference to the unicorn myth, Alta's virginity, and what will happen as Alta's 'innocence' inevitably wanes. In the released version, we simply see Alta's pet tiger turn on her, following a make-out session with Adams. For an account of this and other cuts made to Hume's original script, see Clarke, F. S and Rubin, S (1979: 4–66).

9. Several writers have argued that special effects are the true subject matter of all Sci-Fi cinema. Brooks Landon, for example, claims that spectacular special effects "can be profitable considered as self-reflexive celebrations of film technology itself, as a kind of counter-narrative that often conflicts with the ostensible discursive narrative, and even as a kind of liberatory or utopic moment quite independent from the utopian representations of science-fiction narrative" (1999: 39).

10. This is the estimate provided by art director Arthur Lonergan and effects designer A. Arnold Gillespie (cited in Clarke and Rubin, 1979: 62). While this figure seems unremarkable today, Clarke and Rubin point out that MGM's most expensive picture to date, *Quo Vadis* of 1951, had cost only five million dollars.

11. Clarke and Rubin, op. cit.: 29. MGM executives apparently drew the line at a proposal for specially designed furniture for the Morbius dream home.

12. Hull's influential *Essentials of Behavior* was published in 1951.

13. Ollie Powers identified the transpositional relationship between this latter passage and the earlier Krel-music motif (Powers, op cit: 116).

14. See Freud, S (1919: 217–252).

Chapter Four

THE TRANSMOLECULARIZATION OF [BLACK] FOLK
Space is the Place, Sun Ra and Afrofuturism

NABEEL ZUBERI

We can listen profitably to the futurology evident in black popular cultures and interpret their comments on science and technology as having some bearing upon ethical and even political matters.
(Gilroy, 2000: 341)

Question: *What is the power of your machine?*
Sun Ra: *Music.*
from the film *Space is the Place* (1974)

Space is the Place, *part documentary, part science fiction, part blaxploitation, part revisionist biblical epic. Strange enough in its own time, as the years passed it assumed an even stranger aura of 1970s ideas and affectations and what appears to be the genuinely timeless in Sun Ra's dress and manner.* (Szwed, 1997: 330)

T he low-budget musical Science Fiction film *Space is the Place* was directed by John Coney in Oakland, California in 1972, and produced by Jim Newman for release by North American Star Systems in 1974. Rhapsody Films released it on VHS video in the 1990s. The film stars Sun Ra (1914–1993), the jazz keyboardist, composer, arranger and bandleader of the Intergalactic Myth-Science Solar Arkestra. Though US state documentation registers his birth as Herman Blount in Birmingham, Alabama, for much of his life Sun Ra claimed to be an alien from the planet Saturn.

In *SITP*, Ra visits Earth in a spaceship, time travelling between Chicago 1943 and Oakland, California 1972 where he communicates with local African Americans and tries to convince them to leave with him for a space colony. Ra engages in no less than a struggle for the souls of black folk against an archetypal pimp/mack/player/business figure called the Overseer (Ray Johnson). The medium of combat is a magic card game and Ra's most potent 'tricknology' is his music. The Arkestra performs many pieces of diegetic and non-diegetic music in its efforts to uplift the race to Outer Space. Ra also encounters the largely corrupt media network system, using it to spread his message despite the fact that black radio in the form of announcer Jimmy Fey (Christopher Brooks) is compromised by the Overseer's influence. Ra also contends with the surveillance and violence of the United States government. The FBI kidnaps and sonically tortures him with a recording of the Confederate anthem *Dixie*. Three young men – Bubbles (John Bailey), Bernard (Clarence Brewer) and Tiny (Tiny Parker) – rescue Ra just in time for the Arkestra to perform a concert for the community. During the concert the FBI men try to assassinate Ra at his minimoog keyboard but are again foiled by Bubbles, Bernard and Tiny. Bubbles is shot and killed saving Ra's life but Ra teleports him and his comrades to safety in the spaceship. Ra also teleports the 'black part' of Jimmy Fey just before the Arkestra departs for Outer Space. Like the alien messiah Klaatu played by Michael Rennie in the liberal Cold War Sci-Fi classic *The Day the Earth stood still* (1951), Sun Ra lands on Earth to inform the human race that it needs redemption from its sorry state, and then leaves after relatively little success (Ruppersberg, 1990: 33–37).

The film 'signifies' across and between a number of recognisable film genres and modes such as Sci-Fi, the musical, the urban youth film and the documentary in the style of African diasporic vernacular expression and media production (Yearwood, 1998). *SITP* is one in a series of attempts to translate Sun Ra's music and his concerns with science, technology and Outer Space to the screen. Like much of his oeuvre, *SITP* is concerned with how music can transport black people to other states of being in both material and spiritual terms. In this Science Fiction film, *music is the primary special effect*. The film's sound design incorporates electronic instruments, such as the minimoog synthesiser that became increasingly common in jazz, funk, soul and psychedelic rock in the late 1960s and early 1970s. *SITP* also riffs on the language of black nationalism in the urban African American film of the period. Its dialogue pastiches and parodies the babble of radio and network media. And like many films of the American Vietnam War and Watergate period, it foregrounds the government's audiovisual surveillance of citizens and aliens.

SITP is a molecular milestone in a black music tradition that engages with separation, escape and otherness through the tropes of Science Fiction. Recent 'sampling' of Sun Ra and *SITP* by critics, filmmakers and musicians situates his work in a continuum of African diasporic speculative fiction and Afro-futurism across many media (Thomas, 2000). The exhibition 'Sonic Process: A New Geography of Sounds' that travelled through Barcelona, Paris and Berlin in 2002–03 gives Sun Ra a significant place in its definition of Afrofuturism.

A trend within black popular music, whose paternity is generally attrib-uted to Sun Ra. Transcending musical genres, Afrofuturism draws upon the feeling of alienation inherited from the slavery of American blacks, which it sublimates. In this conception, certain elements of Afro-Ameri-can culture (such as the transcendence of spirituals) are re-imagined and transposed into a new cosmic and legendary perspective, where the alienated becomes extraterrestrial. The most representative artists of Afrofuturism include George Clinton and his various bands (Parliament, Funkadelic, etc.), Lee "Scratch" Perry, as well as Roni Size. (Van Assche, 2002: 21).

This glossary entry might somewhat overstate Ra's (patriarchal) centrality to the genealogy of musical Afrofuturism, but his work manifests some of its key features. Though one can trace many elements of futurology across African diasporic cultures in the near and distant past, the term Afrofuturism has only recently reached critical mass as a formation that codifies, organises and maps an alternative cultural history and critical framework for African American media production. According to Alondra Nelson (2002: 14), the term was first coined and defined by Mark Dery. In his 1993 prologue to a series of interviews with critics Tricia Rose and Greg Tate and Science Fiction writer Samuel R. Delany, Dery writes:

Speculative fiction that treats African–American themes and addresses African–American concerns in the context of twentieth-century technocul-ture – and, more generally, African–American signification that appro-priates images of technology and a prosthetically enhanced future – might for want of a better term, be called 'Afro-futurism'. The notion of Afrofuturism gives rise to a troubling antinomy: Can a community whose past has been deliberately rubbed out, and whose energies have sub-sequently been consumed by the search for legible traces of its history, imagine possible futures? Furthermore, isn't the unreal estate of the future already owned by the technocrats, futurologists, streamliners, and set designers – white to a man – who have engineered our collective fantasies? (1994: 180)

Ziauddin Sardar seems to answer Dery's final rhetorical question with a resounding 'yes'. According to Sardar "science fiction shows us not the plasticity but the paucity of the human imagination that has become quagmired in the scientist industrial technological, culturo-socio-psycho babble of a single civilisational paradigm [western civilisation]" (2002: 1). Sardar emphasises the "colonising, imperial mission of science fiction":

Space, the final frontier, is the recurrent frontier on which western thought has been constructed and operated throughout history, or time. Western thought not only constructed aliens to define itself better, it made constructed aliens essential to fulfilling its moral purpose. (ibid: 16)

Sardar's position historicises Science Fiction, quite persuasively, in our own time of US military-industrial domination, the War on Terror(ism) and Axis of Evil rhetoric. However, his polemic overstates both the Sci-Fi genre's conservatism and the homogeneity of the West. For Science Fiction has also long been part of the radical imagination of 'others' in the West trying to find ways out of its oppressive regimes of power and knowledge. An examination of Sun Ra-in-film can illuminate African American cultural politics as recorded sounds and images pass through various states of diasporic mediation.

In his influential Afrofuturist sermon/summons *More Brilliant Than the Sun: Adventures in Sonic Fiction*, black British cultural critic Kodwo Eshun argues:

So there's this idea of music as this sonic production circuit through which – as Gilles Deleuze was saying – molecules of a new people may be planted here or there. That's very much what Sun Ra's doing: he's using the Moog to produce a new sonic people. Out of this circuit, he's using it to produce the new astro-black American of the 1970s. (1998: A[185])

If we follow Eshun's logic, how might we then understand *SITP* and Sun Ra as material media themselves reconstituted, imagined anew, and remediated in our historical moment?

* * * * * * *

According to John Szwed's exhaustive biography, Sun Ra "followed the rise of science fiction as a child, reading early comic books and seeing the movie serials of Buck Rogers and Flash Gordon; learning its language, incorporating its themes and motifs into his performances" (1997: 131). During the 1950s and 1960s when he was based in Chicago, Ra studied the Science Fiction of the Nation of Islam. Though he didn't subscribe to its cosmology, he was familiar with the Nation's founder Wallace D. Fard's creationist myth in which Yacub, a renegade Imam and scientist, created the diabolical white race as a genetic mutation of the Earth's original inhabitants – the 'Asiatic Black Man'. According to Fard, redemption would come with the arrival of a mother ship made by the original black scientists to destroy "the enemies of Allah" (Szwed, 1997: 132). Fard's successor Elijah Muhammad argued that black people originally came from the moon, which at one time was part of the same planet as earth. Following an explosion caused by Yacub, the two were separated (White, 1985: 105). This permutation of Islam was just was one crossroads in the matrix of African American ideas. Like many 20th Century Afrocentric thinkers Sun Ra studied Egyptology and hiero-glyphics. Steeped in the Baptist tradition, he also read many commentaries on the Bible. Aspects of all these texts made their way into Sun Ra's mythical lexicography.

As a schoolboy Ra had what Szwed describes as a conversion experience articulated in the language of an alien abduction story. Space beings contacted him and told him to join them. He was raised up in a beam of light:

> *it looked like a giant spotlight shining down on me, and I call it transmolecularization, my whole body was changed into something else. I could see through myself. And I went up. Now, I call that energy transformation because I wasn't in human form. I thought I was there, but I could see through myself.* (quoted in Szwed, 1997: 29).

As an invisible man, unlike Ralph Ellison's earthbound black subject, Ra found himself on Saturn. There the aliens instructed him to educate the Earth's people. This spiritual epiphany or revelation reminds me of the prophet Muhammad's first visitation by the Angel Jibreel/Gabriel, the medium for Allah's bio-scientific words: "Recite in the name of your Lord who has created/Created man out of a germ-cell". The prophetic mode was an essential aspect of Ra's musical message throughout his career, and the address of the holy man or imam to the congregation is one rhetorical strategy in *SITP*. At the centre of Ra's gospel, according to Szwed, was Neoplatonism – "the philosophical-mystical tradition in which music is seen as both a model of the universe and a part of its makeup, and where it has the power to bring human beings in line with the cosmos" (1997: 113).

Sound and image were always intertwined in this cosmology. Sun Ra's message was modulated through music, the spectacle of space-age-meets-ancient-Egypt costumes, onstage dancers and the theatre of street marches and black vaudeville. Expressionist lighting effects filtered through live performances. Though trained in the big band tradition of Duke Ellington and Fletcher Henderson (for whom he worked briefly in the early 1940s), Ra was one of the first jazz musicians to use electric keyboard instruments, such as Hammond and Farfisa organs, and synthesisers such as the moog and portable minimoog. The synthesiser's 'strange sounds' became integral to the increasingly elaborate multimedia events or happenings that were the Arkestra's live shows in the late 1960s. The visual aspect of the Arkestra's musical performance was choreographed but allowed for a measure of spontaneity. Before *SITP*, the band appeared in a number of films – *Cry of Jazz* (1958), *Magic Sun* (1968) and *Spaceways* (1968) – and extracts from films were often projected behind the Arkestra during concerts.

Sun Ra came into the orbit of many musical and cultural movements including swing, be-bop and the Beats, free jazz and the Black Arts, psychedelic rock and experimental art music. Yet he always remained peripheral to them, despite influencing some of their prominent actors. By the time *SITP* was shot in 1972, Ra had played for over thirty years around the United States, and had lived as a resident alien and professional musician in Chicago and New York City. The Arkestra had toured in Africa and recently visited

Europe. *SITP* was made in Oakland after Bobby Seale and the Black Panther Party invited Ra and members of the Arkestra to stay in the West Coast city in 1971. In the same year Ra was hired to teach a course at the University of California in Berkeley. His 'Black Man in the Cosmos' syllabus included the suggested student research topic, 'the role of technology in music' (Szwed, 1997: 295). *SITP* was crafted in the confluence of Sun Ra's career as a musician and teacher, the local and national contexts of black nationalism, developments in free jazz and other musical styles, and the emergence of a new black cinema movement marked by Melvin Van Peebles' *Sweet Sweetback's Baadasss Song* (1971).

* * * * * * *

The opening image in the film is the clichéd 'empty but starry space' shot familiar to audiences of the original *Star Trek* TV series in the 1960s. Instead of twinkling keyboard sounds and the woozy theremin-style motif of the *Star Trek* theme, we hear the slow bass-y electronic pulse of a minimoog synthesiser. Instead of Captain Kirk's famous voice-over narration, the electronic ambience is pierced by June Tyson's call: "It's after the end of the world. Don't you know that?" A yellow spaceship resembling a giant, winged seedpod glides into the frame as Tyson repeats her words several times in unison with other members of the Arkestra.

The film then cuts to its only visual evocation of a utopian space 'colony'. Tyson's spoken words fade out. The camera pans across jungle-like vegetation as the electronic pulse becomes fuller and turns into more abrasive atonal sound. As the camera tilts up to capture expressionist tree limbs against a purple-haze sky, deep in the mix a saxophone characteristic of free jazz shrieks and caws like a conference of birds. Sun Ra appears amongst the trees, wearing metallic coloured robes and an ancient Egyptian-style headdress with a golden winged orb on top. His name is superimposed in yellow letters on the screen, the same bright yellow as his spaceship and some of his robes. He walks through this idyllic landscape interacting with cyborganic fauna-flora. These life forms include floating silver spheres with tails, and yellow protuberances pointing to the sky, like the bulbous fingers of hands uplifted in joy and praise during a southern black church service. Ra is accompanied by a hooded figure in monk's robes. We find them standing in a clearing. In medium close-up, Ra hums a refrain to the background music. The film cuts to a close up of the hooded disciple who has a mirror face. Ra directly addresses the camera at a slight angle, like a religious leader pausing in this idyllic setting to address a fellow traveller. The audience is invited into a compact with him as if to meditate on political realities and apply a decisive plan. Ra makes his mission clear:

> *The Music is different here. The vibrations are different. Not like Planet Earth. Planet Earth sounds of guns, anger, frustration. There will be no one from Planet Earth we could talk to who would understand. We'll set up a colony for black people here. See what they can do on a planet all*

their own, without any white people there. They would drink in the beauty of this planet. It would affect their vibrations, for the better, of course. Another place in the universe, up in the different stars. That would be where the alter-destiny would come in. Equation-wise – the first thing to do is to consider time as officially ended. We'll work on the other side of time. We'll bring them here through either isotopic teleportation, transmolecularization or better still, teleport the whole planet here through music.

According to Ra, redemption of black people comes through music. Musical form is a template for society and the body. This statement, the music in the scene and the images manifest a fairly common set of avant-garde ideas in jazz at least since the late 1950s. The music here, particularly the saxophone playing, shares a 'yearning' quality for a utopian elsewhere or 'something else', as suggested in the words of alto saxophonist Ornette Coleman's 1958 album title. Coleman's *Change of the Century* (1959) and *The Shape of Jazz to Come* (1959) evoke the future even more explicitly in their sci-fi titles. Lawrence Kart delineates the main features of avant-garde ideology in jazz as futurism, alienation, antagonism, agonism, improvisation, experiment and "new techniques as a means of more than technical transformation, the work as a transcendental laboratory or proving ground" (2000: 447). These were evident to different degrees and varying emphasis most significantly for jazz historians in the music of Coleman, John Coltrane, Albert Ayler, Eric Dolphy and Cecil Taylor. These players attempted to move beyond metrical form in jazz, to break free of codes and reach other musical forms 'out there'. As Szwed notes, "*Out* in the 1960s carried powerful meanings among certain musicians – an orientation away from an existing music, a certain relationship with society, a kind of musician, a way of playing around chords" (2000: 242). Some outward approaches involved journeys eastward to African sounds, Islamic culture, Indian music and philosophy in the search to create a new 'world' music. This questing can be found in John Coltrane's and Pharoah Saunders' recordings, as well as the orientalist sounds and visual imagery of countless rock musicians and western art music composers.

To achieve 'far-out' sounds in the so-called New Thing, Free Jazz or New Black Music (Jones, 1967), musicians "would use volume, texture, grain, tone color, and other sonic variables to create variation and interest, demanding of the listener a focus and appreciation of sound for its own sake" (Szwed, 2000: 242). This attention to aural texture meant stretching the sonic possibilities of existing instruments, producing dissonance and atonality. Rock music in the 1960s distorted tones and chords through electrical means such as amplification, distortion, and feedback. These experiments were often fed with time-space altering drugs such as LSD. New electronic instruments such as the Moog synthesiser produced peculiar tones outside the parameters of previous listening. The line between noise/sound effects and music in rock, jazz and other popular music styles becomes blurred in this period. Though the eerie, otherworldly sound of the theremin had weaved through thrillers, Science Fiction film soundtracks such as *The Day the Earth stood still* (1951), and the exotica recordings of Les Baxter and others since the 1940s, popular music 'catches up' with Science Fiction noise only in the 1960s, as electronic instruments and the increasingly elaborate manipulations of the studio console commonly permeate the production and sound of music.

In 1968 Wendy (then 'Walter') Carlos used the moog in her popular electronic interpretation of the classics, *Switched-on Bach* and the soundtrack for Stanley Kubrick's *A Clockwork Orange* (1971). According to Mike Berk:

> As the first portable, affordable, and really popular synth, the minimoog made 'synthesist' a viable job description, and the world of popular music was never quite the same again. The minimoog and its immediate successors from ARP, Sequential Circuits, Oberheim, Korg, Roland, and a host of other companies, established the sound of analog synthesis as the sound of synthesis. One or more voltage-controlled oscillators kicked out audio waveforms that were subsequently shaped by a series of modifiers-filters, amplifiers, low-frequency oscillators, ring modulators, and so forth – controlled by the player via a collection of knobs, sliders, switches, buttons, and levers. The sounds they produced were lush, fat, harmonically rich, and curiously organic. (2000: 191)

These sounds and their cultural associations in the late 1960s and early 1970s are semiotically charged with rematerialisation (or transmolecularization, if you will). For example, Trevor Pinch and Frank Trocco describe the appearance of the moog in a "moment of sixties freakout" in Nicholas Roeg's film *Performance* (1970) which stars Mick Jagger as rock star Turner:

> Turner for a moment is the mad captain at the controls of spaceship Moog. The Moog and its sounds are the perfect prop, part of the psychedelic paraphernalia, the magical means to transmigrate a fading rock star into something else...The Moog was a machine that empowered such transformations. The synthesizer for a short while in the sixties was not just another musical instrument; it was part of the sixties apparatus for transgression, transcendence, and transformation. (2002:305)

In 1969 Sun Ra 'borrowed' a prototype of the new minimoog Model B synthesiser from Robert Moog's factory in Trumansburg, upstate New York (Pinch and Trocco, 2002: 72). Moog reports that "more than 12,000 Minimoogs were produced from 1971 to 1981" (quoted in Vale and Juno, 1994: 135). Gershon Kingsley, a musician-engineer who worked with Robert Moog, recorded the electronic albums *The In Sound from Way Out* and *Kaleidoscopic Vibrations* with Jean-Jacques Perrey in the 1960s, had a 1972 moog pop hit with *Popcorn* under the name of Hot Butter and programmed Sun Ra's minimoog for him (see Vale/Juno, 1993: 82–91). But Jon Weiss who worked on the overall design of the moog comments that Ra "had taken this synthesizer and I don't know what he had done to it, but he made sounds like you had never heard in your life, I mean just total inharmonic distortion all over the place, oscillators weren't oscillating anymore, nothing was working but it was fabulous" (quoted in Pinch and Trocco, 2002: 223). This, according to Weiss, made the minimoog "a musical *instrument*, as opposed to a *machine*' (ibid). The two volumes each of *The Solar-Myth Approach* and *My Brother the Wind* recorded by Sun Ra and the Arkestra between 1967 and 1970 explored the moog and minimoog's sonic range (Szwed, 1997: 276–77).

Sun Ra's soundtrack for *SITP*, recorded in 1972, exploits the minimoog's capabilities for a range of alien textures, 'dark' as well as warm tones, rapid keyboard runs and less 'musical' beeps and burps, as well as drones produced through stable sine wave generation. Ra uses the minimoog for discrete sci-fi effects that colour a film scene but are not included on the soundtrack CD release by Evidence. Rickey Vincent points out that "the Moog synthesizer was capable not only of playing low notes, but of stacking a number of bass tones onto one key creating the fullest bass sound ever played" (1995: 246). However, Ra doesn't use the instrument for funk purposes in *SITP*, but paradoxically, the more familiar scary semiotics of alien presence and space in Sci-Fi cinema.

The minimoog joins the piano, Farfisa organ and rocksichord in Sun Ra's keyboard armoury. Ra also plays the Hohner clavinet, used to funky effect in Billy Preston's Grammy-winning Sci-Fi hit *Outa Space* (1972), Stevie Wonder's *Superstition* (1972) and the Commodores' *Machine Gun* (1974). The Arkestra's horns feature strongly in the sound of *SITP*. Brass usually evokes the military and warfare in Science Fiction films, but in the urban action film and road movie, trumpets and saxophones complement the screeching tones of tyres in car chases and the high-pitched whooping of police sirens. In *SITP*, the Arkestra's horns lead the marches of many pro-space anthems, such as *We travel the spaceways* and the propulsive *Watusa*, but also propel the one car chase sequence in the film, in which a run-down old car follows a van. Another strong element in the soundtrack is the polyrhythmic 'Africanist' drumming and percussion of congas, koras, bongos and bells common to other African American genres of this period. Though Ra's soft voice offers monologues, engages in dialogues and 'declamations' (such as "I am the Brother the Wind"), June Tyson's voice dominates with her repeated long phrases, chants, slogans and quasi-jingles for Outer Space travel.

The scene that immediately follows the space colony opening of the film is as close a Sci-Fi example of music as disruptive noise to the regime of 'representation' as Jacques Attali (1985) could wish for. After the relatively muted moog and sax sound of the jungle idyll and Ra's soothing words of utopian promise, we hear tap dancing to a boogie-woogie piano and then cut to a street exterior with the subtitle 'Chicago 1943', then quickly cut again to the interior of a club where a chorus line of African American women, the Ebony Steppers, taps along a stage in unison. The place resembles a low-rent Cotton Club with black and white clientele. Some black punters give the white bourgie-looking customers dirty looks. In this 1970s retro version of the 1940s, Ra sits and noodles at a simple stand-up piano, dressed in, by his standards, a relatively muted wide lapelled jacket with a green zigzag pattern. The Steppers go off stage for a respite. The Overseer appears, though for some time we only see him from behind or the side without the camera revealing his face. We know he's a 'mack daddy', a man of power, because he wears a white suit and Fedora hat, holds a cane and two beautiful women accompany him. A scantily clad 'cigarette girl' rolls and fondles a cigar in her fingers, clips the end off and places it between the Overseer's lips. He thanks her with a greenback tip placed between her breasts. "He sees something he likes he gets around to it" she tells another woman at the bar who looks longingly in the Overseer's direction. The piano player is identified as Sonny Ray, in fact one of Sun Ra's early monikers. The overseer insists to the fawning nightclub MC Jimmy Fey that the piano player "sounds like shit". The Ebony Steppers are due to appear on stage again but Ray avoids playing a dance rhythm so they wait behind the stage curtain uncertain of their cue. Ray suddenly strikes into a regular rhythm and the Ebony Steppers burst onto the stage in relief. However, he soon breaks out of the rhythm with irregular percussive bursts of notes like an angry Thelonious Monk and the dancers can't keep time to the music. As the playing becomes more aggressive and discordant, glasses smash, a chandelier falls to the floor, and a riot breaks out as people try to escape from the chaos. As panic ensues and parts of the club spontaneously combust, a non-diegetic moog's jarring low tones fill the soundtrack, supported by shrieking saxophones. The cacophony creates a force field that throws some people in the club through the air with its gravity-defying power. Ray goes on playing his piano and whipping up the storm. Finally he stops, kicks the instrument away with a final thrashing at the keyboard and the piano careers across the stage like a crashing car. This music machine has caused serious damage.

The scene is an electro be bop paean to Luigi Russolo and the Italian Futurists' art of noises. It captures the Dionysian impetus for entropy entrenched in rock and roll aesthetics and other modernist discourses of art. White noise, white light, white heat. Noise annoys and destroys. Sun Ra brings the noise. In his futurist manifesto for cacophony, Robert Worby (2000: 161) compresses this ideology:

> Distortion is accumulation, overdrive and mutation at the limits of a system and these extremes bring about change, be that in sound or in society. Distortion and feedback in sound cause partials to pile up and collide like molecules in a hot gas – chaos, randomness and entropy are manifested in noise. Noise is entropy; it signifies closure, the end. When society is pushed to the limits, when change is necessary and imminent, when the end of an era is reached, noise blasts through every strand of culture, humanity and life.

We can read the scene in which Ra lands on Earth through this prism. The scene parodies the clichés of the alien arrival from 1950s SF films. The radio announcer stands with a microphone and dramatically proclaims: "This is Jimmy Fey, Channel Five, stone jive, all black station, all black people, with all the news that grooves at noon, live from Oakland, California". A low-angle shot captures television cameras elevated on the top of broadcast vans in anticipation of the spaceship. When it finally lands, with an electronic wow-wow-wow, its inhabitants emerge to meet police sirens and crowd noise. Ra and the Arkestra exit the spaceship and present a wired helmet device to Jimmy Fey. Ra plays a portable keyboard that initially produces several electronic tones that dissolve into white noise, gives Fey some serious pain and leaves him unconscious. Over the din, Sun Ra pronounces, "I am the alter-destiny, the presence of the living myth". The media are rendered powerless here. A siren announcing Fey's departure to hospital is followed by a radio broadcast heard on the ambulance radio in which a woman news reader states in the racist terms of Amerikan media: "Today a party of Negroes claimed to know the secret of space travel, threatening to undermine both the economy and social structure of the strongest nation of Earth and destroy our way of life. They are on the FBI's most wanted list." In *SITP*, the Arkestra's music is mixed and juxtaposed with the sounds of media communication, in particular the blather of Jimmy Fey's radio commentary, the playback of radio sets tuned to his station and featuring Ra's music, news reports in the white media, and secret tape recordings of Ra made by the FBI. Media reportage is closely associated here with surveillance technologies. The two FBI men in *SITP* are shabbier, more incompetent versions of the government operatives played by Gene Hackman and John Cazale in Francis Ford Coppola's *The Conversation* (1973). But Ra's own music often accompanies his surveillance of Earth as an alien. Before he lands on Earth, he sits in a portico in the spaceship at a multimedia control desk that features a keyboard, reel-to-reel tape recorder and a television screen that not only monitors his space dancers but the Overseer in his Cadillac alongside his latest female 'squeeze'.

If, as Vivian Sobchack (1999: 193) notes, the media in traditional Science Fiction films convey crisis information and invoke an 'imagined' national and international community of the human race, by the late 1960s that faith in the airwaves has been undermined. *SITP* parodies the representation of media in Hollywood film while ambivalently acknowledging the power of radio, television cameras, newspapers and magazines to disseminate Sun Ra's subversive message. Ra uses Jimmy Fey and black radio to expose the public to his teachings. In one scene Ra is driven around Oakland and interviewed about the black man's inverted status in society as inner-city residents amusingly gaze at this strangely dressed alien apparition in their midst. The face of Ra appears on the front cover of a daily newspaper and *Rolling Stone* magazine. Bubbles and Bernard argue over whether Sun Ra has been "co-opted and corralled by the corporate Caucasian power structure". The Overseer tries to convince them that Ra is a fraud, dealing in "cold hard cash", not "black magic soul power". Music documentaries like *Gimme Shelter* (1970), which shows the Rolling Stones watching footage of themselves at Altamont on a Steinbeck editing table, illustrate that music cinema of this period was quite reflexive about its status as a medium.

The Arkestra's music accompanies almost all the action in the film but the musicans are rarely in the space of the film narrative. They have clearly been filmed in a recording studio. Close ups of June Tyson in a studded metallic cap and large sunglasses and other medium shots of the Arkestra have a dark anonymous background. Though *SITP* shows the musicians in 'authentic' live performance – common in many post-1950s jazz films from the 1950s onwards and entrenched by the early 1970s after the rock concert films *Monterey Pop* (1967) and *Woodstock* (1969) – here shots of the Arkestra cut back and forth to the story world of Oakland. We are never clear where the Arkestra is – if it's in the space ship or in the sonic motor of the spaceship itself. Only in the rehearsal and final concert at the end of the film do we briefly see the group in Oakland, a generic nod to the backstage musical and youth film in which the culmination of the narrative is the 'kids putting on a show' for the community. The Arkestra also plays over the documentary segments of the film. For example, during its ad campaign for Outer Spaceways Incorporated, the rising Farfisa organ of its introduction ripples as a hand-held camera wanders into the building Ra has secured to sign up people for his space program. The music falls silent for the comic wordplay interludes in which Ra interviews a white former NASA employee afraid of "ending up on [that most dreaded of conditions] welfare" and a drunk who wants to do nothing if accepted for Ra's project. But the horns rise again during shots of African-American men drinking and chatting on a building stoop. June Tyson's memorable and infinitely catchy chorus "If you find Earth boring, just the same old same thing, come on sign up with Outer Spaceways Incorporated" accompanies images of African Americans lined up in a queue against a wall covered with advertising for consumer products.

Sun Ra's visit to an Oakland Youth Development Program is shot in wandering verité documentary style with a deep drone from the minimoog. The audio seems to take the alien messiah's perspective as the camera wanders through the space where young men and women improvise an a capella rendition of a soul tune, *That's the way love is*. The walls are covered with large photographs of African American icons of the Civil Rights and Black nationalist eras – Frederick Douglas, Martin Luther King Jr., Amiri Baraka, Angela Davis, Malcolm X, Huey Newton, Bobby Seale, and Otis Redding. Then we suddenly see Ra from a more objective point of view. He announces himself as an ambassador from the Intergalactic Council of Outer Space. Faced with some youthful skepticism about his authenticity and disparaging comments that he looks like an old hippy, Ra poses the rhetorical question, "How do you know I'm real?" The youths say "Yeah" inquisitively. Ra continues, "I'm not real. I'm just like you. You don't exist in this society. If you did, your people wouldn't be seeking equal rights. You're not real. If you were, you'd have some status among the nations of the world". Close ups of several of the youngsters show that his words have been absorbed. In his own description of this scene, Kodwo Eshun states that, "to listen to Ra is to be dragged into another sonar system, an omniverse of overlapping sonar systems which abduct you from Trad audio reality" (1998: 158). However, Eshun's view of these 'lines of flight' obscures the 'back to the future' aspect of Sun Ra's mobilisation of the big band tradition and its own 'black and tan fantasies'. Eshun also ignores the vocal performance of the soul tune. As I shall argue 'Trad audio reality' is re-mediated rather than escaped from.

* * * * * * *

Szwed describes *SITP* as:

> *part documentary, part science fiction, part blaxploitation, part revi-sionist biblical epic. Strange enough in its own time, as the years passed it assumed an even stranger aura of 1970s ideas and affectations and what appears to be the genuinely timeless in Sun Ra's dress and manner.* (1997: 330).

He gives a brief outline of the plot and circumstances of its production. Initially envisaged by producer Jim Newman as a documentary, Szwed suggests that the film became a mishmash of genres due to the different, often conflicting inputs of Newman, screenwriter Joshua Smith, director John Coney and Sun Ra himself. Many changes and scene cuts were made during the film's production and post-production, some at Ra's behest. Like Szwed, many other brief descriptions or reviews of the film on the World Wide Web represent it as an early 1970s curiosity, a bizarre or camp oddity with a disorganised and almost nonsensical plot. In fact, the film's mix of signifyin(g) humour, space-age prophecy and various generic elements are hardly beyond comprehension.

As a generic hybrid with its musical soundtrack a key element, this slice of Science Fiction might be an example of what African American aesthetic theorist Clyde Taylor (1998: 263) calls "productive imperfection", after Cuban Third Cinema theorist and filmmaker Juan García Espinosa's (1983) manifesto 'For of an imperfect cinema', first published in 1967. Taylor's versioning of the term contends that

> *'imperfect' must be understood as ironical, that is, as depending on a double meaning, twinned with the concept of the perfect that those with the privileges of power/knowledge are eager to impose. The concept of 'imperfect' culture acknowledges this power to define at the same time that it rejects the substance of the definitions. It exposes the irony that resistance will always embrace contraband meanings and values, and these meanings and their carriers will always be framed as unofficial, unorthodox, indiscrete, undisciplined, chaotic, methodologically incor-rect, vulgar, or in a word, imperfect.* (1998: 255)

Taylor goes on to compare this cinematic imperfection to the aesthetics of jazz using Ted Gioia's description of jazz as "the imperfect art". Taylor cites such features as "its call-response relation to its audience, its commitment to improvisation and process rather than to calculation and product, its collective authorship, its irreverence toward tradition, its unabashed populism" (1998: 255). As an example of jazz in film, and Sci-Fi in particular, *SITP* can be considered a generic/genetic mutation in the relatively unprofitable margins of the early 1970s New Hollywood system. In today's information-speak, some might describe the film as a 'bad file' or a (terrorist) virus in the network. However, recent film genre studies of the musical and Science Fiction suggest a more mutable, modular and recombinant sense of genre within which we can accommodate *SITP* and make sense of later re-mediated appropriations of the film and Sun Ra.

In the history of North American cinema, the film plays a small role in the process of what Arthur Knight (2002) calls "disintegrating the musical". In his study of "black performance and American musical film" in the years 1929–1959, Knight (2002: 8–9) uses the word "integration" in more than one sense. Firstly, he means the (vertical) economic integration of the film industry and its consumers as a homogenous market, at the same time that much of the United States was legally and informally segregated along racial lines. His second meaning relates to racial-social integration as the goal of the Civil Rights movement. Knight cites W.E.B. Du Bois' April 1934 editorial in *Crisis* entitled 'Segregation in the North', in which he argued that "it will sometimes be necessary to our survival and ultimate step toward the ultimate breaking down of barriers, to increase by voluntary action our separation from our fellowmen" (ibid). Knight's study is primarily concerned with the musical; but Du Bois' call for separation and his view that there can be "no humanity" (ibid) until the end of economic, racial and national discrimination is a precursor of Sun Ra's own separatist rhetoric and fuels the Science Fiction tropes of alienation and exile in the cultures of the African diaspora. The third sense of 'integration' outlined by Knight refers to formal, aesthetic and ideological aspects of the musical as a film text. The integration of musical sound and spectacle with narrative, and the integration of different subjects and cultures with their own musical forms in the imagined utopian (American) community are both features of the Hollywood musical outlined by a succession of genre critics, including Rick Altman, Jane Feuer and Richard Dyer. Knight argues that, for these scholars, "the integrated musical is a response to the alienating, disorienting, and violently contradictory aspects of mass industrial integration and social distinction" (2002: 15). However, Knight writes that "the creation of the ultimate utopian feeling in the integrated musical relied on an explicit social-racial segregation, and no quantity of formal invention could hide that" (ibid). I quote Knight's next points at some length because they articulate the ambivalence of the musical, and a tension between constraint and freedom that problematises any clear 'up-up-and-away' flight from mediated tradition, form and 'reality', a departure that underpins much of SF discourse:

In its perverse way, through its specifically circumscribed 'utopian' aspirations the 'integrated' musical clarified in narration, song, and dance an important and for African Americans painful American circumstance of long standing. For African American performers and spectators, however, the starkness of the contradiction between a formally expressed desire for integrated wholeness and its manifestation in such critically applauded, even idealized, segregation also offered liberating – or, more accurately, persistently illuminating – possibilities. In the face of the integrated musical, African American performers, spectators, and critics developed methods of dis/integration, sometimes taking Du Boisian advantage of segregation always watching and listening for – and often seeking to create – failures of utopian form and feeling out of which new forms and feeling might emerge, and seldom giving up on the complex possibilities of the 'gift' – sometimes refashioned as joke, assault or evasion – of African American music. (Knight, 2002: 16–17).

Utopian aspirations, jokes, assaults and evasions are certainly elements of *SITP*'s 'disintegrating' power. Though Knight focuses on an earlier period of film history, he contends that aspects of the disintegrated musical appear in a number of later forms such as blaxploitation, pop musicals and music videos (ibid: 234).

Knight's stress on the mutability of the musical genre echoes recent film genre theory and analysis of the SF film. Against the long durée of film cycles and linear historical sedimentation, a more horizontal and hypertextual sense of genre formation has emerged. Genres are now fleeting and mobile formations, ironically conceived in a technological language reminiscent of Science Fiction. In his introduction to the anthology *Refiguring American Film Genres*, Nick Browne states that, "genres, here, are understood to gravitate toward specific assemblages of local coherencies – discrete, heterotopic instances of a complex cultural politics" (1998: xi). This technical-spatial lingua academicus bears the influence of Gilles Deleuze and Félix Guattari; rhizomatic connections and post-Castells network discourse are now recurrent features of genre theory. Genres seem to be less stable. They can disintegrate, dissolve, fall apart and recombine as hybrids or sub-genres. They may have short or long lives. In the same anthology, Rick Altman describes film scholars as akin to nomadic tribes on the Nile in ancient Egypt, raiding settlements of genres for specific purposes. Notwithstanding the dangers of romantic orientalism in this analogy, he argues that, "rather than assume that generic labels have – or should have – a stable existence", we should recognise "the permanent availability of all cultural products to serve as signifiers in the cultural bricolage that is our life" (Altman, 1998: 38).

Recent Science Fiction film studies also reconstitute the genre. With the increasing importance of special effects, scholars emphasise moments and intensities more than narrative. Alongside this turn, genre studies have become more centrally concerned with the *mediality* of film in the digital age. If Sci-Fi already reflects on technologies, theorists insist that the camera and celluloid are Science Fiction because of their ability to manipulate time and space. Critics refigure both apparatus theory and writing on the cinema of attractions through analysis of digital special effects. Brooks Landon argues that study of special effects might produce "a model for what Science Fiction film criticism might discover if it can draw back from its preoccupation with narratives in Science Fiction films and consider the science-fictional story that Science Fiction film production has itself become" (2002: 40). Scott Bukatman suggests that the sensational experiences of special effects are manifestations of the sublime – ways in which both the attraction of powerful technology and our fears about it are articulated within the excess of phantasmagoric spectacle. He writes that:

> The final effect is not a negative experience of anxious confusion, however, because it is almost immediately accompanied by a process of appropriation of, and identification with, the infinite powers on display. The phenomenal world is transcended as the mind moves to encompass what cannot be contained. (2002: 255)

The response encapsulates both 'shock and awe', to borrow the term the US military used for its bombing strategy in Iraq in 2003.

We might extend Bukatman's argument to music's function as a special effect. Sun Ra's central message in *SITP* is, after all, that music is *the* special effect that can transport black people into a higher state of consciousness and being. This seems doubly pertinent in a film that really can't afford expensive visual effects. A discourse of music as special effect, as bodily and mental sensation of musical textures, has gained critical momentum in post-rock electronic dance music DJ culture at the expense of the more narrative-minded analysis of song, verbal meaning and representation that was dominant in rock criticism. We seem to be moving toward what Steve Waksman describes as "a method of musical analysis that is less concerned with sense than sensation, and that recognises the place of sound, as music and as noise, in structuring the varieties of musical experience" (1999: 291). Drugs such as marijuana, LSD and Ecstasy that adjust subjective space and time relations and have played significant roles in music cultures have also contributed to this changed perspective on musical meaning. This is one reason why critics today laud the electronically enhanced psychedelia of the 1960s as one font in a futurism of 'out there' mediated sounds.

One of the strands in current discourse about music and technology, particularly with the rise of digital electronic music, has been a media-centeredness akin to the recent Science Fiction film theory I outlined above. Diedrich Diederichsen argues that music producers and critics articulate "a music only committed to its own mediality – as a strategy of the asemantic" (2002: 35) and that:

> A typical point of argument from the camp of today's digital-music producers is based precisely on media theory. This fixes in place all

significant differences regarding the digital status of (almost) all cur-
rently available sounds and defines one's own production as the one that
– even in a somewhat 'critical' sense – displays digitality, makes its
special effects audible, and, in contrast to other music, does not just use
digital sound manipulation to optimise already known musical practices.
(ibid: 34)

This modernism of sound production – the shock of the new and its non-representational materiality as mediated noise – underpins why Sun Ra's use of electronic instruments and the generic fusions – jazz-funk, jazz-rock, art rock and so on – of the late 1960s and early 1970s have become privileged points in an emergent techno-centric discourse in popular music studies. Even back in the 1970s, Val Wilmer claimed that:

Sun Ra's use of it [the moog synthesiser] is inspired and original. His
work epitomises Marshall McLuhan's thesis that electronic media herald
a rebirth of tribal conditions. McLuhan has pointed out the Afro-Ameri-
can talent for making audible the new possibilities of electronics, and
Sun Ra, along with Stevie Wonder, it should be said, has done for the
synthesiser what Jimmy Smith did for the organ and Charlie Christian
did for the electric guitar. (1992: 79)

* * * * * *

If we are to use Science Fiction texts in order to be more reflexive about the technologies in which they are mediated, then how might we consider *SITP* and Sun Ra from our present vantage point? Let us consider how *SITP*, as a generically unstable film that dis/integrates the musical is itself under erasure and reconstitution in its remediation in new contexts. The film and Sun Ra's audiovisual presence have been looped, sampled, appropriated, and re-voiced in a number of forms that contribute to the contested formation of Afrofuturism. Ra remains a ghostly echo in the mix, as in Theo Parrish's inspired murky funk track *Saga of Resistance* (2003), where the Arkestra's horns and percussive movement dissolves into a slow drawn out shuffle beat.

Angela Y. Davis points out the "fragility and mutability of historical images, particularly those associated with African American history" (1998: 23). Like Sun Ra, Davis taught in the University of California system. She laments that photographs taken of her in the late 1960s and early 1970s now define her in media culture and popular memory as 'the Afro'. She draws attention to a March 1994 *Vibe* magazine spread entitled 'Free Angela: Actress Cynda Williams as Angela Davis, a Fashion Revolutionary'. This 'docu-fashion' spread incorporates the stereotypical sartorial elements now associated with the black nationalism of the period, such as black leather jackets and sunglasses. Davis worries how media texts grounded in a serious politics of the past travel and mutate into apolitical commodity-signs in the postmod-ern present. David Crane (2000) argues that images of black people, science

93

and technology together are not always empowering but are often used in popular culture to mediate 'proper' uses of technology in a manner that fetishises the 'urban authenticity' of African Americans. Given *SITP*'s place at the intersection of black nationalism, blaxploitation and Sun Ra's musical theatre of alienation, the film's 'cult' and camp status risks us not taking its humour and other elements seriously. At the same time, we might remain wary of Ra's sanctification by his followers.

SITP and Ra have disintegrated into a number of other texts, resurrected through modular traces in various arguments since his death in 1993. Kodwo Eshun uses *SITP* and Ra to argue for a positive sense of alienation which rejects the sociological imagination and realism: "Everywhere, the 'street' is considered the ground and guarantee of all reality, a compulsory logic explaining all Black music, conveniently hearing anti-social surrealism as social realism" (1998: 00[-004]). While I agree with Eshun that analysis of black music is often couched in the limited, literal terms of documentary and ethnography, his argument risks evacuating a consideration of the social, political and economic contexts in which it is produced, distributed and consumed. In his enthusiasm for a posthuman dissolution of the human within the machinic and technological, he tends to elide the way that the 'human' might still be a useful category.

In the film *The Last Angel of History*, John Akomfrah and the Black Audio Collective insert images of Sun Ra in *SITP*'s space colony alongside interviews with many cultural practitioners (including Eshun and Sun Ra expert John Corbett) to sketch a history of popular Afrofuturism that explores the line "between Science Fiction and social reality". Citing the chant that opens *SITP* – "It's after the end of the world, don't you know that yet?" – Corbett argues that for Ra, Lee Perry and George Clinton, "the possibility of this impossible alternative futurity rests on reconfiguring the past, on the construction of vast, transformative, science-fictional mythologies, on looking back at the end of history – not a romantic terminus but the historical truncation endemic in the white 'uprooting' of black African civilizations" (1994: 22). To this end, Ra took up "the task of global pedagogy – as a supersonic cosmo-science sermonist" (ibid: 169). Indeed, Ra can be found in more didactic mode in Robert Mugge's 1980 documentary *A Joyful Noise* than in the relatively narrative-driven *SITP*.

Ajay Heble (2000: 117–139) takes off from the pedagogical element in Ra's work to meditate on Ra and *SITP*, and indeed jazz, as templates for postcolonial critique and new forms of knowledge. However, he also points out that Ra's desire in the film to leave for a 'colony' remains within the logic of imperialism. Heble alludes to John Gill's critique of Ra's silence, and the silence of his admirers, about his queer sexuality: "Sun Ra died and was buried... a plump elderly heterosexual in a Mardi Gras frock and the queer Herman Blount was duly Disappeared in the obituary columns" (1995: 61). *SITP* also betrays the patriarchal ideology of early 1970s' black nationalism, encapsulated in the track *When the Blackman ruled the world, Pharaoh was sitting on the throne*, ironically voiced by June Tyson. Apart from Tyson's powerful shamanic presence, women are mostly signs of male power in the film. Tellingly, only black men get to go to Outer Space with Ra. While Ra believed in the group improvisation process in his big band format of the Arkestra, he also stressed strong leadership and autocracy. Szwed notes that Ra voted for Richard Nixon and George Bush and was going to vote for Ross Perot when he died (quoted in Hargus, 1997). In fact, Kodwo Eshun approvingly refers to Ra and other African–American alien musicians as 'despots' because they are anti-human, since human is "a really pointless and treacherous category which has never meant anything to African-Americans" (A[193]).

In a chapter entitled 'Third Stone From the Sun' (named after a song by the Jimi Hendrix Experience), Paul Gilroy (2000: 326–356) reminds us of the possibilities of vernacular futurisms but also warns of the rise of apocalyptic, military–authoritarian and racially essentialist Science Fictions. He is critical of the Nation of Islam but also the nationalist and familial Science Fictions of *Independence Day* and *Men in Black*. Gilroy concludes his book *Against Race* with a call for "more powerful visions of planetary humanity from the future into the present and to reconnect them with democratic and cosmopolitan traditions that have been all but expunged from today's black imaginary" (2000: 356). Alexander G. Weheliye also believes that we might not want to ditch the notions of human and humanism just yet: "in proclaiming the historical moment of the posthuman, we might do well to interrogate 'other humanities'... and thus ameliorate the provinciality of 'humanity' in its various Western guises" (2002: 40). That way, I believe, we might be nearer to reaching the spaces and the places that The Streets suggest in their utopian chorus, "Weak become heroes and the stars align".

I should like to thank Tom McCourt for access to his Sun Ra archive.

Chapter Five

NOSTALGIA, MASCULINIST DISCOURSE AND AUTHORITARIANISM
in John Williams' Scores for *Star Wars* and *Close Encounters of the Third Kind*

NEIL LERNER

1977 was a major year for Hollywood, ranking with 1915, 1927 or 1939 as a year of particularly significant 'event' films[1]. The release of both *Star Wars* (back when it was just called 'Star Wars') and *Close Encounters of the Third Kind* (again, before it had any 'special' or 'collector's' edition amendments to its title) prompted Larry Gross to describe the moment as "the Year of Our Lord 1977" especially in relation to blockbuster action films (1995: 7)[2]. Gross goes on to trace a genealogy of what he calls "the Big Loud Action Movie", positioning *Star Wars* and *Close Encounters* as key influential films standing between *2001: A Space Odyssey*, the James Bond films and the Irwin Allen disaster movies, on the one hand; and then, on the other hand, leading to "Big Loud Action Movies" like the *Die Hard* trilogy or *Batman Forever*[3]. *Star Wars* and *Close Encounters* are also identified as significant, although not as groundbreaking as *Jaws*, in the important essay entitled 'The New Hollywood' written by Thomas Schatz (1993). Schatz cites the economic and marketing factors that transformed Hollywood filmmaking in the mid-1970s, most notably its turn towards the production of blockbuster films that, through front-loading and saturation marketing, were capable of generating massive profits for the industry. While both Gross and Schatz agree that several elements of production come together to make the New Hollywood blockbuster a cultural event, neither seem to regard music as an especially significant factor in the films' multiple successes. The films' successes can be measured in many ways: in terms of economics, they can be seen as successful at generating revenue[4]; as entertainment for audience members, the massive ticket sales speak to the numbers of people desiring that filmic experience; and as rhetoric, these films must surely be respected for their success at conveying any number and type of values, the full implications of which we may never comprehend.

Yet music, and specifically the orchestral scores of John Williams, has become an important part of the New Hollywood. Williams' scores of the mid-1970s have been hailed as a kind of renaissance or re-emergence of symphonic music for cinema (Palmer and Marks, 2001). At the same time, the symphonic score never completely disappeared from Hollywood, and Jerry Goldsmith is one of several who might be annoyed to hear that Williams 'restored' the type of score he and others had been writing through-out the late-1960s and early-1970s. It would also be inaccurate to suggest that the symphonic score led to the removal of more popular musics from Hollywood's soundtracks. More than just returning to an older way of making musical sounds (using a symphony orchestra), Williams' scores are remarkable for their rhetorical power. At the heart of Williams' wildly successful scores for *Star Wars* and *Close Encounters* is an effective blend of memory, nostalgia and manipulative power for the films' less obvious arguments. Just as both films give the illusion of looking to the future while offering up reactionary arguments steeped in a desire for the values of the past, the two scores similarly resist radical musical languages in favor of the familiar sounds of the late 19th and early 20th centuries. What I want to offer in this chapter is a reading of these two film scores that reveals their seductive and, at least to some, unsavory arguments: in *Star Wars*, a particular (and central) melodic motif reinforces the film's overall masculin-ist imagery and focus; with *Close Encounters*, the dialectic between the modern and antimodern styles supports those critics who find the film's rhetoric authoritarian or even fascist.

Musical Codes and Masculinity in *Star Wars*

Williams' score for *Star Wars* sits at the heart of one of the great, unremarked paradoxes of the film and its reception. It is contrapuntal in the sense that the music does not, in certain ways at least, reflect the images. While Lucas's mise-en-scene was roundly praised for its illusion of a gritty realism – for example, the space ships and robots show evidence of wear via scratches and scuffs, equipment sometimes needs repairing, the menacing space station has a smelly trash compactor, and so on – the music could hardly be called 'realist' in any sense. As performed by the London Symphony Orchestra and channeled through a Dolby sound system, this music connotes something without grit; on the contrary, it gleams and shines. Williams employs a musical style that has long been encoded with associations of precision, power, and bourgeois subjectivity: namely, the post-romantic orchestral style of composers like Richard Strauss or Erich Wolfgang Korngold. That such a musical language felt natural for this film was no accident, given its clear connections back to the adventure films of the 1930s, like the Errol Flynn swashbuckling costume epics (scored by Korngold) and the *Flash*

Gordon and *Buck Rogers* serials[5]. Randall Larson (1985) is one of many who have observed that Williams eschewed electronic or avant-garde music, choosing not to equate 'alien landscape' with 'alien style', the mode used so often in 1950s SF soundtracks, where unfamiliar timbres like those of the theremin worked to destabilise a sense of familiarity[6]. Often contemporary reviewers spoke of the score as Wagnerian, or of the film as a 'space opera', and James Buhler's perceptive essay on the *Star Wars* score (2000) locates in Williams' use of the leitmotif the restoration of the mythic qualities lost in most film music, a loss identified and lamented by Adorno[7]. Still, the *Star Wars* score borrows from sources beyond Wagner; it is, as Kevin Donnelly (1998) has noted, a pastiche comprised of many styles and languages (Stravinsky, Holst, and Korngold are but three of the other influences that can be heard[8]).

Much has been made of *Star Wars'* obsession with the past. In his famous 1983 essay 'Postmodernism and Consumer Culture', Fredric Jameson speaks of the "nostalgia film", a type of film about the past whose style depends upon a pastiche not from high culture but rather mass culture. After marking Lucas's first financial success, *American Graffiti* (1973), as one of the inaugural nostalgia films, Jameson goes on to complicate the category by suggesting that *Star Wars* is also, metonymically, a nostalgia film:

> Star Wars *reinvents this experience* [of the Saturday afternoon serial] *in the form of a pastiche: that is, there is no longer any point to a parody of such serials since they are long extinct.* Star Wars, *far from being a pointless satire of such now dead forms, satisfies a deep (might I even say repressed?) longing to experience them again: it is a complex object in which on some first level children and adolescents can take the adventures straight, while the adult public is able to gratify a deeper and more properly nostalgic desire to return to that older period and to live its strange old aesthetic artifacts through once again. This film is thus* metonymically *a historical or nostalgia film: unlike* American Graffiti, *it does not reinvent a picture of the past in its lived totality; rather, by reinventing the feel and shape of characteristic art objects of an older period (the serials), it seeks to reawaken a sense of the past associated with those objects.* (Jameson, 1983: 116)

Just what was so attractive about that older period, though? *American Graffiti*, to cite but one example, used rock music to evoke "a culture before the Beatles, the Kennedy assassination, Vietnam, and Watergate" (Smith, 1998: 179), in short, a time before the loss of innocence that so traumatised the generation of the US baby boomers. Calling the 1940s and 1950s a 'golden age', a time before a loss of innocence, is to overlook the many positive changes that happened concurrently with the disillusionments of Vietnam and Watergate. To name but one, I would point to the altered social and political roles permitted to women in the United States. The setting of *Star Wars* is "a long time ago, in a galaxy far, far away" with regards to its gender roles, for the central focus in this narrative – made clear for us by the music – is the coming-of-age of Luke Skywalker.

That the female experience is omitted, marginalised or recast into traditional subservient roles is an observation that commentators quickly made about *Star Wars*. Dan Rubey wrote about the film's foregrounding of the male relationships and male-oriented viewpoints:

> *Women exist primarily to provide motivations for male activity, to act as spectators, or to serve as mediators between different levels in the male hierarchy. When Luke's aunt isn't stuffing artichokes into the Cuisinart, she serves as a mediator between Luke and his uncle and then as a motive for revenge when Luke returns home and finds her charred body... Princess Leia, despite her attractive spunkiness and toughness, basically fills the same male-oriented roles. She is the traditional damsel in distress – it is her capture by Darth Vader which begins the film and provides the motivation for Ben Kenobi's return and Luke's rescue mission. Although she does grab a laser at one point and fire a few shots, she is dependent on her male rescuers, and the only action she initiates during the rescue almost gets them killed in the garbage crusher. Her most memorable line, repeated over and over by her holograph image, is "Help me, Obi-Wan Kenobi. You are my only hope." (1978: 18)*

The boys' club was not limited to the fictional world of the film. In his unauthorised biography of Lucas, Dale Pollock reports that Carrie Fisher, often the only woman on the set, was required by Lucas to flatten her breasts with electrical tape in an effort to conceal her femininity; and Pollock also quotes Lucas as saying that Leia was "'sort of a drag and she's a nuisance, just like most little sisters" (1983: 165). And in case Lucas's screenplay did not make clear Leia's role as a relatively passive object, Williams' motif for her (slow, alluring, with the rising major sixth suggesting a passionate longing) further confirms that her character is associated with these reactionary gender roles: Leia's motif, quite unlike Luke's, undergoes little transformation or development[9].

In contrast, it is made apparent from the opening moments of the film that Luke is at the centre of *Star Wars*, as Williams' score presents the heroic title theme, a melody that becomes Luke's leitmotif throughout the film. Commenting on his motif for Luke, Williams has said that he "composed a melody that reflected the brassy, bold, masculine, and noble qualities I saw in the character"[10] (quoted in Matessino, 1997: 11). Certainly as we first hear it, during the opening credits, when it is not yet clear that the motif will represent Luke, the music sounds brassy, bold, noble and, even, masculine. The martial duple rhythms, the trumpet timbres for the melody and the leaping, disjunct quality of the melody's shape (ascending first a fourth, then a fifth and finally, twice, up a seventh, before coming to a resting point) are all ways that many composers have earlier connoted masculinity through music. Many of the features of the *Star Wars* main title music resemble the main title music in Korngold's score for *Kings Row* (1942). While the films' diegetic settings are literally worlds apart, they both share an important similarity: both films are coming-of-age narratives about a male protagonist, and both scores imply that character's importance by adopting the character's motif as the film's title music[11]. Many commentators have remarked on the similarity between the Luke and Parris motifs – see, for example, Adams, (1999); Flinn (1992); Gilliam (1999b), Lerner (2001) and Scheurer (1997) – and Williams follows Korngold in using different forms of the motif to represent varying stages of the character's development. In one of Korngold's most efficient examples of leitmotific technique and character development, Parris, the main character from *Kings Row*, walks over a turnstile, away from the camera, as a child. Then, after an elliptical edit covering the passage of ten years, he walks back towards the camera and over the same turnstile only now as an adult. His motif is heard first in the woodwinds, slowly, softly, without a clear sense of pulse, and thinly orchestrated. Then the adult Parris's footsteps follow, underscored by the brass, in a much louder and rhythmically decisive fashion. The shifts in tempo, rhythm and, most importantly, timbre subtly alert the audience to Parris's maturation.

Williams extends that technique throughout *Star Wars* where Luke's motif goes through considerable development. The motif occurs several times beyond the opening titles. As we first see Luke, and hear his name called out by his aunt, his motif occurs in the French horn, slower and more smoothly than during the main title. The melody comes back in later scenes (for instance, as Luke sells his landspeeder), often in the woodwinds, as Luke is defined as immature and whiny. During the scene where Luke and Leia escape from stormtroopers by swinging across a chasm, the motif returns as it did in the title music, loudly and heroically, with the melody back in the trumpets, where it creates one of the most euphoric moments in the film (could some of the excitement be from the kiss – "for luck" – that Leia gives Luke right before leaping over the abyss?).

Luke's motif also figures prominently in the music accompanying the rebels' attack on the Death Star, where Williams sometimes shifts it to the minor mode. Both in terms of the narrative, as well as through its visual symbols, the attack on the space station marks the final step in Luke's growth as a man in this film. The earlier rebel briefing scene, where the pilots are shown a film instructing them how and where to place their missiles, bears an odd resemblance to a sex education film, showing as it does how one tiny but precisely-delivered missile can set off the chain reaction that can bring about the explosive climax of the relatively huge and spherical Death Star. The symbolism is barely symbolic: X and Y material (X-wing and Y-wing fighters)[12] are sent off to the giant sphere/ovum; and we watch the faces of the all-male pilots scrunch up and grimace as they enter the Death Star's trench. Some of them deliver their missiles prematurely and externally, and thus ineffectually since they do not penetrate. But Luke, with the help of Han and the coaching of Kenobi, remains in the trench long enough to send the missiles to their destination, which causes his face to relax as he takes long, heavy breaths in the afterglow created by the Death Star's massive detonation[13]. Williams' music – building, sequencing, ultimately climaxing – conspires with the images to announce this significant step towards Luke's achievement of (one type of) manhood.

It is not hard to imagine why this preoccupation with manhood and masculinity would have been so popular in 1977, so shortly after the patriarchal power structures in the United States were challenged both domestically and abroad. The success of the music in *Star Wars* is not just in the way that Williams revived the dormant swashbuckling sounds of Korngold and Hollywood's 'golden age', but more importantly, the ways that the music works so seamlessly with the rest of the film to sate a nostalgic appetite for so-called simpler times[14]. Film and score return us to a time of unproblematic masculine dominance.

Politics, Science Fiction and Aesthetic Modernism in *Close Encounters of the Third Kind*

Close Encounters was *Wünderkind* Steven Spielberg's follow-up to the industry-transforming *Jaws*, the 1975 film that nearly single-handedly established and defined the emergent New Hollywood marketing practices of the front-loaded summer blockbuster (Schatz, 1993). Coming out in mid-November 1977, only a few months after the first US release of *Star Wars* (late May), *Close Encounters* engaged rather different conventions of the Science Fiction genre than its light-sabre-wielding neighbor. *Close Encounters* offers up a type of spectacular cinematic salvation in response to a middle-American suburban life that is represented as banal, materialistic and claustrophobic – in a word, alienating. The film acknowledges its generic ancestors, particularly the alien invasion (or Bug Eyed Monster – B.E.M.) Science Fiction film so popular in the 1950s. Indeed, Spielberg's early working title for the film was 'Watch the Skies', the closing lines from 1951's *The Thing from Another World*, an early and important alien invasion film[15]. One of Spielberg's more radical transformations of the genre followed upon the important model of Stanley Kubrick's *2001: A Space Odyssey* (1968), which presented the optimistic possibility offered earlier (and rarely since) in 1950's *The Day the Earth stood still*: that humans were being watched by benign extraterrestrials, heavenly creatures who care and just want to get to know us better. As the tag-line went on promotional posters and in trailers, 'We are not alone'[16].

The initial release of *Close Encounters* sparked two divergent responses: as the film enjoyed commercial and financial success, being cheerfully consumed by millions of filmgoers, a relatively small group of writers were quick to draw attention to Spielberg's manipulative cinematic techniques. Robert Entman and Francie Seymour turned to Susan Sontag as they outlined a number of authoritarian or even fascist traces in the film's ideology (Entman and Seymour, 1978; Sontag, 1975). They noted connections between Weimar Germany and the Carter-era US in the film's attacks on the governing authorities, its resignation to authoritarianism and elitism and its elevation of irrational dogma over scientific reason. Tony Williams took the argument further, memorably referring to *Close Encounters* as "a Disneyland version of *Triumph of the Will*" (1983: 23). A study of Williams' remarkable score can enrich this ideological critique.

Although it is not normally read as a critical aesthetic manifesto, Steven Spielberg's film (and John Williams' score for) *Close Encounters* contain, among other things, a familiar rendering of a certain kind of musical modernism that encodes that which is meant to be perceived as 'alien'. Music plays a significant role in the film's diegesis, acting as the most important of several nonverbal languages, teasingly connecting some characters while alienating others (in ways not at all unlike the alienation of some listeners with concert hall modernism). The film has already been fruitfully inter-preted as one of several post–Watergate, post–Vietnam texts appearing in the middle and late 1970s, offering up a US middle class distrustful of the government, the military and patriarchal authority in general – a populace ripe, as several have argued, for an authoritarian message. Classed generi-cally as a Science Fiction film, *Close Encounters* addresses some of the traditional questions of the genre – questions of moral and metaphysical speculation, of cultural identity and one's position in the cosmos (or, at least, the suburbs) while projecting and personifying collective anxieties onto the easy target of an alien. It is a Science Fiction film that is aware of its generic ancestry, for in it we can find a number of references back to earlier films, including the genre-transforming *2001: A Space Odyssey* as well as a host of alien invasion films from the 1950s. Beyond, or underneath, the film's political and metaphysical discourse, however, lurks Williams' richly eclectic music, persistently pulling us towards the film's infantalisingly epiphanic conclusion.

The *Close Encounters* score employs several characteristic techniques of high musical modernism, including aleatoric passages and the use of tone clusters, in addition to the overarching modernist musical eclecticism championed by Richard Strauss in 'Der Rosenkavalier'[17] (Gilliam, 1999a: 89). A close analy-sis of Williams' score for *Close Encounters* can enhance our understanding of the overall cinematic text. Spielberg's seemingly inevitable movement from darkness to light, from mystery to enlightenment, from suburb to celestial paradise, is powerfully underscored as the music shifts stylistically from cues with a pointed lack of melody early in the film (emulating the progres-sive/modernist tone cluster pieces of György Ligeti and Krzysztof Penderecki) to later cues featuring a clear, familiar melodic theme (frequently Disney's *When You Wish Upon a Star*), harmonised with a post-Romantic tonal language. The score thus sets up the more experimental musical style as strange by associating it with the aliens, and ultimately it rejects this modernist musical language, substituting tonality for atonality just as it substitutes a non-descript heavenly existence for middle-American materi-alist banality. As a film existing in several versions and rich in intertextual allusions, *Close Encounters* offers up a peculiarly disturbing response to life in the United States of the 1970s. To look past the visual and musical spectacle of the film's conclusion is to realise the extent to which Spielberg infantalises both the diegetic and the non-diegetic viewers and inscribes an authoritarian (or to some, fascist) ideology. The stylistic metamorphosis present in Williams' score – the movement from a high modernist vocabulary towards a more familiar melodic vocabulary – serves as a powerful semiotic, rhetorical, and critical strategy.

Besides its obvious Science Fiction antecedents, the film also has less obvious roots in the genres of the religious epic film popular in Hollywood in the 1950s and 1960s and in the Disney magic film, especially *Pinocchio* (1940) but also, to a certain degree, *Peter Pan* (1953). A number of writers have noted, in one way or another, the film's religiosity and its theological tone – see Entman and Seymour (1978), Torry (1991) and Williams (1983). The central lesson of the parable of Roy Neary is, like Peter Pan, to dismiss the adult world of responsibility in order to chase one's childhood dreams. Indeed, it serves to underscore the relative profundity of the moral lesson in Spielberg's next alien film, *E.T. The Extra-Terrestrial* (1982), which is conveniently if not necessarily simple: to "be good." Some examples of the Judeo-Christian religiosity in *Close Encounters*: Roy behaves as a sort of Moses figure, leading his chosen people out of the suburbs and to an important promised encounter at a mountain (in his first scene, the crossing of the Red Sea sequence from the film *The Ten Commandments* is playing on Roy's television set)[18]. Roy is also configured as a kind of Christ figure (Moses's typological equivalent). His very name, Roy, contains an old Shakespearean pun ('Roy' = 'roi' = 'king', *Henry V*, iv.1.49), hinting at his regal character while also creating certain ironies as both a 'king' (he is an ineffectual, even impotent patriarch within his family) and as someone 'near' (he is alienated from job, wife, and family). Spielberg's decision to include part of the Budweiser jingle 'Here comes the king' was a financially costly one, according to Fred Karlin, who saw its presence only as a way to increase an illusion of realism (1994: 137). However, it was also a clever way to reveal Roy's kingly status and also his connection with material consumer culture – we hear "The king is coming, let's hear the call/When you've said Bud you've said it all" just a moment before Roy has his televisual epiphany that connects his living room mountain with Devil's Tower, the site of the aliens' arrival. One of the 'disciples' running up the mountain with Roy succumbs to the army's sleeping gas, like the sleeping disciples in the garden of Gethsemane. Roy is selected from a group of twelve red-suited 'pilgrims' and led, arms extended, in the shape of a cross, up to his ultimate communion with the heavens. Other biblical stories invoked in *Close Encounters* include: Saul's conversion experience on his way to Damascus (Roy too is lost on the path and the blinding light burns and transforms him); the Tower of Babel and the issues of communication (the government workers are ineffectual in reaching up to the heavens, in part because of their language barriers, while characters like Roy and Barry are able to intuit messages from the aliens); and the parousia-like return of the dead as acted out by the Mothership's returning of the abductees.

Roy's earlier enthusiasm to take his children to see *Pinocchio* follows Spiel-berg's Christological narrative. A Christ figure, the character of Pinocchio finds himself uncomfortably torn between two worlds, that of being a wooden puppet and that of being a 'real' boy. After wishing upon a star, his father gets his wish that his (only begotten) son be transformed from wood into flesh. Along the way, Pinocchio faces the temptations of Pleasure Island, the acting life and that nagging conscience in the form of Jiminy Cricket, who sings the most famous song from the score, *When You Wish Upon a Star*, a melody that was later adopted by Disney as the theme for their weekly *Wonderful World of Disney* television series. The melody appears diegetically in *Close Encounters* (a music box plays some of it in the Special Edition) and also non-diegetically, as Williams quotes it several times in the final scenes (as well as in the closing credits of – only – the Special Edition). In early drafts of the screenplay, Spielberg intended to have Ukelele Ike's original version of the song from *Pinocchio* playing as Roy entered the Mothership. Spielberg's novelisation of the film makes clear something that may not be as obvious from the screenplay or finished film: the song *When You Wish Upon a Star* is what Roy is hearing as he enters the Mothership (Roy "was thinking and hearing a song in his head" and it goes on to print the words)[19]. The fact that the music is intended to be heard within Roy's head is but one example of how Roy's experience and positioning is strongly set up as the intended subjective positioning of the audience – we are all supposed to be Roy.

The music participates in the film's authoritarian rhetoric; it leaves little ambiguity as to how the film demands that it be read. Williams' score masterfully manipulates the audience through its careful use of a number of widely understood musical codes, some of which are quite old. A recurring chase motif in the film consists of obsessive, Herrmannesque repetitions of the first part of the *Dies irae* chant (a melody Williams used before briefly in *Star Wars* as Luke and Obi-Wan find the charred remains of Luke's aunt and uncle, the moment of the famous allusion to John Ford's *The Searchers* [1956]). This motif is sometimes blended together with an alternating (rocking) two chord pattern (often a D-flat major with an added sixth to a C seventh), privileging a rising tritone melody. This music accompanies most of the early observations of the recurring shape that will eventually become identified as the United States' first national monument and site for the close celestial encounter, Devil's Tower. Could Williams have purposefully at-tached the old *diabolus in musica* (the tritone) to Devil's Tower?

Beyond using ancient religious musical codes for the satanic (the tritone and the *Dies irae* melody), Williams also plays with certain modernist vocabular-ies in order to emphasise the frightening nature of the aliens (before we learn their true benevolent intent, they are set up as mischievous and even menacing: they mess up our refrigerators and steal our children). In inter-views, Williams speaks of two musical vocabularies, one atonal and one Romantic (Bouzereau, 1998). Hollywood's stylistic hegemony of musical vocabularies has generally avoided avant-garde modernist practices except when underscoring horror and Science Fiction (there are exceptions to that as well). The horror film in the 1930s and the Science Fiction film of the 1950s both turned to modernisms of timbre. Kubrick's famous temp track/score for *2001* brought the post-tonal tone cluster sound of Ligeti to a wide audience, implicating that sound with images and ideas of the profoundly unknown and unknowable (the alien). Williams' tone cluster cues for *Close Encounters* follow that precedent. Referring to the most (traditionally) frightening scene in the film, where Barry is abducted from his mother's house[20], music editor Ken Wannberg has recalled that, "the one piece I remembered that it was temped with was the Penderecki" (quoted in Bond, 1998: 28). Even though Wannberg does not name it, it seems plausible and likely that the specific work was Penderecki's famous and heavily anthologised *Threnody for the Victims of Hiroshima* (1960), whose tone clusters and non-traditional string playing techniques can be heard in Williams' abduction music. Extreme dissonance, unfamiliar timbres and atonality have long been associated with representations of negative states and emotions, and Williams' use of this post-serial atonal vocabulary here acts only to heighten the sense of terror associated with the abduction[21]. This scene (and its music) marks one of those points where Science Fiction and horror conventions are identical.

Like many carefully crafted verbal arguments, the score's most powerful rhetorical maneuvers occur right at its conclusion. In general terms, the music in this film progresses from a more abstract, melody-less atonal language (the 'alien' modernism) to one that is more familiar, melodic, and tonal. The visual motif of darkness and light, perhaps representing a drive towards spiritual enlightenment, finds a musical parallel in this movement from melody-less music towards a music of clear, even famous, melody. Formlessness yields to form; the threatening yields to the familiar as Penderecki yields to Disney. The closing scenes depict Roy's assumption to the heavens, as the government officials who originally prevented his attendance at the event mysteriously decide to include Roy among the twelve other red-suited 'pilgrims' and as the child-like humanoid aliens choose Roy from the group as the sole human who will ascend with them.

The music begins in the style of the earlier abduction scene but Williams gradually interpolates the melody from *When You Wish Upon A Star* into an increasingly tonal and melodic symphonic section that rhapsodises through postromantic harmonies and satisfyingly familiar voice-leading and cadences. Early drafts of the screenplay reveal Spielberg's diegetic placement of the song and his early conception of Roy as a sort of Pinocchio figure. Spielberg later wrote that when Roy Neary walks up the ramp to the Mothership, "he becomes a real person. He loses his strings, his wooden joints, and he goes on that ship knowing what he's doing" (quoted in Durwood, 1977:118). The extra scenes in *The Special Edition* let us, along with Roy, gaze upon the womb-like interior of the Mothership. Williams' music for this sequence in *The Special Edition* repeats the larger progression from abstract to melodic, actually juxtaposing the two vocabularies during a tilt shot showing the aliens behind windows. Since one of the main

105

connecting themes in Disney films of the 1940s and 1950s (such as *Pinocchio*, *Peter Pan*, and *Dumbo*) is the constant reassurance of the comforts of familial and particularly parental bonds, the music of Disney and Pinocchio makes rhetorical sense here. The radically different style of the anti-melodic modernist tone cluster music resonates strongly as the appropriate music to accompany the abduction of a child, the disruption of the familial bonds, for it sets itself in opposition to melodic, tonal music (the music associated with the Disney model of family). After Roy's ascension to the Mothership, the music becomes lovingly tonal and melodic. Williams crafts a new melody here and harmonises it through chromatically-inflected tonality; he also brings back other melodies from the score, including the five-note 'communication' motif. Furthermore, the 'Mountain' motif refers back to Hollywood's characteristic timbres for representing epic religiosity and grandeur: harps and textless female choirs[22]. By the final scenes in the film, Williams' music demands that we regard the extraterrestrials as not only benevolent but both familiar and familial. Beyond simply suggesting an anti-modernist critique of the tone-cluster modernism of Ligeti and Penderecki, Williams' score for *Close Encounters* brings together the traditional musical signifiers for that which is alien next to the signifiers of epic religiosity. Williams' brilliantly effective music for *Close Encounters* fortifies the film's authoritarian rhetoric and helps to prepare the way for Reagan's 1980s.

It is important to note, however, that Williams, like virtually all composers working within the commercial film industry, provides music that fits the specifications of the director. Hollywood composers almost never get to rewrite screenplays or dictate issues of editing or cinematography. If one composer does not or cannot provide the music desired by the director and/or producer, another composer will be brought in who can supply the desired effect. What is so remarkable about Williams' scores – and they are considerable achievements in the history of musical style – is the way that they so effectively limit any oppositional readings of the films they accompany. In *Star Wars*, the music makes it difficult to identify any other character besides Luke as the central hero, and in *Close Encounters*, the music communicates no sense of dread or remorse over Roy's abrogation of his duties as husband/father. In this way, both scores contribute to what Robin Wood has termed "The Lucas-Spielberg Syndrome" (1986: 162–174). Wood stresses the centrality of the concept of reassurance in this syndrome – the reassurance that comes, for instance, from repetition and retreat into a child-like perspective. Williams' sweepingly nostalgic music reassures, persuades, and above all else, lulls us into being uncritical.

Special thanks are due to Tay Fizdale who first introduced me to the politics and rhetoric of *Close Encounters* in his film lectures at Transylvania University.

Notes

1. *The Birth of a Nation*, *The Jazz Singer* and both *Gone with the Wind* and *The Wizard of Oz* were the important event films of those years.
2. A brief note on editions: by *Star Wars*, I will in this essay be referring to the film that is

now known as *Star Wars Episode IV: A New Hope*. When pertinent, I will distinguish between *Close Encounters of the Third Kind* (1977) and *Close Encounters of the Third Kind: The Special Edition* (1980). These films now exist in multiple forms, sometimes with significantly different scenes, edits, and musical scores. In the Newer Hollywood of Lucas and Spielberg, any film is now subject to continual and constant revising and updating, as budgets and technologies progress. The director may claim that issues of quality motivate these revisions, but it also provides for a planned obsolescence (and the consequent repackaging and reselling of the original text) that leads Gregory Solman (2002) to equate "movie" with "software".

3. Gross categorises the influential innovations of Lucas and Spielberg into four points crucial to the new action movie: 1. B movie genre plots are elevated into elaborate and expensive production; 2. narrative complexity is reduced; 3. the Cinematic, the Image and Technology dominate the narrative experience; 4. self-deprecating humor. There is a subdued elegaic tone behind Gross's analysis, one that is perhaps not unlike 'The Silver Swan'.

4. Jeff Smith reports that:
the overwhelming success of *Star Wars* would help to revive the commercial fortunes of the classically styled film score. Released by 20th Century-Fox's record subsidiary, the *Star Wars* soundtrack sold over four million copies and made a household name of its composer, John Williams. (1998: 216)

5. Richard H. Bush (1989) describes the 'tracking', or stock, music used in the *Flash Gordon* and *Buck Rogers* serials that Universal Pictures produced between 1936 and 1940. Besides using many of the late Romantic works that had become standard fare during the pre-synchronised sound era (Liszt, Tchaikovsky, and Wagner all surface with regularity), there was also considerable recycling of existing film scores such as Franz Waxman's *The Bride of Frankenstein* (1935).

6. Almost all Science Fiction films from the 1950s deployed some sort of electronic timbres (often the theremin) to signify the 'alien'. The practice extends to Elmer Bernstein's score for *The Ten Commandments* (1956), where the music accompanying the plagues contains theremin and novachord.

7. Buhler rightly draws attention to the binary sunset sequence, where Luke stares out dreamily at the Tatooine horizon and we hear the Force/Ben theme. Buhler finds that moment remarkable since at that point in the film, the Force theme has not been explained. Although the Force motif has been heard once already (in the opening sequence, as Leia loads the Death Star plans and her plea for help into R2-D2), the musical signifier is still undefined in relation to either the Force or Obi-Wan Kenobi, and so Williams returns to the musical-dramatic techniques of Wagner (2000: 44). Irene Paulus (2000) has also written of the connection between Wagner and Williams.

8. Donnelly uses two scores by Danny Elfman, *Batman* and *Batman Returns*, to note the presence of pastiche in what he calls the post-classical film score. He refers as well to Williams and writes that, "both composers [ie Elfman and Williams] could to some degree be dubbed neoclassical in that they value the classical and use it as a model while also differentiating their music from it" (Donnelly, 1998: 150). He further delineates them by writing that "while both composers' music could be characterised as neoclassical, John Williams' work is best described as a pastiche of classical film scoring, and Danny Elfman's music for the Batman films as a parody of the film music of the past" (ibid: 151).

9. Leia's motif is nearly always played by woodwinds and reflects the ways that timbre has become loaded with gendered associations and meanings; woodwinds can suggest the feminine or the unmanly. Consider this speculation: "you can even imagine that if Princess Leia played an instrument, it would be a flute" (Kendall, 1997: 23).

10. Williams has also been quoted as describing the Luke theme as "flourishing and upward reaching, idealistic and heroic.... a very uplifted kind of heraldic quality. Larger than he

is. His idealism is more the subject than the character itself I would say" (quoted in Adams, 1999: 22).

11. Michael Pisani noted that the Luke motif has become the signature music for the entire *Star Wars* film series – in that every film opens and closes with that music – in a paper entitled "Building an EMPIRE: Levels of Communication in John Williams' Film Music," presented at the national meeting of the Society for American Music, March, 2003, in Lexington, Kentucky.

12. I am grateful to Jim Herrick for sharing that observation with me.

13. Further examples of this thinly-veiled psychosexual imagery come from the obsessively repeated symbolic castrations, in the form of arms being forcibly removed from masculine bodies (C-3PO and the would-be assailants in the bar both lose their arms, as Luke and Vader will, in later films, lose their hands), and Buhler has noted the fetishising of the phallus that occurs with the light sabre, a "relic of the Father" (Buhler, 2000: 49). Jane Caputi has written about the pervasive negative masculine qualities of *Star Wars*, noting that it presents "an all-white, all-male world and, like the Westerns and war movies it is modeled on, [it] reserves its principle commitments for violence, male bonding, and war." (1988: 496) I am grateful to Paul Miller for introducing me to that essay.

14. The musical language that Williams develops in *Star Wars* finds its way into later films like *Superman: The Movie* (1978), *Raiders of the Lost Ark* (1981) and their sequels, as well as numerous derivative scores by other composers.

15. That Spielberg's ambition was to be "the Cecil B. DeMille of Science Fiction" was reported by *Firelight* crewmember Jean Weber Brill (quoted in McBride, 1997: 463).

16. It is likely a coincidence that this five-syllable phrase could fit with the five-note 'communication' motif. Spielberg was insistent that the melody not be too long, like the seven notes of *When You Wish Upon A Star*, but rather something more compact, like a doorbell chime; Williams generated somewhere from 250 to 300 melodies until Spielberg settled on the one that made it into the film (Bouzereau, 1998).

17. Gilliam's observations about Strauss's modernist ahistoricism, his disinterest in stylistic uniformity, rings true for Williams as well, as when he writes that with Strauss, "we may see a composer who keenly recognised the disunities of modern life and believed that such incongruities should not be masked by a unified musical style" (1999a: 89).

18. The rampant allusions to earlier films by many Hollywood directors in the 1970s is discussed in Carroll (1998), and although Carroll only mentions Spielberg's references to cartoons in *Close Encounters* (the "flying saucers [that] zip along the highway like Road Runner") or the ways the ending "feed[s] off the 'Night on Bald Mountain' sequence of *Fantasia*") (251), the significance of *The Ten Commandments* to *Close Encounters* should not be underestimated.

19. The song appears in Roy's head in both the original novelisation of the film (Spielberg, 1977) and the revised 1980 novelisation, *Close Encounters of the Third Kind: The Special Edition* (Spielberg, 1980).

20. It might be argued that the final scenes of infantalised scientists and government officials, frozen with wide eyes and slack jaws in the presence of a mysterious higher power, is in fact the most terrifying image from the film.

21. Williams employs a similar dualistic score, setting atonality in opposition with tonality, in Robert Altman's *Images* (1972), described as "one of film music's outstanding creations" by Royal Brown (178). At present, this film is hard to find (although copies sometimes appear on eBay), and facsimiles of a few pages of the score are reproduced in Bazelon (1975: 303–307).

22. Debussy and Holst are two composers who earlier used wordless choirs to similar effects.

Chapter Six

SOUND AND MUSIC IN THE *MAD MAX* TRILOGY

REBECCA COYLE

In the beginning, my approach was very straightforward. I saw film purely as visual music and I became fascinated as to how we take little bits of celluloid and join them together like notes on the piano. For me, my first feature Mad Max *was a piece of visual rock and roll. I cut* Mad Max *like a silent movie trying to get the rhythms working just for the eye. Only later did I add the sound.* (George Miller, interviewed in the documentary *White Fellas Dreaming* [1993])[1]

In the above quote, director George Miller suggests that his first feature film – *Mad Max* (1979) – was edited without sound. Yet, despite this emphasis on an original 'silent cut', premised on durational elements of action and visual rhythm[2], sound is a key (and foregrounded) aspect of the film and its sequels *Mad Max 2* (1981) and *Beyond Thunderdome* (1985, co-written and co-directed with George Ogilvie). The *Mad Max* film trilogy has been widely reviewed and critiqued. Curiously, the music and sound of the films are rarely mentioned, much less analysed in depth[3]. Yet the film sound tracks, apart from serving the visual and narrative elements, significantly construct their own narratives, refer to their own generic conventions, and have their own production stories. These, in turn, contribute to the aesthetic aspect of their operation in the audio-visual texts. Furthermore, as reflected in Miller's comments quoted above, musical concepts and metaphors have influenced the director's oeuvre, commencing with the aesthetics that informed the production of the first *Mad Max* film in the late 1970s, and which developed in its sequels.

Miller was born in 1945 and raised in Chinchilla, a small town in rural Queensland. Although television was introduced in Australia in 1956, Miller recalls that it was a rare commodity in his town until much later and that film screenings at the local cinema were a more significant influence on his development. As a child, Miller habitually sneaked under the cinema building to experience films that he was not allowed to watch, where he huddled beneath the speakers, "content just to listen" (quoted in the *White Fellas Dreaming* documentary). This audio awareness of films may have informed his later approach to sound, music and movies as visual music.

Miller has claimed that, "[o]ur movies are the songlines of white fellas' Australia and, like the songs of the Aboriginal creation fathers, they sing us into being" (ibid). In what follows, I will tease out several points arising from Miller's comments, including the 'movies as visual music' aesthetic informing the *Mad Max* series, the construction of sound in the trilogy, and connections of the sound and music to Australia. This chapter analyses specific sequences and sound usages in each film and draws on these to characterise the role of sound and music in constructing the films' central protagonist, the narratives arising from his actions and motivations and broader filmic themes, issues and ideas. Extending Harley's analysis of the films' music (1998), this essay concentrates on the film sound tracks more generally, and particularly as they construct Science Fiction narratives.

The film narratives, I will argue, interweave various generic conventions that are threaded into futuristic scenarios. The accumulation of sound elements in the films provides elements of an historical overview of technologies of sound recording and playback. It also allows a revision of modernist euphoria around the sound-producing elements of industrialisation. The chapter discusses the sound of objects, atmospheres, speech and music in the films. While the audio components of films are generally clustered under headings of sound, music and voice, it is impossible to strictly abide by these categories, given the ways in which sounds are used as music, musical elements are used as sound, voices contribute to melodies, and so on. As such, this chapter offers a critique of production-informed approaches that use such divisions of film sounds as their starting point. Instead I will show how these elements only generally form sound clusters, and integrate to form aural sensory environments.

I. Background and Trilogy Overview/Overhear

The first *Mad Max* film directed by George Miller and released in 1979 was (and continues to be) significant for Australian cinema. The film became a box office hit in Australia, Europe and Japan and grossed more than AUS$150 million worldwide and recouped costs to the extent of being listed in the *Guinness Book of Records* as the most profitable film on a cost-to-revenue basis (King and Guilliatt, 1999: 68). Produced on a shoestring budget of AUS$380,000, *Mad Max* was funded via corporate sponsorship rather than supported by government funding agencies. At a time of Australian cinema's concentration on social realism, art movies and historical costume dramas, *Mad Max*'s apocalyptic scenario and mythic hero presented a distinctly different model for national cinema. *Mad Max* challenged filmmaking formulas in its rhythmic editing style, camera movement and punk-influenced visual motifs. The film was the first in Australian cinema history to be filmed in wide-screen format, compressing the perspective of roads "stretching to infinity" (Byron Kennedy quoted in King and Guilliatt, 1999: 68) and emphasising the sparse landscapes. In addition, while tackling universal themes such as good overcoming evil, the film retained sufficient references to Australian geography and lifestyles to be culturally resonant to Australians (and/or Australiaphiles). But, in addition to the direction, editing and narrative, the impact of *Mad Max* was also achieved via its sound track, particularly in comparison to the relative conservativism and/or stylistic inexperience of Australian film sound in the 1970s. In a highly critical review published after a preview of the film in May 1979, former Australian film producer, industry adviser and critic Philip Adams describes being "shaken with revulsion 12 hours later" (1979: 38). While he associates this feeling with the violence depicted onscreen and states that Miller's "diabolic opus" has "all the moral uplift of Mein Kampf" (ibid), it is likely that the full-on sound and music of the film contributed to its impact[4].

Post-production on *Mad Max*'s sound was completed over an extended period of five months full-time. Miller and co-producer Kennedy chose to use Armstrong Studios in Melbourne, a facility that specialised in sound for advertising and music recordings, rather than the established film sound facilities then based in Sydney. This choice of mixing venue enabled the producers to develop a complex mix, synthesising many diverse elements in a then-experimental style, giving the sound track "much more body – more oomph!" (Kennedy quoted in unattributed, 1979: 368). This included harmonising tracks via digital time delays and simple effects units like Marshall time modulators, and adding further sound effects as the mix was built up[5].

Mad Max was followed by *Mad Max 2*, produced on an AUS$4 million budget and released in 1981. Marketed as *Road Warrior* in the US, where the first film had not been a major hit, the box office success of the sequel stimulated audience awareness of the central character and assisted in the efficient marketing of the third *Mad Max* film, *Beyond Thunderdome*, released in 1985[6]. As a result, and helped by a $13m budget and star roles performed by Tina Turner and Mel Gibson, the third film achieved high attendance rates in the US, taking US$30 million in its first three weeks.

Mad Max 1 was marketed as a road movie, although the film references generic conventions of horror as well as car action, bikie and cop films. Ventkatasawmy *et al.* (2001:4) identify it as a "sci-fi apocalyptic" road movie to distinguish it from other hybrid forms of the 'road movie' genre developed in Australian cinema. Miller claims that the film was originally located in a contemporary setting and later shifted to a short period into the future:

> *Halfway through the script, it occurred to me that it didn't lend itself to realism, it was too hyperbolic. And I remember saying to [producer] Byron, I'm thinking of setting it a few years in the future, even though*

111

> *we didn't have the budget to make it too far into the future. That was the licence that enabled us to maintain our enchantment in the world, and yet not have too many contemporary references. It allowed us to push out into another place.* (quoted in King and Guilliatt, 1999: 67)

In some senses, the first film is set in a transitional period in which there are elements that resemble features of Australian lifestyles of the time, especially 1960s Australian car culture when "deserted roads were used as much for sporting arenas as they were for transportation and there was a disproportionate number of highway casualties" (Miller quoted in Peary, 1988: 208)[7]. The narrative tells the story of a taciturn cop, Max Rockatansky (Mel Gibson), who fights the forces of evil represented by gangs who rule the Australian highways. Tim Burns, who played the biker character Johnny the Boy, argues that the original *Mad Max* script had impact for him due to its contemporary themes:

> *It was the only script I'd ever read that got the essence of what I'd grown up with as a teenager in the Southern Tablelands of NSW – that hunger for speed, some kind of visceral experience that could break you out of the ennui of suburbia.* (quoted in King and Guilliatt, 1999: 67)

Mad Max 2 refers to a transitional period after a global war that destroyed fuel sources and left survivors to scavenge in a wasteland. Shot around the outback mining location of Broken Hill, *Mad Max 2* was influenced by observations of Australian communities threatened by an energy crisis, specifically the petrol rationing due to oil shortages and subsequent social behaviour in the 1970s. Here Max has become a lone wanderer who has not yet recovered from the death of his wife and child in the first film and negotiates between those optimists rebuilding communities and those living by a survival-of-the-fittest credo. The third film was released four years after *Mad Max 2*, by which time Max had achieved cult hero status. *Beyond Thunderdome* is located in a post-apocalyptic period when some semblances of community have developed along different lines, ranging from the desert-dwelling children assimilated to their oasis environment, to the cut-throat commercial operators in isolated Bartertown. These aspects are summarised in Table 1 overleaf.

The films are not generically clear-cut and are influenced by Miller's and (the late) Kennedy's fascination with Westerns, road movies and action films as well as "obsession for the pure kinetics of chase movies" (Miller quoted in Peary, 1988: 208). Morphett argues that the first two films "belong to a growing genre: the vigilante film" (1984: 41). *Mad Max* reflects some of the principles espoused by the Italian Futurists, who declared a love of speed, science, mechanisation and universal dynamism that would disrupt the complacency of middle-class society. *Mad Max*'s cops, while ostensibly ridding society of evildoers like the Knightrider (Vincent Gil), find themselves enticed by the same love of speed and machines. The film is steeped in the

TABLE 1: MAD MAX TRILOGY – COMPARATIVE SUMMARY

FILMS	NARRATIVE	GENRE ASPECTS	FUTURIST SCENARIO
Mad Max	Max police officer. Campaign to clean up roads. Goose burned, wife and son killed. Max wreaks revenge on biker gang.	Action. Road, biker, car chase. Cops and criminals. Max as 'conventional hero'.	Some years in future. Road terrorism. Extremities of Australian car culture.
Mad Max 2 Road Warrior	Max lives in car on road. Gyro Captain shows refinery and gang. Max helps the Papagallo community to escape to new world. Defeats Humungus gang.	Western. Road movie. Max as 'anti-hero'.	Transitional – post Doomsday. Petrol a scarce and valuable resource. New world for Northern Tribe.
Mad Max 3 Beyond Thunderdome	Max nomadic. Goes to Bartertown for camels. Defeats Master Blaster but exiled. Saved by Oasis children. Helps children return to destroyed city.	Action. Adventure. Science Fiction. Max as 'legendary hero'.	Post-apocalyptic. Bartertown use of pigshit ethanol as fuel. Oasis Children new approach to future based on past.

sound of vehicles: "screeching tyres, layers of metallic sounds and engine roars punctuated by lonely gusts of wind" (Harley, 1998: 23) contrasted with those scenes of Max at his beachside home, where his wife Jessie (Joanne Samuel) plays the saxophone, or at the beachside idyll where the car is serviced (again) to the sounds of waves on the beach, birdsong and baby gurgles. After his wife and son are killed by Toecutter's (Hugh Keays-Byrne's) biker gang, Max abandons his consideration for human life and methodically eliminates the gang leaders, ostensibly creating a new world order of a kind consistently linked to the Science Fiction genre.

II. Back To The Future

The love of speed, science and mechanisation in *Mad Max* invites comparison to the content of various manifestos published by the Italian Futurists – spearheaded by Filippo Marinetti (1876–1944) – around the First World War.

The Futurists euphorically adopted the latest inventions and technologies then becoming available (including media forms such as radio broadcasting and cinema) and had ultimate faith in these technologies and their perceived ability to transport humankind universally into a better world. The creation of such a 'brave new world' was a radical and confrontational project and the fascist connections of the Italian Futurists have been well documented (see, for example, Perloff, 1986). Like the Futurists, Max and the police force aim to cleanse the world of self-serving elements (such as Toecutter's gang), supposedly in order to create a more positive society. Max relies on machines to do this, carefully planning the destruction of the gang leaders using the souped up Interceptor car. The Futurists' machine euphoria was connected with their rejection of mass in favour of elements like energy and motion. However, the machines so beloved of the Futurists contributed to a sound-saturated world. Indeed, Luigi Russolo, who made a significant contribution to the Movement with his 'Art of Noises' manifesto published in 1913[8], emphasised this by devising a noise maker machine and *intonarumori* ('noise instruments') that combined with the sounds of everyday life and human activity to create 'noise music'. Consistent with such a manifesto, *Mad Max's* sound design is steeped in machine noises, often in competition with one another and with composer Brian May's music. Peary argues that *Mad Max* is "less interesting as a story about people than as a marriage between a filmmaker's machines (his camera, his editing tools) and the motor-powered machines (cars, motorcycles) that he films" (1988: 206). Following the death of Max's wife and child, Max retreats into action with even less verbal communication, and his dialogue is reduced to telegraphic language. This idiosyncrasy is developed in *Mad Max 2* where no dialogue is heard at all for the first ten minutes of the film.

Mad Max 2 references generic conventions used in Westerns (especially, Peary suggests, *Davy Crockett, King of the Wild Frontier* [1955])[9]. This is clearly evident in the film's central scenario, which involves a group of oil-refining compound dwellers being surrounded by a gang of 'savages' led by The Humungus (played by body-builder Kjell Nilsson) and his thug, Vicious Wez (Vernon Wells). But despite the conventions suggested by the narrative, May's music from the outset suggests a thriller genre, with cues based on stabs of brass and featured percussion. This mixture is further diversified by the sonic bombardment provided by the eighty vehicles used for the film (many of which have their own sound characteristics) and which further broaden the film's generic possibilities.

By *Beyond Thunderdome*, the approach to sound has changed considerably. There are more subtly defined machine noises, a different approach to music by Maurice Jarre and fewer of the aggressively noise-producing elements that suggest a post-industrial soundscape. The grunting and snuffling of the energy-producing pigs, the wind/bird/dingo nondiegetic sounds in the desert and human calls in Bartertown's marketplace are more significant aural elements than the machine sounds that (re)appear in the final chase scenes (and reference similar sequences in the earlier films). Here the vehicles used by the fleeing Oasis Children and Bartertown pursuers have different kinds of aural profiles, with the clanking and dull rumbling of the train intermingled with a variety of adapted motors differentiated by a range of high-to-low sounds and differently textured noises. The sound track rejects the Futurist euphoric adoption of machines and machine-like objects used in everyday life and the workplace. Instead it presents two different approaches to alternative lifestyles: the dictatorship of Bartertown powered by alternative energy sources and governed by simple slogans, contrasted to the self-sufficient lifestyle and ululations of the Oasis community. Constructivists like Naum Gabo explored light and motion without the glorification of mechanisation and argued that modernist speed need not be associated with noisy analogues. In 1920, with Anton Pevsner, he claimed:

> *ask any Futurist how does he imagine "speed" and there will emerge a whole arsenal of frenzied automobiles, rattling railway depots, snarled wires, the clank and the noise and the clang of carouselling streets ... does one really need to convince them that all that is not necessary for speed and for its rhythms ... Look at a ray of sun ... the stillest of the still forces, it speeds more than 300 kilometres in a second ... behold our starry firmament ... who hears it ...?* (quoted in Bowlt, 1976: 211–212)

III. Sound and Soundscapes

The second part of this chapter explores the soundscapes of individual sequences in *Mad Max* films. In using the word soundscape, I am, in part, drawing upon the global theories of social theorist Arjun Appadurai but also upon the work of Canadian composer and sound theorist R Murray Schafer. Both theorists draw on the notion of 'scapes' as an abstraction from 'landscape'. Just as the *Mad Max* films are not generically clear-cut, they are not particularly fixed in time and place (see Table 1 above). In this sense, they can be read against the 'scapes' (of people, images, technologies, finance and ideas) presented by Appadurai (1996) who argues that, crossing borders and time zones, such social operatives can create disjuncture when placed in new contexts and domains around the world. As I will detail, the *Mad Max* films feature items with sound signatures that derive from the past and are recycled and functionally transformed in the present to create new futures. In relation to sound, in the 1960s Schafer commenced teaching and writing about music as part of a "soundscape of life" (1967: 3) and these ideas were brought together in his influential book for electroacoustic artists, *The Tuning of the World* (1977). Schafer talked of the world as a macrocosmic musical composition and took his lead from John Cage's definition of music as sounds, as well as practices of *musique concrète* artists composing music from the sounds of life. Schafer developed the idea of the soundscape as any acoustic field of study, meaning any event heard rather than merely seen, and was involved in the World Soundscape Project that studied acoustic ecology and anti-noise procedures around the world[10]. This project led

Schafer to the conclusion that noise pollution could be 'solved' in two ways: first; by citizens (especially children) undergoing "ear cleaning exercises" (1967) to improve "the sonological competence of total societies" (1977: 181); and second, by a worldwide energy crisis, that would decrease machine-produced noise. The second point Schafer argues by noting the manner in which people in industrialised countries suffer from "an overpopulation of sounds; there is so much acoustic information that little of it can emerge with clarity" (ibid: 171). Schafer argues for the development of a high fidelity (or hi-fi) sound environment where "discrete sounds can be heard clearly because of the low ambient noise level" (ibid: 43). The quiet ambience of the hi-fi soundscape, Schafer claims, allows the listener to hear "farther into the distance" and aligns this with the hi-fi soundscape of *rural* locations contrasted with the lo-fi *urban* (industrialised) environment.

Projected against these sets of arguments, the *Mad Max* films use sound to carry significant narrative and aesthetic content. While largely shot in rural or outback Australian locations, the sound components refer to the detritus of civilisation and, by *Beyond Thunderdome*, to approaches to an energy crisis that precipitates new environments and sound ecologies. In what follows, I will discuss the films according to how the sound components operate as acoustic fields. These fields I have generalised as 'musicscapes', 'voicescapes' and 'noisescapes'. I am using this model as an alternative to a chronological approach to analysing the three films. It should also be emphasised that my model does not strictly abide by technical film sound definitions and categorisations according to music, voices and sounds, given the way in which they overlap and inter-relate. Rather, following Harley's argument that the music and related sounds "function to build sonic characters within a sonic narrative" (1998: 22), I want to emphasise how the films can be *heard* along the lines of broader arguments about the representation of the future and of Max as a mythic hero figure. These scapes can be summarised in the table overleaf.

IV. Noisescapes

Schafer has noted how meanings of the word 'noise' have changed in recent times, shifting from a broad area of unwanted sound, unmusical sound, any loud sound or a disturbance in any signaling system to a subjectively limited term suggesting unpleasant or unwanted sound. In my discussion of noisescapes below, I am drawing upon the word as a way of emphasising that, unlike the soundscapes referred to by Schafer, sound effects, atmospheres and noises used in film sound tracks are all deliberately and carefully sculpted into the audio visual package. While location sounds are part of the recording process, the sound mixer chooses whether or not to incorporate all of those sounds into the film sound mix. These noises are also inevitably connected with the other sounds deliberately recorded during the shoot, so that the noise may well form a backdrop for the voice recordings. In Australia, ADR (the studio recording of dialogue in post-production) tends to be avoided, in preference for preserving a spontaneous vocal performance (as discussed in

TABLE 2: MAD MAX TRILOGY SOUND MAP

FILMS	VOICESCAPE	NOISESCAPE	MUSICSCAPE
Mad Max	Max – mostly laconic (US accent). Goose verbose. Knightrider screams.	Cars. Bikes. Max's V8 Interceptor.	Brian May thriller style. High in mix, loud. Brass, drums, etc. Music competes with SFX. Max's theme + saxophone
Mad Max 2 Road Warrior	Max bitter. Gyro Captain verbose. Papagallo rational argument. Humungus screams. Feral Kid mute.	Music box plays 'Happy birthday'. Humungus vehicles. Wind. Boomerang whiz. Refinery machinery. Gyrocopter swishes. Dog whines, barks and growls.	Brian May thriller style. Spaces for dialogue & SFX. Max's theme.
Mad Max 3 Beyond Thunderdome	Max cryptic phrases. Bartertown: Aunty Entity melodious. People slogans. Oasis children: onomatopaeic, fragments of the past, storytelling (esp Savannah Nix).	Whistle. Saxophone. Underworld pig grunts, snuffles. Children's calls – ah-aaah-ah. Oasis: chimes, Bugs Bunny, Victrola, etc.	Maurice Jarre atmos + themes for places and people. Didjeridu, ondes martenot, sax, etc. + Tina Turner songs at beginning & end: *We Don't Need ... + One for the Living*

the voicescapes section below). In addition to hearing the noises of the *Mad Max* films, it is worth observing the sections of film where a lack of obvious noise is particularly apparent.

The *Mad Max* films draw upon technological artefacts that represent a series of timeframes, although the relics so central to those timeframes are shown to be both redundant and overlaid with nostalgia. Over the three films, the time periods represented in the narratives move further into the future although this is not fixed. Indeed, the films work on imagined futures that are not strictly post-apocalyptic or post-nuclear but, rather, "heightened, caricaturized futuristic worlds" (Miller, in Peary, 1984:281). According to Miller, the films were not intended to be speculative but rather allegorical, revealing "truths about human nature through their depiction of people and their problems in a particular place and time" (ibid):

> *It occurred to us sometime after we completed the [first two] films that they are more medieval than futuristic. The time is the future, yet it is a*

117

very regressed world, where the ground rules that hold society together are quite rudimentary. The normal interractive [sic] society has given way, and you have a much more futile, scavenging, hierarchical society. (ibid)

The kind of advanced technology often eulogised in Science Fiction films is not present, rather the films refer to technological forms of the past, all of which have sonic profiles. *Mad Max 1* is oriented around the cars and bikes used by both the cops and the gangs, and these machines are significantly rendered via their signature sounds. In *Mad Max 2*, the first moment we see Max express slight bemusement is when he hears the sound of a tiny music box mechanism that he finds in the hand of a dead lorry driver. The music box is reduced to its sound-producing mechanism (a tuned steel comb plucked via raised pin heads in a cylinder), stripped of any fancy housing and with nothing to enchant the eye. Later in the film he plays the mechanism for the Feral Kid (Emil Minty) who reacts with delight and, when Max gives the trinket to the kid, he creates an ally who later saves his life. The music box mechanism plays *Happy Birthday to you*[11] (which, by the 1980s, was one of the three most popular songs in the English language[12]). Another sonic component in *Mad Max 2* is the sound of the deathly metallic boomerang as it flies through the air (used by the Feral Kid to attack the Humungus gang – slicing off the fingers of a gang member at one point). The boomerang is an Aboriginal wooden hunting weapon, roughly V-shaped and designed to fly in an arc and return to its sender. The flight of the Feral Kid's metal boomerang is accompanied by a rhythmic swishing and concludes with a thunk as it lands.

In *Beyond Thunderdome*, other sound-producing objects are used for critical scenes. Max defeats his opponent in the ring with the blast of a whistle. Aunty commands one of her minions to play "something tragic" on the saxophone to signal the test of Max's abilities. Later Max challenges the Oasis children's view of the world by playing a record on an old-style player. Up to this moment, the record has been used mnemonically to recall the SOS radio calls made by the pilot who originally took the children out of the city. The children hang the record (which they call 'sonic') from a string, rotate it, and intone "Delta Fox X-ray … Can you hear me? … Come in … Is anybody out there? … Can you read me Walker?" while another of the teenagers pulls the string on a bugs bunny toy to create a personal call: "Awww … what's up doc? … Say – take me with ya". The record has become a fetish object. Once its aural content has been revealed to the Oasis children, the record takes on entirely different properties.

V. Musicscapes

Woven into the overwhelming sounds of vehicles and violent action in the first two films, the music scores draw on a combination of instrumentation, arrangement and mixing. The music scores for *Mad Max 1* and 2 were composed by Brian May and are musically dense (the former having 50 minutes of music, and the latter having 57 minutes). Born in Adelaide in 1934, May studied piano before undertaking formal training at Adelaide's Elder Conservatorium. During army service, May composed music for brass bands, the influence of which is apparent in the *Mad Max* scores, which feature brass instrumentation for many of the cues. In 1968 May became musical director for the Australian Broadcasting Corporation (ABC), arranged music for symphony orchestras and choral music for the Adelaide Singers, and directed the ABC Show Band with which he made several recordings. The ABC then brought May to Melbourne to form the Melbourne Showband, a multipurpose television and record-making unit, but it was May's symphonic arrangement of the musical *Hair* in the early 1970s that led him to film composition via director Richard Franklin. May's film credits include scores for Australian features like Franklin's *The True Story of Eskimo Nell* (1975) and *Patrick* (1978) prior to working on *Mad Max*. The commercial success of *Mad Max* (and AFI awards for, amongst others, Original Music) enabled the production of the sequel, which was also scored by May (and won an Australian Performing Rights Association Golden Award in 1985)[13].

While influenced by his experience in symphonic music, and the powerfully motific style of Bernard Herrmann's scores, May's approach was also affected by working on US television music prior to *Mad Max 1* and his observations of music mixing in this context. He noted:

> *Americans have a definite commitment to music, and when they want it to be there, they mix it in such a way that the music is right up front. We* [Australians] *tend, I feel, to follow the British tradition and the score is sometimes unable to make its effect.* (quoted in Hutchinson, 1978: 32)

This production approach is reflected in the mix for *Mad Max*. The music score draws largely on musical stabs orchestrated with brass, strings and percussion, and stingers to highlight (often violent) action. The timbral qualities of the brass and percussion instruments are featured high in the mix and orchestrated in thick, often atonal, arrangements to support and add to the mechanical sounds. The score introduced two main musical ideas for Max and for the bikie gang. A short motif dominated by trumpets characterises Max (and this is adapted for the two sequels). The bikie gang and the threat it poses is linked to a low rumble of drums, strident brass and pulsating, dissonant strings highlighted by the sound of clashing steel blades. May argues that,

> Mad Max 1 *was a strongly energised score in the violence/action department, and for that they wanted a totally non-melodic score. It was very jagged and shearing, and George particularly wanted me to antagonize the audience by making them feel uncomfortable.* (quoted in Flanagan, 1983: 23)

However, for *Mad Max 2*, regarded as an "optimistic picture" (ibid), May was

119

asked to suggest vastness and space and devised the score in terms of "soaring French horns" and used "deep basses, cellos, and lots of short motifs that were not totally melodic but were just enough to be unified" (ibid).

For the third film, Maurice Jarre was commissioned to compose the music, much to the chagrin of May's supporters[14]. Jarre, born in Lyon (France) in 1924, first developed his musical interests by playing percussion in an orchestra and subsequently studied composition and non-western music at the Paris Conservatoire. Jarre was employed as arranger and conductor for theatre companies (including the Théâtre National Populaire) and composed theatrical scores, ballets and concert works. In the 1950s he composed scores for director Georges Franju but Jarre's international reputation as a film composer was secured when he scored and, in 1962, won an Academy Award for, David Lean's *Lawrence of Arabia*. He also won Oscar Awards for original music in Lean's later films, *Doctor Zhivago* (1965) and *A Passage to India* (1984).

The score for *Beyond Thunderdome* incorporates symphonic arrangements, percussive rhythms and dissonances, rather than identifiably melodic cues, and is performed by the Royal Philharmonic Orchestra with orchestration by Christopher Palmer, Jarre's assistant for ten years. Miller attended the score recording sessions in London and, after an unpublicised preview in Phoenix, Arizona, contributed to a remix of some of the sound. The locations and sensibilities of Bartertown and the Oasis are reflected in musical themes that merge with leitmotifs for the central female antagonists in these communities, that is, Aunty Entity and Savannah Nix. Bartertown is introduced with a harsh riff and the distinct tone colour of the ondes martenot. A vibrating synthesiser sound is used in conjunction with hammering and clanging anvils, leading to a raunchy saxophone solo that is adopted by an orchestral arrangement with strings and ondes martenot. The Oasis Children are represented by a delicate arrangement of shakers, flutes, high strings and cello around a six-note melodic motif that falls, then rises, to suggest youthful optimism.

Having effectively used the ondes martenot as a solo instrument in *Lawrence of Arabia*, the instrument, played by Jeanne Loriod, Cynthia Millar and Dominique Kim, is used to create an otherworldly effect in the *Beyond Thunderdome* score. The ondes martenot was devised in its original form by cellist and radio telegraphist Maurice Martenot in 1928. Influenced by the Russian designer of the theremin, Lev Termen, Martenot aimed to produce "a versatile electronic instrument that was immediately familiar to orchestral musicians"[15] using a vacuum tube oscillator as a sound source. Later versions of the instrument, still used today, have a keyboard and a fingerboard strip control for glissando and vibrato that make it accessible to keyboard players. As Paul Théberge notes, this enabled it to move out of the realm of a novelty electronic device (a mere 'invention') to become "an 'innovation' of considerable musical import, if only within a limited sphere" (1977: 45) which was incorporated into works by composers such as Olivier

Messiaen. *Beyond Thunderdome's* score also uses the didjeridu (played by respected performer Charles McMahon[16]) mostly to accompany sweeping landscape shots. The association of the instrument (and Australia's indigenous population) with the Australian landscape has been frequently exploited in filmmaking practices (see Kibby and Neuenfeldt, 1998). In addition, drawing upon the narrative presence of the saxophone, played by one of Aunty Entity's minions, Jarre features the instrument in the score, and saxophone solos (performed by Tim Cappello) are also included in the two songs used for the credit sequences.

May's scores for the first two films have been largely overlooked and/or dismissed by critics. Reviewer David Chute, for example, asked Miller why he chose to adopt "traditional, horror-adventure scoring" when the movies "cried out for rock 'n' roll on the soundtrack" (1982: 30). As Jeff Smith observes, in the post-1975 period, the film industry (particularly in the USA) was dominated by the buzzword 'synergy' to describe "the phenomenon of successful film and music cross-promotion" (1998: 186). Such 'synergy' often resulted in the production of film sound tracks that centred on remixed or 'needledrop' material (frequently pop and rock items) and the promotion of films via their songs. Miller's response to Chute distanced him from this phenomenon:

> We're continually being told that we should have rock scores, because the movies already have something like the feel of rock. They're visual rock 'n' roll, in a way. But I don't think I've ever heard a rock score that really coalesces with the visuals, or that didn't stand out as something apart. (quoted in Chute, 1982: 30–31)

In light of these debates, however, *Beyond Thunderdome's* musicscape represents a compromise insofar as the score sequences originally composed and recorded for the opening and closing sequences of the film (described by Stoner, 1986/87) were later replaced by songs featuring Tina Turner's vocals. This approach, Smith argues, serves "both artistic and commercial interests by combining the traditional musical language favored by composers with the more contemporary styles favored by record labels and publishers" (1998: 218). The marketing of *Beyond Thunderdome* included promotion via Turner's single *We Don't Need Another Hero* (written by Terry Britten and Graham Lyle, and produced by Britten). The single reached number 5 in the Australian ARIA[17] chart at the time of the film's release (after being widely screened on television music programs) and number 3 in the UK charts[18]. The accompanying music video featured scenes from the film and other scenes shot by Miller with Turner in Los Angeles and a further video was released for Turner's second song, *One for the Living* (written by Holly Knight, produced by Mike Chapman) that is used in the opening film sequence.

VI. Voicescapes

Miller characterises the *Mad Max* films as "montage" films in which "performance and dialogue are secondary to the work of the camera and editing" (paraphrased in Pollak, 1985: 11), as distinct from "mise-en-scène" films in which "the camera simply records a powerful dramatic interplay" (ibid). A film, according to Miller, is "sound and pictures – not talking and pictures" (ibid). Yet Miller's use of language in the *Mad Max* films is as much about script and performance as it is about sound and screenplay. Furthermore, his exploration of language and performance makes the *Mad Max* films, especially *Beyond Thunderdome*, exceptional within the film genre of Science Fiction. As Vivian Sobchack observes (with specific reference to US films):

> *Surely, one of the most disappointing elements of SF cinema is dialogue. How can a genre which so painstakingly tries to awe and surprise us with imaginative images seem so ignorant and careless of the stiffness, banality, pomposity, dullness, and predictability of its language.* (1999: 150)

Miller's interest in the orality of Aboriginal Dreaming (a complex set of stories handed down through generations and outlining Aboriginal history, law and social ritual) and his fascination with voice and textural elements of language and vocal performance are demonstrated in the *Mad Max* films[19]. In each film, Max's voice and vocal mannerisms are contrasted with eloquent, effusive or verbally dexterous characters or, alternatively, mute or non-linguistic characters, (for example, the mute Feral Kid in *Mad Max 2* or the childlike Blaster in *Beyond Thunderdome*). Max's voice becomes more textured and rough and the warm intimacy in the *Mad Max* scene with Jessie where he recalls his father, is gone by the third film, by which time his tone is generally sardonic, cynical or bitter. Miller explains his reluctance to give Max too much dialogue by referring to film language per se:

> *I think the great filmmakers were people like Buster Keaton or Harold Lloyd. They really understood that images were film language. They didn't rely on the spoken word.* (quoted in Broeske, 1982: 482).

In the first film, Max is given little dialogue prior to the family tragedy. This is consistent with the horror, action and western film genres that *Mad Max* references, but minimal speech is also perceived to be a masculine trait, particularly in relation to Australian masculinity. For the US market, key dialogue scenes were dubbed with American voices, reflecting Miller's desire to attract US audiences. Richard Fox, then President of Warner Bros International, argued that while the first two of the trilogy were considered "foreign movies", the box office success of *Beyond Thunderdome* meant that it was not considered "foreign" and speculated that the fourth Mad Max movie would be "as American as apple pie" (quoted in Maddox, 1985: 17).

Antje Ascheid has discussed the nature of voice dubbing in cinema and argued that:

> *Film, as an example of a languaged cultural commodity... provides an*

122

> *allegory for any product's cultural function, working on problematic
> notions of identity, dependency and equivalence.* (1997: 39)

The Australian male speech style has been characterised by linguists as a
non-effusive speech voiced through semi-closed lips which uses short cryptic
speech grabs rather than complex sentence structures[20]. Indeed, in Australian cinema, effusive speech is generally allotted to weaker, effeminate
and/or disturbed male characters. Furthermore, this laconic male speech
style is linked to the lack of ability in male characters to openly declare
emotion or passion. Sarah Kozloff notes how Hollywood film tends to
prioritise action over words but argues that this stems from "larger or
stronger cultural forces" denigrating speech (2000: 9). Furthermore, she
continues, "talkativeness has traditionally been allied with femininity, terse
action with masculinity" (ibid). In the *Mad Max* trilogy, Max's voice is
associated with the sound of his vehicles. This is established from the outset,
where we see little of Max as he listens to the opening confrontation between
the cops and the Knightrider. His first words are a response to Goose's call
for help, using a low-pitched monotonal speech style, and he uses telegraphic
queries with little rising intonation to indicate questions: "Go ahead", he
says, then "You okay?" to indicate concern for his mate and, later, "Much
damage?" to change the direction of the conversation. While critic Sandra
Hall (1982) was disturbed by the lack of dialogue, Barbour argues that "in
the futuristic, nightmare world, life has been reduced to stark survival,
restricting most characters to essential communication only" (1999: 30).

After Max's best mate, Goose, and his wife and child are killed by the biker
gang, Max becomes even more reticent and the angry roar of his V8
Interceptor car effectively becomes his voice. Midway through the film, this
specially constructed vehicle was introduced to him by Goose who, frustrated
with Max's reservations, exclaims: "Come on Max. You've seen it, you've
heard it, and you're still askin' questions?" The car's sound is the most
complex voice of the vehicles used in this film, drawing on a combined low
bass rumble, roughly-textured mid-range roar and a high-pitched whine. In
the next film, we are once again introduced to Max via the V8 Interceptor
and its signature sound and, in fact, do not hear Max's spoken voice until
ten minutes into the film. Max throws off the snake that guards the Gyro
Captain's aircraft but he is ambushed by the Captain who demands fuel from
Max's V8 Interceptor. Max warns him: "Booby trapped. Touch those tanks
and kerboom!" Max's choice of vocabulary is reminiscent of the word-as-text
aesthetics of Marinetti and the Dada-ist sound poetry connected with Kurt
Schwitters (particularly his *Ursonata* written in 1924 in which
onomatopeaic, often monosyllabic, words are relied upon to create sound
images in an imaginary, non-representational yet aurally coherent language).

In *Mad Max 2*, the two voices adopted to 'speak' for Max are the Interceptor
car and his dog, which communicates in a variety of whimpers, whines,
growls and barks. The Gyro Captain's manic and effusive speech, voiced in

a high-pitched fast-paced manner, is embroidered with whoops and giggles and hiccups. In order to persuade Max, the Captain resorts to mimetically onomatopoeic phrases. For instance, when he wants to impress Max with the sheer volume of the precious petrol being refined, he describes it as "kchoong kchoong kchoong". In contrast, Humungus's speeches, as Barbour (1999: 32) notes, are a curious combination of biblical and Shakespearean rhetoric drawing upon phrases such as "unleash my dogs of war" and "the valley of death".

In *Beyond Thunderdome*, Max's taciturn grunts are highlighted through the notable vocal characteristics of Aunty Entity, Savannah Nix and the high-pitched screeches of the diminutive Master. In contrast to Aunty's procla-mations over Bartertown's loudspeaker system, Savannah Nix calls "ah-aaah-ah" to the Oasis children across the wasteland. In addition, she has a musical 'voice' in the theme that accompanies her onscreen presence, created by the instrumentation and melodic sounds used in the score. It is not insignificant that Aunty is played by Tina Turner, a singer recognised for her vocal dexterity and power. Her vocal accomplishment enables her to use a widely varied pitch range in her speaking voice (when, for example, she tells her story of how she was a nobody made good in the post-apoca-lyptic era). As Anne Cranny-Francis (1988) notes, while Aunty is associated with a languorous melodic line on saxophone, Savannah is 'heard' through the 'organic' wind and percussion theme used for the Oasis children.

The two opposing communities that have grown up out of the destruction of the old world each have their own voices. The Bartertown residents are taught to think in terms of slogans akin to commercial marketing and advertising, which they often chant repetitively, such as "Two men enter, one man leaves" (to describe the ethos of Thunderdome), and "Bust a deal, face the wheel" (to direct the non-conformer to subsequent action). Aunty's dominant character is foreshadowed in the film's opening sequence by Turner's vocals on the song *One For the Living*, which urge a 'survival of the fittest approach to life'[21]. Aunty operates as a dictator in her eyrie, situated high above the market streets. The choice of the name 'Thunderdome' for the gladiator ring-type battle ground associates it with threat through the reference to a sound often feared by children and this is reinforced when, in her role as MC for Max's battle against Blaster, Aunty Entity declares:

> *Remember where you are. This is Thunderdome. Death is listening and will take the first man that screams.*

Ultimately it is not a scream that draws the battle to a close but the sound of a whistle, a high-pitched sound intolerable and disabling to Blaster.

Miller's original intention was to develop an altered language akin to that used in Stanley Kubrick's 1971 film *A Clockwork Orange* (based on Anthony Burgess's 1962 novel)[22] for the Bartertown residents: "then we realised that it would be the kids that spoke it since they hadn't been in school, so we kept it for them" (quoted in Pollak, 1985: 13). The Oasis Children represent another approach to survival, living in a fertile 'crack in the earth' and relying on hunting for food. They have organically devised their own language, which is learnt by repetition of fractured memories of verbal phrases used in the past, and from the older children who tell a version of their history by oral storytelling. Linguist Daniel Long has identified that the Oasis community's language uses a set of standard variationist devices (pc July 2003). These include modifying Standard English language's subject-verb-object (SVO) order for an object, subject, verb one (OVS) (eg "this you know") and conversion, that is, making nouns out of verbs (eg "the tell"). These are mixed with aspects such as colloquial features (eg "gonna"), altered agreements (eg "you hears"), regular non-standard dialect features (eg "we seen" rather than the standard "we have seen") and the creation of unusual past tense forms (eg "we knewed")[23]. Long contends that these elements combine to "give the feeling of an exotic language without its being incomprehensible" and also offset the exoticism with a folksy colloquial feel (ibid).

Miller argues that the "tribe of kids" lived according to a "fractured mythology" and were "very short on knowledge but very big on belief" (ibid) enabling Max's compassion and an optimistic scenario to be revealed. Max's first question addressed to the children "Who are you?" is repeated back to him in an echoic fashion, as are his commands for "quiet" and "shut up". This pattern of listening and repeating is replicated later when a French language instruction record is played on the Victrola gramophone and the children repeat, as requested:

> Welcome. Open your book at page one. Now repeat after me. Bonjour... Good Morning ... Ou allez vous? ... Where are you going? ... Je vais chez moi ... I'm going home ...

The Oasis Children's record is from a time much earlier than the film's setting and prior to the development of the long-playing (LP) record in the 1950s. The 78-rpm record retained as a totem by the children holds recorded material produced for the niche market of those learning to speak French. The Victrola gramophone discovered amongst the objects in Master's train carriage is an example of technology that has since been surpassed by several more recent items[24]. The reference to now-defunct sound equipment highlights Miller's interest in newly developing technologies and recalls his argument (in King and Guilliatt, 1999: 70) that the anticipated *Mad Max* 4 would only be possible with the latest digital filmmaking equipment.

Conclusion

Theo van Leeuwen argues that, while the industrial age featured 'rough' sounds that characterised the urban environment, the current era features more cushioned sounds and these are often invoked in Science Fiction films (1999: 132). The *Mad Max* films eschew this approach to SF film sound, but are instead steeped in gritty, grainy textured sound. Paradoxically, these sounds are often linked to items that featured in lifestyles previous to that of the narrative. *Beyond Thunderdome's* final narrative sequence is set in a partly-destroyed warehouse back in the ruins of Sydney where the Oasis children are gathered around Savannah Nix who cuddles a young baby (in a "madonna and child" tableau, according to Cranny-Francis, 1988: 164) and retells the story of the journey back to the city:

> *This you know. The years travel fast. And time after time I done the tell. But this ain't one body's tell. It's the tell of us all. And you gotta listen and 'member. Cos what you hears today, you gotta tell the newborn tomorra.*

> *I's lookin' behind us now, into history back. I sees those of us that got the luck and started the haul for home. And I 'members how it led us here and we was heartful 'cos we seen what there once was. One look and we'd knewed we'd got it straight. Those what's gone before had the knowin' and the doin' of things beyond our reckonin' – even beyond our dreamin'. Time counts an' keeps countin'. And we knows now – findin' the trick of what's been and lost ain't no easy ride. But that's our track and we gotta travel it and there ain't nobody knows where it's gonna lead.*

> *Still an' all, every night we does the tell so that we 'member who we was and where we came from. But most of all we 'members the man who finded us – him that came the salvage – and we lights the city not just for him but for all of them that're still out there. 'Cos we knows there'll come a night when they see the distant light an' they'll be coming home.*

The sound and the sound producing objects highlighted in the *Mad Max* narratives are firmly rooted in a revision of the past. Viewed in isolation, *Mad Max 1* presents a negative scenario of human nature and our tentative balance between good and evil that inevitably leads to social disintegration. However, viewed as a trilogy, the *Mad Max* scenario and perspective on the future is altered somewhat and we are left with at least two models for social operations of the future – the pragmatic market-driven world of Aunty Entity's fiefdom and the idealistic new world proto-socialism espoused by Savannah Nix in the city remains. The soundscape of the third film makes an argument for a future scenario where communities value sounds and sound-producing objects from the past and the present. The core of the community is that of organic storytelling and revision of the past, a kind of 'whitefella dreaming'. While the first *Mad Max* film was dominated by noises of dysfunctional civilisation, by the end of the third film, we are left with the sounds of voices echoing in the spaces where the children are building a new way of life. After ensuring the hand-over of Master to the Oasis children (and thus providing them with the 'brains' of Aunty Entity's dominion), Max returns to his nomadic existence and we are left with a vision of the future that, in its imagery, seems merely the detritus of the past. However, it is the film soundscape that, if not trumpets, at least *sounds* the future, filling the void and producing a new form of communication that learns from the nostalgia of the past to create a brave new world. Max's violent physicality and cryptic communication style, representing the horrors of the past, has no role in this scenario and the credit sequence rolls to Turner's voice, accompanied by the Kings House School Choir, singing "We don't need another hero/We don't need to know the way home/ All we want is life beyond Thunderdome".

Notes

1. George Miller, quoted in *White Fellas Dreaming* (1993), a documentary on Australian cinema made as part of the British Film Institute documentary series that commemorated 100 years of world cinema.

2. In the same way that sounds can evoke images in a listener's mind, images can also draw upon characteristics also common to sound – eg durational elements like rhythm.

3. A notable exception is Ross Harley's chapter in Coyle (ed) (1998).

4. In 1972 Miller made the satirical short film *Violence in the Cinema Part I*. Miller's treatise on cinematic violence featured an actor (Arthur Dignam) who reads a lecture previously given by Adams. Despite being shot in the eye, disembowelled, run over by a car and set on fire, the lecturer continues to drone on. Following this film Miller actually avoided including much violence onscreen and, indeed, most of *Mad Max*'s violent acts are implied as offscreen activities, reinforcing the role of other elements – such as sound – in creating dramatic impact. Significantly, fourteen years later Adams commented on the "promiscuous power" of film music, which, he argues "sneaks up on you" (1993: 8) in the cinema.

5. The work invested in the sound track resulted in, among other awards, an Australian Film Industry award for Best Sound in 1979. *Mad Max 2* also won an AFI award for Best Sound in 1981.

6. In 1985, the first two films were fourth and fifth in all-time box office rentals of Australian films in Australia.

7. Miller trained as a medical practitioner and, as an intern, worked in the emergency ward of an inner city Sydney hospital where he dealt with those injured in motor vehicle accidents.

8. See Appollonio (1973: 74–88) and Russolo's eponymous 1916 book.

9. Although, in a July 1988 Newsweek survey, *Road Warrior* made it into the list of top ten movies in the Science Fiction category (Barbour, 1999: 38).

10. The project examined by-laws from over 200 communities internationally in order to study the question of what constitutes 'noise' or unacceptable sounds in as many varied cultures as possible.

11. This celebratory song dates from 1893 and was originally written as a classroom greeting by two Louisville teachers, Mildred J Hill (an authority on Negro spirituals), who composed the melody, and Patty Smith Hill (professor of education at Columbia University), who wrote the lyrics as 'Good Morning To All'. 'Happy Birthday To You' was first copyrighted in 1935 (quoted in http://www.ibiblio.org.team/fun/birthday – accessed September 2002).

12. Along with two other special occasion songs, the Scottish-English *Auld Lang Syne* and *For He's A Jolly Good Fellow*.

13. In 1983, May became the first Australian composer to work in a major Hollywood production company when he was offered a contract by Universal Studios to work on Franklin's *Cloak and Dagger*.

14. See, for example, Daniel Ryall Penton's web page eulogising "the heavy percussion and

strong brass of a Brian May composition – you know, the kickass songs that drive the Mad Max films" at www.geocities.com/Hollywood/Hills/4367/ accessed March 2002.

15. http//:www.obsolete.com/120_years/machines/martenot/ accessed accessed September 2002.

16. McMahon's work is discussed in Homan (1997: 123–137).

17. Australian Record Industry Association – representing the major record labels in Australia.

18. Smith notes that the song was more useful for promoting Turner's character in the film than the film was for improving the song's chart performance, and the song's success was "largely attributable to Turner's star power" (1998: 219).

19. Also in subsequent films, for example, the 'voices' given to the animated animals in the Babe films for which he has writing credits (Babe, 1995, directed by Chris Noonan, and Babe: Pig in the City, 1998, directed by Miller).

20. See early prescriptive studies such as Turner's anthology (1972) compared to later collections of socio-linguist studies such as Collins and Blair (1989).

21. However, in the closing sequence, when she sings We Don't Need Another Hero, Turner is separated from her diegetic role as Aunty Entity and speaks for the Oasis children.

22. See the discussion of these as Science Fiction offered by Chapman, 1999.

23. Substituting the past tense for the past particle ["we'd known"] and, simultaneously, creating a double past, adding the regular past "-ed" ending to an already past-marked verb.

24. The gramophone succeeded Louis Glass's uses of the phonograph for cylinder recordings of musicians and comedians at first in phonograph parlours and later in a portable form for home use. In the late 1890s the phonograph was supplanted by the gramophone, which used recordings on discs.

Chapter Seven

"THESE ARE MY NIGHTMARES"
Music and Sound in the Films of David Cronenberg

PAUL THEBERGE

I awoke in the early morning hours to what sounded like pieces of wood being wrenched apart and, somewhat more distant, the hollow sound of water dripping: in the ceiling above me there appeared to be a number of large cracks and water was beginning to penetrate my home. I felt strangely vulnerable, physically threatened by the widening cracks and, more than anything, by that sound. The feeling was so overwhelming that it took several moments for me to realise that I had been dreaming.

Experiencing the films of David Cronenberg is a bit like that dream: the borders between the real world and that of the dream, the hallucination or fantasy are fluid and constantly shifting, as are the boundaries between the self, the body, and the external world. Themes of penetration, disease and decay are present throughout Cronenberg's work and all of this is deeply troubling for most audiences: 'disturbing' and 'abject' are adjectives typically used to describe his work. And indeed, my dream had been provoked by Cronenberg's films: I had been watching them, one after the other, late at night while preparing to write this chapter. My dream made me realise that this analytic exercise was perhaps having a cumulative effect on me that I had not anticipated.

Cronenberg's films have such an effect on audiences because the stories that he tells are themselves disturbing (and, in his early films, often horrific) and because he uses every technique at his disposal- from set design, to lighting and cinematography, dialogue, sound, music and editing – to shape the story in cinematic terms and, equally important, to disrupt the normal expecta-tions of the audience. Of course, as much as Cronenberg has been described as an *auteur*, the films are shaped by many hands: to his credit, Cronenberg, in interviews, has often acknowledged the importance of his longstanding relationships with a number of collaborators. And for my purposes here, none of these relationships could be more important than the one that Cronenberg has enjoyed with composer Howard Shore: their collaboration, which spans more than two decades and includes ten feature films and a number of shorter projects, has been remarkably productive and is second to none in the history of cinema. Indeed, one might argue that the disturbing atmosphere that pervades much of Cronenberg's work is as much due to the musical contributions of Shore as to any other single element.

In this chapter, I want to explore the various ways in which dialogue, sound, and especially music contribute to the construction of Cronenberg's film narratives. While I will concentrate primarily on his work in the horror and science fiction genres, I will also make some reference to a number of his other films as well. However, because the nature of the various sonic elements and their relationship to narrative and genre are so important to my discussion, notions of authorship and genre will also be examined.

[NB Unless otherwise attributed, all quotations attributed to William Beard, David Cronenberg and Howard Shore in this chapter originated from telephone interviews with the author conducted in July–August 2002.]

Dreaming Together

In many ways, David Cronenberg epitomises the popular (and critical) conception of what an auteur is supposed to be: although a number of his films operate within established 'American' genres and have enjoyed considerable box-office success, he is thought of as an outsider to Hollywood, preferring to make his films, whenever possible, in his home town, Toronto; his films are often considered as 'difficult' in that they deal with problematic social and cultural issues and often do not follow narrative convention; and, taken as a whole, they exhibit a remarkable thematic and stylistic consistency. But most important, Cronenberg's work is considered as the product of an individual with a "vision": "an outstanding example of a body of work, signed by a single person, that manifests an incredibly tight and consistent group of subjects, themes, and attitudes as well as an identifiable style" (Beard, 2001: ix). Indeed, the elaboration of Cronenberg as *auteur* is the guiding assumption and explicit organisational principal of much of the critical work that deals with his films (most recently exemplified in the work of Beard [ibid], and Grünberg, 2000).

But while Cronenberg is likely not averse to the idea of considering himself as an auteur (and, in principal, neither am I), it is that notion of "a body of work, signed by a single person" – so at odds with the actual ways in which he works – that makes this underlying assumption of auteur theory so difficult to apply in this instance. It is not simply a recognition of the multiple contributions to the film-making process that should lead one to question the validity of the notion of the auteur: such a recognition has never been sufficient to challenge the primacy of the role of the director in the past and, indeed, watching the voluminous credits roll by at the end of any contemporary film, if anything, tends to reinforce the feeling that such a diverse mass of labour must be guided by some kind of individual "vision" if a film is to make any sense at all. But in the case of Cronenberg, one cannot help but notice the value he places on working with a small and consistent group of collaborators: in particular, production designer Carol Spier, cinematographers Mark Irwin (from *The Brood*, 1979, through to *The Fly*, 1986) and Peter Suschitzky (from *Dead Ringers*, 1988, to the present), composer Howard Shore, and editor Ronald Sanders, among others. Sometimes referred to as 'the Cronenberg crew', the work of this tightly knit group of creative individuals – from conception through production and post-production – must be regarded as having a significant impact on the look, feel, sound and pacing of every Cronenberg film and, indeed, on the evolution of what has often been referred to as 'his' style.

Certainly, it could be argued that other filmmakers have also relied heavily on the creative relationships they have developed with various collaborators and it has seldom interfered with their claim to sole authorship. If one considers the area of the musical soundtrack alone, as an example, one notices not only a wide range of potential approaches to the issue of collaboration but also, a variety of ways in which film-makers can assert their control. Hitchcock, who had enjoyed a long, highly productive relationship with composer Bernard Herrmann, did not hesitate to throw out Herrmann's score to *Torn Curtain* (1966) when it did not suit his purposes (studio pressure appears to have been a factor in his decision but, whatever the reasons, his act ultimately ended their creative relationship). Similarly, more contemporary auteurs, such as Stanley Kubrick, have been known to abandon scores in favour of pursuing their own, individual (and even idiosyncratic) approaches to soundtrack construction: his famous pastiche of prerecorded music employed in *2001: A Space Odyssey* (1968) is a case in point. Martin Scorsese has employed a variety of approaches to his soundtracks, including the use of popular songs, the adaptation of pre-existing musical scores, and commissioning specially composed music. Arguably, his work as a whole does not exhibit any particular consistency as regards soundtrack construction but, nevertheless, his uses of popular music have been regarded as highly personal and have tended to enhance his reputation as an auteur. Thus, even within a realm of high specialisation such as the production of music – a realm, unlike cinematography and other aspects of film production, where few directors have any direct knowledge or practical skill – film-makers can assert a significant degree of control, if they so choose, and thereby enhance their claim to authorship.

But it is precisely in the working relationship that Cronenberg has developed with his co-contributors that one finds the key to understanding the nature and significance of their collaboration. Cronenberg routinely sends out his scripts to the members of his creative group almost as soon as he has finished writing them, actively soliciting their comments and input. Composer Howard Shore is among the first, if not *the* first to receive a copy (personal interview with Cronenberg). This practice is highly unusual: conventionally, composers are seldom brought into the filmmaking process until the post-production stage, when the film has already been brought to a rough cut. From the outset, Cronenberg is involved in discussions with Shore (and other members of the production team) about the film, the ideas that underlie it and its characters. And these discussions continue throughout the filmmaking process: for example, Shore likes to visit the sets, when his schedule permits, while filming is taking place (personal interview with Shore). In general, however, they do not talk about details concerning the music itself – this, Cronenberg considers to be Shore's contribution to the film and he does not interfere. Even later, during the spotting and music recording sessions, in which Cronenberg takes an active interest, he seldom questions Shore's judgement.

This openness of approach is evident in other areas of the film-making process as well: for example, Cronenberg often does not make use of a storyboard, preferring to let his films evolve during shooting and editing, thus maximising the potential for his contributors to have creative input (personal interview with Cronenberg). The level of respect and trust Cronenberg places in his creative relationships is attested to in comments made by various members of the creative group, including Shore, Spier and Suschitzky, when they have been interviewed about their relationship with him. Indeed, it is one of the factors that have led them to continue working with him on project after project. If the world created within a film is like a dream, then the dream world created in Cronenberg's films must certainly be considered a *collective* dream – the result of a finely tuned and highly nuanced collaboration between a small group of creative individuals.

There is another sense in which Cronenberg's films can be considered as a 'collective dream': the sense in which they are related to conventional film genres. His early films, in particular those leading up to and including *The Fly*, consistently operated within the Horror and Science Fiction genres and have been analyzed in relation to genre conventions by a number of critics (see, for example, Handling, 1983). And Cronenberg, at least until the mid 1980s, often identified himself as a maker of Horror films, citing the structure of *The Brood*, for example, as a 'classic' model of the Horror genre (since then, he has been much less inclined to describe himself, or his films, in this way). Of course, the Horror and Science Fiction genres are closely related to one another and have often been treated as such by genre theorists (eg, Neale, 2000: 92–104). J.P. Telotte has argued for the use of the term "Fantasy" film to encompass both genres and devotes an entire chapter of his book, *Science Fiction Film*, to a discussion of Cronenberg's *The Fly* as a prime example of a work that crosses the boundaries between Horror and Sci-Fi genres (2001: 179–195). Elsewhere, Jonathan Crane (2000) has argued that even in the films that most closely fit within the Horror genre, Cronenberg's resuscitation of the figure of the scientist – the figure of Dr. Frankenstein – moves his films in the direction of Science Fiction: these figures include, for example, the pharmacologist, Dr. Ruth, in *Scanners* (1981), psychologist Hal Raglin, in *The Brood* and, most prominently, Seth Brundle, in *The Fly*.

But what interests me most here is the degree to which genre can be considered as an *enabling* factor in Cronenberg's films: that is, the way genre functions as a cultural and discursive context in which various thematic topics can be explored. In this sense, Cronenberg draws on a set of collectively shared devices, strategies and syntaxes for making his films and, equally important, audiences bring to the films certain generic expectations that allow them to interpret the significance of events within the film text (Neale, 1990). Freed by the expectations associated with the Horror and Science Fiction genres, Cronenberg is able to explore, for example, the idea of technology as an extension of the body, in films such as *Videodrome* (1983), in ways that would be impossible in genres bound by the type of authenticity and cultural *verisimilitude* demanded by conventional realism (ibid). And in this regard, Linda Williams' (1991) notion of Horror, Pornographic and Melodramatic films as "body genres" is significant: not only is the subject matter of the film related to a certain spectacular relationship to the body – a relationship characterised by a kind of 'excess' – but its treatment is also intended to evoke a visceral reaction from the viewer (ibid – interestingly, the horror evoked in Cronenberg's films is often closely related to the unleashing of sexual desire). Similarly, in *eXistenZ* (1999), the multiple, shifting levels of reality represented within the film can only be understood within the context of a non-realist genre such as Science Fiction.

The figure of the scientist is only one type of character that is explored by Cronenberg: often, their victims are the more central characters in his films; and in the case of *The Fly*, they are simultaneously scientist *and* victim. The emphasis on victimisation, on emotional suffering and its (often horrific) outcomes, marks Cronenberg's films as more than simply Horror films: as William Beard has argued, as early as *The Brood*, Cronenberg's films represent a shift towards a complex blending of the Horror genre with Melodrama (2001: 91–92). Beard refers to this as the "melodramatization" of the genre, a process, which "enables the film to examine personal trauma and personal grief, to feel them, while retaining the tools of shock and horror," (ibid: 92). As I will argue in more detail later, this cross-genre tendency in Cronenberg's films influences how he makes use of voices, sounds and music.

The influence of genre codes and expectations can also be regarded as an enabling factor in Howard Shore's approach to scoring Cronenberg's films as well. Upon learning that *The Brood* (the first film that he worked on with Cronenberg) would be a Horror film, Shore says that he immediately thought of the use of avant-garde music in Horror films of the late 1950s and early 1960s (personal interview). This freed him to experiment with a number of compositional techniques that he had not previously had opportunity to employ in his career as a musician in popular music, television and theatre.

And equally important, it allowed him to search for a type of musical expression that would complement the complex physical and psychological horror that was central to the film. The reliance on such stylistic codes and expectations can, of course, quickly degenerate into cliché: for example, the sound of the theremin, in conjunction with prominent, angular melodic lines in many Science Fiction film scores of the past quickly became overused, a parody of itself; while seldom found in feature film scores today, it is still routinely used to introduce children to the genre (eg, in children's television programs, such as various episodes of *The Magic School Bus*, or in recent feature films such as *Jimmy Neutron: Boy Genius*[2001]). To his credit, when Shore has used the theremin, as he did in the score to *eXistenZ*, he has done so in a more subtle fashion, burying it within the orchestral texture such that its sound is more felt than heard. As Cronenberg's films became more melodramatic in character, the musical range of expression demanded of Shore also became greater: for *The Fly*, Shore has described his approach as "operatic" (personal interview), and his use of the symphony orchestra both reflects this operatic intent and helps to articulate the film, sonically, with melodrama.

In these ways, the notion of David Cronenberg as *auteur* needs to be tempered by an understanding of the collaborative nature of his working methods, on the one hand, and the empowering influence of the non-realist Horror and Science Fiction genres, on the other. While Cronenberg's work has often been cited for its visual style – especially its stylised use of lighting, special effects and gore – the aural style manifest in his films has received far less attention, and it is to this set of stylistic features that I would now like to turn.

Dreaming Voices

The characters that inhabit Cronenberg's films often have a complex and ambiguous relationship to one another and to their own personal identity and it is through the use of the voice that this complexity is often most clearly manifest. For Cronenberg, the voice is "the kernel," "the essence" of identity and shifts in vocal quality (due to aging, frailty or other causes) can be more significant and more shocking than physical changes in appearance (personal interview). Changes in ways in which characters make use of the voice, or changes in the ways in which they are recorded and manipulated, should therefore be regarded as indices of a more profound shift at the level of their individual identity or their relationship to the film narrative.

Unlike his lengthy and ongoing working relationship with composer Howard Shore, Cronenberg does not appear to have a singular relationship of the same duration or creative depth in the area of sound design, having worked with a variety of location and post-production sound personnel during his career. During his early years, however, Cronenberg cited the importance of location recordist, Bryan Day, to his filmmaking (Rodley, 1992: 72). At the time, Cronenberg regarded him as an integral part of his creative team and, indeed, Day worked as a regular member of the 'Cronenberg crew' on eight different films (including *The Brood*, *Videodrome*, and *The Fly*, among others) in the period between 1979 and 1993. Cronenberg also appears to encourage his sound people to experiment with manipulating voices and sound effects, choosing those variations in sound that he feels are appropriate to the "psychological reality" of particular film sequences (personal interview).

It is difficult to assign responsibility then, in any precise manner, for the various ways in which voices are conceived, performed and recorded in his films, but it is clear that a certain sensitivity to the cinematic potential of the human voice has been evident in Cronenberg himself from his earliest filmmaking experiments. Due to their low budgets, Cronenberg's early forays into the world of Science Fiction – *Stereo* (1969) and *Crimes of the Future* (1970) – were shot without synchronous sound and made extensive use of voice over narration. The voices tend to be detached, clinical in character and often appear strangely cold and ironic in relation to the sometimes sexual and violent events depicted in the film images. The effect of this counterpoint, with its intense imagery and indifferent commentary, is especially unsettling in *Stereo*, where a number of distinct voice-overs (both male and female) describe a series of research experiments involving telepaths. The telepaths themselves are, not surprisingly, silent; but their interactions with one another are intimate, intense, and ultimately destructive. The sheer number of voice-overs, delivering what is essentially the text of a clinical report describing the experiments, lends a strange, de-centred character to the 'voice' of science and emphasises the anonymity, detachment and domination inherent in the relationship between scientist and research subject.

In his later films, however, voice-overs are only used on rare occasions and it is in the relationship of the voice to personal identity and inner transformation that one finds Cronenberg's most consistent preoccupation. Interestingly, the manipulation, detachment or displacement of the voice remains among Cronenberg's most powerful techniques. For example, in the final scene of *Scanners* (1981), the two principal characters – Vale and Revok (who are, again, telepathic) – are engaged in a deadly struggle: after an argument in which it is revealed that they are actually brothers, they turn their mental powers against one another in a battle to the death. As in *Stereo*, dialogue is abandoned at this point and the telepaths engage one another in silence (or rather, to the powerful accompaniment of electronic sounds and music – a point to which I will return later). As the struggle draws to a close, each character having undergone the most hideous physical pain and disfigurement, the evil Revok lets loose a powerful roar: it is as if his last remaining inner power and spirit has been brought forth, projected outward through the voice – whether it has been brought forth in dominance or defeat is not yet clear. A few moments later, Kim (whom Vale has earlier befriended) enters the room to find the charred remains of a body. When a figure then reveals itself from a corner of the room, it is Revok, or rather, the body of Revok who speaks with the voice of Vale: "Kim, we've won, ... we've won".

The implication here is that, although we *see* Revok, it is, in essence, Vale (represented only by his voice) who has been victorious.

While the use of audio dubbing to create the effect of this voice/personality substitution is obvious enough, it is nevertheless quite effective in the context of the film where other post-production audio special effects have been similarly employed. For example, when pursued by security guards in an earlier scene, Vale and Kim unleash their telepathic powers in an effort to divert them: as if in response to the mental pain to which they are being subjected, the voices of the guards become first distorted and then lowered in pitch. In this instance, various analogue post-production techniques are employed – especially changing the speed of the audio tape – to make manifest, in aural terms, a form of internal anguish which is essentially invisible (elsewhere in the film, Cronenberg resorts to spectacular visual special effects to achieve an impression of the power of telepathic assault, as in the case of the famous exploding-head scene).

In other films, Cronenberg's use of the voice can be more subtle[1]: for example, in *The Fly*, the body of scientist Seth Brundle is gradually taking on the physical characteristics of a fly as a result of an accident in an experiment in teleportation. While in the original production of *The Fly* (1958) we are immediately confronted with the horror of the transformation that has taken place, in Cronenberg's *Fly*, the progression of the metamorphosis is slower and, initially at least, Brundle appears somewhat bemused and even fascinated by the changes in his physical appearance and in his new-found powers (eg, in his unusual strength). However, as he begins trying to reverse the process of the transformation, his voice becomes increasingly agitated and somewhat higher in pitch. Initially, this change is virtually imperceptible but is made evident to the audience when Brundle attempts to activate his computer via voice recognition. When the computer's security software fails to recognise his voice, forcing him to over-ride the system, we become aware, for the first time, that the transformations which Brundle is experiencing are not only irreversible but that they are also no longer confined to his physical appearance alone: it is through the changes in his voice (ironically, validated by the objectivity of the machine), that we gain knowledge of the transformation that has begun to take place within him as well.

In a similar fashion, Cronenberg sometimes uses dialogue or modes of address as a means of hinting at sub-textual elements within the film. For example, in *Videodrome*, when we are first introduced to Dr. Oblivion during a television interview, the *non sequitur* character of his response to the interviewers questions alert us to the fact that something isn't quite right: only later, do we learn that he is actually dead and speaking from a pre-recorded video tape. Surprisingly, Oblivion still appears able to address Max (the central character in the film) directly, even via what appears to be a pre-recorded video. In this latter sequence, we realise, along with Max, that the boundaries between the real world and the hallucinatory world of the Videodrome have begun to blur.

Changes in vocal quality, achieved primarily through acting, are also employed in an extensive manner in Cronenberg's Science Fiction thriller, *eXistenZ*, and are, in this instance, more central to the script as a whole. In *eXistenZ* we are thrust into an organic game world where the boundaries between reality and the game dissolve. At various points, the players say things that appear inappropriate, indicating that they are not entirely in control, that they are speaking through their game characters. Elsewhere, we are made aware of the heavy accents of the programmed game characters (all of whom appear to be otherwise quite 'real'). When questioned about one of them, Allegra Geller (creator of the game) says that she finds his accent and dialogue to be "disappointing," an indication that he is "not a very well drawn character," thus emphasizing the artificial, constructed nature of the game and its inhabitants (and, by extension, the film itself). Sometimes the players encounter a glitch in which programmed characters get caught in a kind of loop, constantly repeating themselves or not responding at all; the players must then find something to say that will be appropriate to the game context at that particular moment in order for the game to continue. It is in the final scene, however, where we discover that, in fact, the entire film has itself been yet another level of the game: *all* of the players are then revealed to us in their 'natural' voices and accents, each quite different from the game characters' voices that we have heard up until this point in the film. Thus, the voice becomes a key element in the unravelling of the various levels of identity and reality depicted in the narrative as a whole.

In most Horror-oriented genre films, however, where the scream is the privileged mode of expressing fear and terror (both within the film and for the audience), subtlety in vocal production is seldom a requirement. In a sense, the scream is a sign of the horror's excess, the moment when terror forces expression to become irrational, inarticulate and primal. And this would appear to be as true for some of Cronenberg's early Sci-Fi/Horror films as for any other in the genre: certainly, screams are a central component of the soundtrack in films such as *Shivers* (1975), as are the semi-articulate ravings of sexual depravity found in *Rabid* (1977). But in *The Brood*, a particular form of inarticulate expression – that of rage – becomes thematic. In *The Brood*, rage is physically externalised through a process of psychological therapy; in its most extreme form, this externalisation takes on the character of independent beings – the brood children. And while the children of rage show signs of physical deformity – their faces are misshapen, they have no navels, and they are destined to die once their rage has been vented on their victims – their physical appearance seems far less startling (especially compared to some of Cronenberg's other creations) than the sound of their voices. Because of various deformities of the mouth and voice box, the brood children cannot speak and are thus forced to express themselves through an animal-like repertoire of hisses, grunts and screeches. And it is the sound of their screeching (together with Howard Shore's music) that is perhaps the most terrifying feature of their vicious attacks on other characters in the film. What strikes us then in *The Brood* is not so much the hideous

137

"shape of rage" (the title given to the psychologist's book in the film) as the 'sound of rage' – the inarticulate and terrifying sounds produced by the brood children.

Dreaming Sounds

Strangely, if voices become inarticulate in Horror films, reduced to the most primal forms of expression, sound effects can often reach new levels of articulateness: in both Sci-Fi and Horror films, sound effects share the burden of making fantastic worlds seem real, on the one hand, and transforming real worlds into surreal ones, on the other. Furthermore, when key sound effects are used thematically (as opposed to functioning as simple, environmental cues) they can make significant contributions to the narrative structure of film. Given the emphasis on the body and on technology in many of Cronenberg's films, it is not surprising that both organic sounds and technological sounds should be given special prominence and treatment in his soundtracks; indeed, in some cases, the two sound worlds merge together as one.

In many Science Fiction films, it is the sound of electricity- in its various forms ranging from the low hum of 60-cycle alternating current to the loud crack of lightning striking – that is the privileged conveyor of the power invested in technology. In *The Fly*, for example, Cronenberg uses a powerful cracking sound reminiscent of lightning in sequences when experiments in teleportation are conducted. In this way, he draws on the generic conventions of Science Fiction that have often depicted scientists' attempts to harness the power of electrical forces in instigating significant physical transformations of one kind or another: for example, one finds various uses of electricity in the key moments of transformation depicted in the many films associated with the Frankenstein myth, in the silent film classic, *Metropolis* (1927), by Fritz Lang and, more recently, in Sci-Fi comedies such as *Back to the Future* (1985) where the power of lightning is employed to hurtle one backward and forward in time.

But Cronenberg's uses of electronic sounds can also be more subtle. Again, in *The Fly*, when Brundle works feverishly at his computer we hear not only the familiar clicking sound of his fingers on the keyboard but also a soft, electronic sound that accompanies the appearance of text on the computer monitor. The sound has a searing quality, almost as if the texts were being burned onto the screen: while such an effect could hardly be regarded as 'realistic', it lends a subtle feeling of psychological intensity to these sequences that they might not have otherwise. Similar exaggerations (or fabrications) of sound effects associated with computers occur in Cronenberg's film *Scanners*.

In *Scanners*, however, the most significant uses of electronic sounds take place in relation to the theme of telepathic power: as this power is essentially invisible, Cronenberg must turn to sound in order to make it manifest. Indeed, it is through sound that the scanning power is not only made manifest but, also, given the kind of physical intensity that justifies its enormous effects on other individuals and on the external world. Typically, the sound of the scanning tones (derived from sustained raw oscillator sounds and other effects associated with the 'classic' electronic studio of the 1950s and 1960s) increases in intensity until its power is suddenly unleashed and its effects made visible in the cinematic image: in one such sequence, Vale is able to transmit his mental power via the telephone, literally burning up the wires in the process and causing an enormous explosion in the computer facility of the corporate headquarters at the other end of the line.

I will return to the use of electronic sounds in *Scanners* later in my discussion of music, in part, because composer Howard Shore was largely responsible for their creation. However, it is worth mentioning here that Shore's use of electronic sounds in *Scanners* has clear generic precedence in other Science Fiction films. Most significantly, his use of electronic sounds, both stylistically and thematically, is not unlike that found in *Forbidden Planet* (1956): while the 1950s classic makes more extensive use of electronic sounds throughout its soundtrack, the specific use of electronic sounds to depict the externalisation of the inner, psychological monster – the 'Id' – is of particular relevance to *Scanners* (see the chapter on *Forbidden Planet* elsewhere in this volume).

Technological sounds of a different order figure prominently in the film *Videodrome*, and in this instance, they are combined with sounds of the body: the opening sequence, for example, contains the sounds of television static intercut with a voice from the television, the close-up sound of a clock ticking, a coffee steamer, and the exaggerated sounds of Max (James Wood) eating. Max's first tentative introductions to Videodrome broadcasts are similarly marked by static and intermittent reception. Later, as Max tries to learn more about (and becomes increasingly enmeshed within) the hallucinatory world of the Videodrome, he watches a video of Professor Oblivion: at various moments, both the video tape and the television set begin to move and change shape to the accompaniment of breathing and low growling sounds. The sound of breathing is especially prominent, thus animating the video technology and lending it a disturbing, almost organic character that is in keeping with the main theme of the film: the merging of subject and object, viewer and video transformed into "the new flesh" (and it should perhaps be noted here that, in the dialogue track, this theme takes on a repetitive, mantra-like quality later in the film). Similarly, in a famous scene where Max inserts his entire hand, which is holding a pistol, into an opening that has appeared in his abdomen, his breathing is heavy, simultaneously full of surprise, fear, and disgust. In these moments, Max is as much a spectator as the film audience: powerless to control what is happening, his gasping breath reflecting (or perhaps leading) that of the audience as well.

The sound of breathing has a special status within *Videodrome* as it also links the world of sexuality and sexual perversion with the ultimate, deadly violence of this surreal televisual world. When Max and Nikki (Deborah

Harry) have sex, the image goes into slow motion and the sound of their passionate breathing is made to reverberate throughout a large, empty space, reminiscent of the Videodrome broadcasts. The hallucination is cut off, however, when we hear what sounds like a gun shot: the shot is very processed, almost unrecognisable with most of the low register attenuated and the sound heavily reverberated, but noticeably unlike the whips and other sadomasochistic sounds associated with the Videodrome broadcasts viewed up until this time. The scene ends with a final close-up of Max's face and this suggests that we are to take the sound of the gunshot as a kind of hallucination, or perhaps a premonition of the violence that he will eventually inflict on other characters, and himself, by the end of the film. Indeed, in the final minutes of the film, Max's suicide is repeated: performed first on television, with Nikki urging him to merge with the "new flesh" (her urging taking on sexual overtones, "Come to me Max"), and then, immediately after, in Max's 'actual' suicide. The earlier hallucination containing the sound of a single, reverberated gunshot should thus be understood as existing within a larger set of premonitions and repetitive structures within the film. The reverberation serves a dual function here: together with the slow-motion images and extreme close-ups, it is used as a common cinematic device suggesting that the sound is to be heard as part of Max's interior, psychological or hallucinatory world; but it also serves to extend the sound in time through the use of acoustic reflections, thus suggesting the idea of repetition.

The merging of the organic and the technological is treated in a more elaborate fashion in Cronenberg's later Science Fiction film, *eXistenZ*, where gaming technology essentially becomes a kind of living organism connected directly to the player via an umbilical cord. In *eXistenZ*, as with the breathing TVs and videotapes in *Videodrome*, the game 'pods' move in an organic fashion and even purr when stroked. Their assembly, in a factory operation known as the "trout farm", is accompanied by all manner of machine-like noises and the fleshy, liquid and squelching sounds associated with animal dissection. And once again, the bio-technology of the game world of *eXistenZ* is associated with sexuality and violence: when the game novice, Pikul (Jude Law), is fitted with a game "port" it is "installed" with the explosive discharge of a shot-gun; later the ports are treated erotically, as sexual orifices.

It is in the scene that takes place in the Chinese restaurant, however, where the relationship between biotechnology and the violent game world is perhaps given its most salient treatment. The so-called "gristle gun" – a pistol made up of animal parts which fires what appear to be human teeth – is assembled by Pikul out of various bits and pieces of the meal he is eating at the restaurant; he then uses it to murder the Chinese waiter who has brought him his meal. The scene is significant within the film as a whole because the gun surfaces, like a kind of leitmotif, in many different sequences in the film, changing hands between various characters and moving between different levels of reality. In linking it to Pikul at its apparent point of origin, it gives the audience a hint as to Pikul's true role in the narrative – a role that will not be fully revealed until the very last moments of the film. The sonic treatment of the sequence is therefore given special care: first the sound of Pikul eating, and then every movement and fitting of a new body part to the gun, is accompanied by the most grotesque and sickening body sounds – the close-up sounds of flesh being torn and mashed and bones being cracked; these sounds subtly become more metallic in character, culminating in the violent discharge of the gun when it is fired at the waiter and the sound of the tooth/bullet tearing into his flesh.

Although it has been seldom remarked upon, the graphic violence and gore with which Cronenberg's films are often associated is, in many ways, matched in the sound track by the attention given to sonic details such as those found in the Chinese restaurant in *eXistenZ*. But more important, the sounds often do not function simply as a form of sensational counterpoint to the graphic images: insofar as they serve to underscore or create signifi-cant links between the general, thematic elements present within the film narrative – especially themes associated with the body, technology, sexuality and violence – then the attention given to the crafting of sound effects must be regarded as a significant component within Cronenberg's overall cine-matic strategy.

Dreaming Music

Perhaps more than any other sound element, music has been a significant factor in the shifting relationship of Cronenberg's films to genre conventions, to the expression of various thematic elements, to the structure of his films, and to the overall evolution of his filmmaking style. His long, creative relationship with composer Howard Shore is thus of the utmost importance in understanding not only the role and use of music in his films but, perhaps also, to the progress of his work as a whole.

In this regard, it is interesting to note that Cronenberg's earliest, experimen-tal Science Fiction films did not use specially commissioned music (a result, no doubt, of their low-budget financing). In the case of *Stereo*, no music is employed at all, the soundtrack being given over entirely to the multiple voiceovers. But with *Crimes of the Future*, and in keeping with many other films in the genre, Cronenberg used electronic music to evoke his Science Fiction world. However, in this instance, while his use of repetitive electronic sound patterns do contribute an overall sense of mood to individual scenes, they tend to *accompany* the film, in a general kind of way, but do not appear to be otherwise closely related to the development of the narrative.

In his first feature films, Cronenberg and his collaborators attempted to introduce a greater degree of coordination between music and narration but with mixed results. In both *Shivers* and *Rabid*, producer Ivan Reitman (who is also credited as Music Supervisor for the films) provided a soundtrack consisting entirely of pre-recorded, stock music. While it must be said that this 'needle-drop' approach to scoring works, in some ways, remarkably well within the context of the films – for example, the dissonant, avant-garde character of much of the music creates an unsettled feeling, complementing the bizarre and horrific events portrayed in the films – it is still not capable of producing the same degree of subtlety usually found in specially-composed music. In particular, because the music is pre-formed, 'spotting' (the placement of the music in relation to the editing of film sequences) tends to be awkward: the music often appears to enter and exit in a rather arbitrary fashion and musical phrases are not always precisely coordinated with visual events. Furthermore, the music sometimes appears exaggerated in character: for example, in the opening sequences of *Rabid*, the innocence of the young couple prior to the motorcycle accident is suggested by a gentle flute melody, the effect of which is perhaps overly sweet, cliché in its pastoral and idyllic associations (see Tagg, 1983). While the music is meant to contrast with the more ominous, avant-garde music that follows, it does so in an obvious way and there are no thematic, tonal or other ways to link the musical passages at a more subconscious, structural or narrative level.

Much of this changes, however, with the arrival of Howard Shore on the production team of *The Brood*, the first film in which Cronenberg was able to engage a composer. As mentioned above, Shore, had come to film music from a background in popular music (having written, performed and recorded for several years with the Canadian band Lighthouse), theatre (in both radio and stage performance, where he had even tried his hand at directing), and television (as the first Musical Director of *Saturday Night Live*, from approximately 1975 to 1980). But it was in film music that Shore felt that he could realise his most creative and expressive potential as a composer: although he had been thoroughly trained in composition during his student days at the Berklee School of Music, in Boston, Shore had not fully pursued his interests in composition, in part, because he felt the possibilities of getting his music performed would be limited (personal interview).

Shore's background and personal attitude towards film music is significant in that it may account, in part, for the experimental approach that he has taken to the medium. Unlike earlier generations of film composers, many of whom had come from classical music backgrounds and sometimes felt that their work in film was compromised by the commercial nature of the industry and by the demands of the medium itself (eg, composers such as Korngold and, to a certain extent, even uncompromising individuals such as Bernard Herrmann), Shore appears to have consciously moved towards film scoring as the most viable creative outlet for his musical ideas. Indeed, it is in the Science Fiction and Horror genres and in psychological thrillers – genres that often allow for a degree of experimentation and an increased expressive range – where Shore has achieved some of his greatest success, having scored not only the majority of Cronenberg's films, but also some of the most stylised and disturbing psychological thrillers of the past decade: films such as Jonathan Demme's *The Silence of the Lambs* (1991), David Fincher's *Seven* (1995), and Tarsem Singh's *The Cell* (2000)[2].

It was precisely with this intention of exploring the creative possibilities offered by the film medium that Shore approached the score to *The Brood*: as mentioned earlier, in equating the Horror genre with avant garde music (much as Cronenberg and Reitman had already done), Shore allowed himself to experiment with a number of compositional techniques – including atonal dissonances, glissandi, and serial techniques – that he would have otherwise had little use for in his earlier career. Shore's score reflects a certain impulsive energy that, in large part, derives from this experimentation with musical ideas designed to meet the demands of *The Brood*'s psychological themes and shocking imagery. This impulsiveness is evident in the diverse range of stylistic influences present in the score: including the string quartets of Bela Bartok, serial techniques, and the music of Bernard Herrmann. While certainly less cohesive than many of his later scores, Shore achieved some degree of consistency by virtue of the relatively austere, monochromatic use of strings: while his decision to score the film for 21 strings was, in part, based on budgetary constraints, it also allowed Shore to create a more intense, unified sound than would have been possible with a small orchestra of varied instrumentation (personal interview).

But perhaps more significant, are the generic resemblances evoked by this use of strings, and in particular, the apparent reference to Bernard Herrmann's music to the film *Psycho* (1960): in each of the attacks by the brood children, the sound of their screams is accompanied by a high, chromatic figure in the violins, similar to the screeching violin sounds used by Herrmann in the earlier film's famous shower scene (such an association is reinforced by the fact that one of the attacks of the brood children takes place in a bathroom). The musical figure would no doubt be recognisable to audiences familiar with not only the score to *Psycho* but other, later films in the horror genre that made use of a similar figures: as in the music to Brian de Palma's *Carrie* (1976), released three years before *The Brood*.

It is difficult to account for why such a musical figure should become so prominent within these films but its significance, I think, goes beyond simple inter-textual reference to *Psycho* as a prototype within the genre (if indeed, such a reference was intended). It seems to me that the recurrent use of this figure by composers associated with horror films suggests a musical/theatrical relationship that is as much gestic as it is sonic or generic: that is, the murderous bodily movement – the slashing knife in the case of *Psycho*, the hammering blows in *The Brood* – is virtually identical to the movement of the violinist's bow arm in producing the repeated *martelé* strokes (literally, 'hammered' stroke) used to create the short, intense screeches in the high register of the instrument. In this sense, at those moments when action within the horror film takes on its most intense and distilled form, gesture and music become one (not in the sense of 'mickey mousing', but as a non-synchronous, analogous gesture that gives musical expression to the main action).

At a more semiotic level, the screeching violins can be read as a sign of horrific excess: like the vocal screams of the brood children (with which they are often paired), the high-pitched screeches are a sonic signifier of the irrational.

In this regard, it is interesting that Shore precedes each of the attack scenes with a series of slower glissandi, often beginning in the low strings: whereas tonal and atonal music are both equally subject to the rational organisation of the twelve chromatic pitches of the Western tuning system, the glissando escapes this background organisational logic and becomes the ultimate expression of the irrational in the domain of musical pitch. It is perhaps no accident then, that glissandi appear in similar sequences elsewhere in Shore's film scores – scores that are otherwise stylistically very different from one another: for example, string glissandi immediately precede the moment when Brundle-fly kidnaps Veronica in an attempt to prevent her from aborting their child, in *The Fly*, and also precede the murder of the Chinese waiter and the burning of the diseased game pod, both intense, irrational moments in *eXistenZ*.

While the score to *The Brood* includes one musical cue containing electronically produced sounds, they appear less integrated with the rest of *The Brood*'s score than is the case in the use of electronic sounds in Shore's music for some of Cronenberg's most well known science fiction films, especially *Scanners*, produced two years after *The Brood*. In *Scanners*, Shore relies heavily on raw oscillator sounds and the use of editing and looping techniques common in 1950s and early 1960s tape music. Given the fact that Shore was an early adopter of sophisticated digital technologies such as the synclavier, his use of these older sounds and techniques might appear somewhat anachronistic. However, the sound palette suggested by the analogue sounds is completely in keeping with the conventions of earlier Science Fiction films, thus placing his work firmly within those generic boundaries.

Indeed, as mentioned earlier, the sound palette of *Scanners* has much in common, both sonically and stylistically, with Louis and Bebe Barron's soundtrack to the 1950s Sci-Fi classic, *Forbidden Planet*. The electronic sounds in *Scanners* are primarily associated with the telepathic powers of various characters and are thus perceived, at least initially, as sound effects rather than music. Shore made use of orchestral instrument sounds for the film's main theme and background music thus relying on a more conventional division of soundtrack labours than was the case in the Barrons' work, where the electronic sounds did double duty as both sound effect and music (for a detailed analysis of the soundtrack to *Forbidden Planet*, see Rebecca Leydon's contribution to the present volume). One of the benefits of Shore's more conventional approach was that it allowed for less ambiguity in terms of how the different sonic elements operated within the narrative but it also enabled him to produce a more complex, textural layering as well. This layering has implications for both the overall structure of the film as well as the ways in which we derive meaning from the narrative.

At the structural level, Cronenberg's films seldom adhere to the tidy conventions of Hollywood narratives: that is to say, there is often little resembling a conventional unfolding of the plot and action towards a climax and denouement. At the end of his films, narrative conflicts typically explode rather than resolve themselves and this tendency is no doubt one of the elements that have contributed to his films being labelled as hopeless or 'abject'. This places a significant burden on Shore, I would argue, insofar as he must control the pacing and structure the score so that it will contribute its greatest force to these final sequences within the films.

In the case of *Scanners*, each of the scanning sequences builds in intensity during the course of the film, paralleling the increasing strength of Vale's telepathic powers and his ability to control them. Shore not only saves his most complex electronic texture to the final sequence in which Vale and Revok battle one another to the death but he also layers it with a dense orchestral score, each sonic layer vying for our attention. Finally, just in advance of Revok's hideous vocal roar, we hear the extended sound of the roar slowed down and lowered in pitch. In fact, because the slowing of the tape extends the sound in time, it both precedes, and is layered with, the 'normal' sound of Revok's voice, doubling its effect. While this technique is in keeping with the tape manipulations of the dialogue track heard earlier in the film, it is the first time that such a complex layering has occurred: because of the processing involved and its placement in the mix, the pitch-shifted voice in this instance becomes more a part of the general texture of electronic sounds and music than a part of the dialogue track. At this penultimate, climactic moment of the film, Shore has brought each element of the soundtrack – dialogue, sound effects, and music – to their most complex development, both individually and in combination with one another, thus achieving an excruciating level of intensity demanded by Cronenberg's narrative and images[3]. A short time later, after Vale's voice speaks triumphantly through Revok's body, Shore plunges the listener back into the dissonant orchestral texture as the final credits roll: denying the possibility of a 'happy ending', the music suggests that nothing has been resolved by Vale's victory, achieved through the agency of his superior telepathic powers. Indeed, earlier in the film Vale appeared to take some enjoyment in his ability to inflict pain on others but, in the final moments of the film, it is only Shore's music that alerts the audience to the ambiguous nature of power and the unresolved character of the narrative.

With Shore's pitting of the orchestral and electronic sounds against one another during the final moments of *Scanners* (and in this regard, it is important to note that the two layers of sound do not merge with one another but remain essentially two separate textural planes), one is tempted to read the sonic layers as a kind of symbolic battle between Vale and Revok, between good and evil. While such a reading is certainly supported by the narrative context I'd like to suggest an alternate interpretation. Shore has commented that when he works with orchestral and electronic sounds or, together with the sound engineers, with industrial and environmental sound elements, he feels that the expressive character of musical performance captured through live recording has an essential 'human quality' that comes through even after processing and complex mixing (audio commentary to the DVD edition of *Seven* (1977). In this sense, the orchestral sounds in

Scanners could be taken as signifying something essentially human, and perhaps physical in character, versus an electronic texture that has been so clearly associated throughout the film with the mind and with supernatural powers.

Such an interpretation can be supported, I think, in relation to some of Cronenberg's later horror and Science Fiction films and may be one of the ways in which Shore's music contributes to the increasing "melodramatization" of these genres. Indeed, the final moments of *Videodrome* are similar to those of *Scanners* insofar as they both concentrate on individuals, on the plight of the main characters in the films: the music's role in these instances is, in part, to allow us to *feel* the intensity of these moments of personal trial. While Max's suicide (in *Videodrome*) is more clearly 'tragic', the music nevertheless lends his transformation into "the new flesh" a certain transcendent character: through the quasi-religious tone set by the use of organ textures, prior to the scene of transformation, and by an almost romantic striving suggested by the constantly rising melodic line that leads up to the moment of suicide. For William Beard, it is only with *Videodrome* that Cronenberg's characters actually achieve a sense of being full "human subjects" (2001: 106), and it is perhaps, in part, the ability of the music to focus the emotions of the audience that allows the quality of subjectivity to emerge.

The focus on the human subject within Cronenberg's Horror and Science Fiction films is perhaps most clearly felt in *The Fly* where the personal, subjective transformation of Brundle is as essential to the narrative as his physical transformation. Not only is Shore's score to the film essentially orchestral and, in his own words, "operatic" in character, but there is also a clear division made between electronic sounds – associated most often with technology in the film – and music, which is associated with the flesh and the human. In this regard, the electronic sounds are most often cast in the role of sound effects and are associated with the computers and "telepods" but, even here, subtle distinctions are made. For example, when Brundle first demonstrates his teleportation machine to Veronica, using one of her nylon stockings, the sounds of the machines and the background music are entirely synthetic. However, when a baboon is used for experimental purposes (or when Brundle himself later enters the machine) the accompanying music is orchestral – suggesting a link between the instrument sounds and things of the flesh (throughout the early parts of the film, Brundle's main problem is to get the machine to work not simply with inanimate objects but also with complex, animate beings). Diegetic music is relatively rare in Cronenberg's films and it is significant that in two sequences in *The Fly* Brundle is shown playing the piano or singing: the most poignant of the two sequences occurs when Brundle, already hideously disfigured by his slow physical transformation, sings the children's song 'There was an old lady who swallowed a fly'. Shore's music exits as he trails off with the final phrase "... perhaps she'll die." In the final sequence of the film, after Brundle undergoes his last attempt at teleportation, the explosions, bursts of electricity, and electronic

146

sounds associated with the pods are faded out entirely and only the orchestral music, along with Veronica's sobs and Brundle's animal-like groans, are heard as he wordlessly begs for her to kill him. In all of these instances (and very much unlike the uses of music and electronic sounds in the earlier films), the sounds of the human voice and instrumental music in *The Fly* are used to underline, in melodramatic fashion, the suffering of the human subject, while electronic sounds are relegated to the realm of technology.

Conclusion: Waking Up

Following *The Fly*, Cronenberg has made few films that could be classified strictly within the genres of Horror or Science Fiction, turning instead to a the complex psychological dramas and hallucinogenic worlds of films like *Dead Ringers* (1988), *Naked Lunch* (1991) and, most recently, *Spider* (2002). In most of these films, Shore has continued to use primarily instrumental music as the basis of his scores. However, electronic sounds and, more importantly, the electronic processing of instrumental sounds are a significant part of Shore's sonic palette as is evidenced in the score to *Crash* (1996), with its six electric guitars, each processed individually and panned within the stereophonic array. Only *eXistenZ* fits comfortably within the fantasy world of Sci-Fi but, even here as noted earlier, the electronic sounds are fused within an overall texture that is principally orchestral in character (which, it could be argued, is entirely in keeping with the shifting levels of reality and the bio-technology theme of the film).

It must be said, however, that all Cronenberg's films are marked by an abiding interest in the world of fantasy and dream and, in this sense – his films represent a highly complex relationship to experience and the notion of 'reality'. Indeed, the worlds of fantasy and reality are intertwined in both his thought and his films: "Things that happen in our daily lives come to us in our dreams in a transformed way; and then when we come out of those dreams, those things are transformed for us in our daily lives. They now have a different meaning, they have resonances from our dreams that they didn't have before the dream" (Cronenberg's audio commentary to the DVD edition of *eXistenZ* [1999]).

If we think of him as an auteur, then comments such as "after all, these are my nightmares, not theirs" (Cronenberg, personal interview), would seem justifiable. But as I have argued throughout this chapter, the expression of Cronenberg's dreams on film are not simply 'his': they are also the result of a collective process in which a number of highly talented individuals participate, on the one hand, and engage with the genre conventions at their disposal, on the other. They too, in this sense, inhabit that same dream when they work: "[film] is a little dream-like. So you want to get into that dream, and you want to sort of stay in there and ... and kind of wake up occasionally and write down some notes" (Howard Shore, audio commentary to *Seven* DVD). But equally important, is the impact that Cronenberg's films have on his audiences, the potential for his films to enter into our daily lives and transform them, changing our notions of what is real and what is fantasy. In that sense, these worlds of sounds and images, of fantasy, horror and science fiction are not simply 'his'. These are our nightmares too.

Thanks to director David Cronenberg, composer Howard Shore, and Professor William Beard for graciously allowing me to interview them. Thanks also go to Kristine Paznak, a graduate student at Carleton University, for assisting me in tracking down some of the source material used in this chapter.

Notes

1. A fascinating use of more recent, digital signal processing (DSP) technology to achieve changes in the pitch of the human voice can be found in the film *M. Butterfly* (1993). In his role as Song Liling (Butterfly), actor John Lone's voice is pitched up slightly, placing his voice in a more female register. Unlike analogue techniques, digital pitch shifting does not result in a change in the temporal dimension of sound, thus maintaining image synchronisation and more "natural" speech characteristics (and in this way, the technique does not break with the more conventional codes of realism predominant in the film). By not having to ask him to resort to a falsetto when filming, Cronenberg was able to retain the full expressive potential of Lone's acting voice (personal interview). One only becomes aware of this subtle manipulation (if one becomes aware of it at all) in the final scenes of the film when Song confronts Gallimard with his deception in a police wagon: here, Lone adopts a more aggressive, male voice (his own) in alternation with the more submissive tones of Butterfly (manipulated via DSP in post-production).

2. It should be noted that Shore's experience as a film composer has not been limited to the particular genres that are the primary focus of this essay: indeed, during his career he has scored an enormous range of films, from conventional drama to comedy. But I would nevertheless argue that his most characteristic work has been found in the more complex genres of Horror and psychodrama. Even his most publicly acclaimed work, such as the score to Peter Jackson's *Lord of The Rings: The Fellowship* or *The Ring* (2001) – his only score, to date, to have ever been nominated for (and to have won) an academy award – exists in the Fantasy realm, where a certain anti-realism and expressive "excess" are often expected.

3. As mentioned earlier, Shore was responsible for the music of the film as well as much of the electronic "sound effects." Whenever possible, he also likes to work closely with the sound engineers and mixers on Cronenberg's films. So while it may be difficult to determine, with any certainly, who was ultimately responsible for the decision to use the pitch-shifted voice in the way described here, Shore would no doubt have participated in that decision-making process.

Chapter Eight

AMBIENT SOUNDSCAPES IN *BLADE RUNNER*

MICHAEL HANNAN AND MELISSA CAREY

Ridley Scott's *Blade Runner* (1982) is a complex film that poses funda-mental questions about what it means to be human through its exploration of the interaction of humans and human clones (known in the film as 'replicants'). Although its bleak vision and ambiguous message arguably explained the film's moderate box office performance when first released, it has since emerged as a cult film for film critics, academics and fans alike. Apart from the wide-ranging philosophical issues raised by the film, com-mentators have also been attracted by the rich layering of visual symbolism and the interplay of film genres (Science Fiction and film noir). Bruno (1990) focuses, for example, on the film's postmodern architectural pastiche. Telotte (1990) explores the quality of desire in the world of the human double. Pyle (1993) interrogates the opposition of the human and the clone, the contra-dictory use of Christian symbolism and the ironic use of film noir conven-tions. Byers (1990) ruminates on how the popular culture film can stimulate debate on the dehumanising tendencies of late capitalism. Deftereous (1998) deals with photos and memories, Saini (1996) with the symbolism of the eye and seeing, Guokas (1996) with the symbolism of the eye and televisual monitors and Scott (nd) with misogyny and film noir critique.

Although there is no lack of literature treating the philosophical ideas and narrative devices of *Blade Runner*, very little attention has been given to the role that music and sound play in the construction of the film's interplay of meanings. Sammon's (1996) book on the making of *Blade Runner* provides little information about the actual score. He classifies the score as "futuristic nostalgia", describing it as "a dizzying mélange of unabashed romanticism, ominous electronic rumblings, gutter level blues, delicate celestial shadings, and heartbreaking melancholy" (1996: 273) but offers little more in the way of analytical detail about the music and its relationship to the narrative. Stiller (1991: 196–200) provides the best available analysis of the score and provides some insights into the function of the music, particularly in relationship to the theme of nostalgia. A feature of Stiller's account is his discussion of the extreme use of reverberation for the score and sound effects (ibid: 199). Bukatman's monograph on *Blade Runner* also makes similar references in the few words devoted to music and sound:

> *The score by Vangelis, more tonal than melodic, evokes a poignant melancholia. Sometimes the film even seems to be taking place underwater: reflections play off the walls, liquid sounds are exaggerated and in the final battle water drips down the walls of the Bradbury Building.* (1997: 40)

The focus of this essay is on the way the music and sound effects of *Blade Runner* are responsible for reinforcing the main narrative ideas and images of the movie. The functions and structure of the music and sound cues are described with reference to film music and film sound theories articulated by Gorbman (1987), Brown (1994), Huckvale (1990) and Chion (1994). The integration of music and sound effects on the soundtrack is analysed focusing on the electronic and ambient nature of both elements.

For the purposes of this study, the version of the movie under discussion is *Blade Runner – the Director's Cut* (released in 1992) in the DVD format (released in 2000). In this version the voice-over narration (a classic film noir device) has been removed and Ridley Scott's original pessimistic ending restored (the studio had insisted on changing Scott's ending for the film's US domestic theatrical release in 1982). There are a number of other versions of the film including the workprint (1982), the US San Diego sneak preview (1982), and the international European/Asian theatrical release (1982). Reference is made throughout the article to titles of music cues that appear on the 1994 soundtrack album. Most of the main cues that appear in the film are given titles that are useful to refer to in the discussion of the film score. The relevant cues from the soundtrack album are *Main Titles, Love Theme, One More Kiss, Dear, Blade Runner Blues, Memories of Green, Tales of the Future, Blade Runner (End Titles)* and *Tears in Rain*.

Plot summary

In order to understand the following analysis of the score and soundtrack in relation to the narrative and the philosophical themes of *Blade Runner* it is necessary for the reader to have some idea of the plot. Set in 2019 in Los Angeles, *Blade Runner* depicts a world whose sustainable environment has been destroyed by humans, many of whom have now moved to off-planet colonies. The plot revolves around Deckard, a former 'blade runner' (cop/assassin) who is coerced by his former boss (Bryant) to hunt down and 'retire' some renegade replicants who have returned illegally to earth and have already killed a currently employed blade runner (Holden). There are four replicants still on the loose including two females (Pris and Zhora), Leon (who had escaped after killing Holden) and Roy Batty (their leader).

Deckard encounters a fifth replicant at the Tyrell Corporation when he is asked by Eldon Tyrell (the mastermind of replicant design) to run a test (the Voight-Kampff test) on Tyrell's personal assistant, Rachael. As Deckard discovers from the test, Rachael is a replicant but she doesn't know it because Tyrell has programmed her with memories based on the life of his niece. A love interest begins to develop between Deckard and Rachael.

Using an Esper machine (a kind of image analyser that even allows the viewer to see around corners), Deckard discovers an image of Zhora in a photo discovered in Leon's hotel room. When investigating the origins of an animal scale (also found in Leon's room) Deckard discovers it is from an artificial snake that is used by Zhora in a lewd performance act at a night club (the Snake Pit Bar). After a backstage encounter at the bar Deckard chases Zhora through the crowded streets and shoots her dead but Leon has witnessed the shooting. Leon tries to kill Deckard but is saved by Rachael. Working through Tyrell's genetic designer employees, Chew and J.F. Sebastian, the other replicants (Roy and Pris) are able to get to Tyrell. Roy kills Tyrell after he says he can't do anything to halt their approaching deaths (replicants have a life span of only four years).

Deckard tracks Pris to J.F Sebastian's apartment (in the Bradbury building). They fight but she is eventually shot by Deckard. Roy arrives and discovers that Deckard has killed Pris. Although he is in a position to kill Deckard, he gives him a chance to escape and then follows him. In the desperate chase Deckard is about fall to his death from the top of a building when Roy saves him at the last moment. At this point Roy dies. Deckard returns to his apartment and finds Rachael asleep. He wakes her and they hurry to leave with the intention of escaping the authorities.

Music and sound effects: overview and context

Vangelis was the first composer to win an Oscar for a completely synthesised score – for *Chariots of Fire* (1981). His score for *Blade Runner* is also a largely synthesised one featuring [synthesised] orchestral textures associated with dramatic Hollywood cinema and more abstract electronic music textures. The use of synthesisers to create entire scores for feature films was not common until the invention of user-friendly instruments such as the moog analogue synthesiser that was famously used for much of the soundtrack of *A Clockwork Orange* (1971). A problem with early synthesisers was that they could not convincingly simulate orchestral sounds, although they were easily able to produce broad range of weird sonic effects like those in *Forbidden Planet* (1956), the first entirely synthesised score. The quality of the orchestral simulation in *Blade Runner* was a breakthrough even when compared to later scores such as Maurice Jarre's music for *Witness* (1985) which involves unconvincing attempts at copying specific instrumental sounds (although Jarre's score does also includes inventive cues that exploit the uniqueness of synthesiser sonorities). Vangelis's scoring for *Chariots of Fire* is not focused on simulation of orchestral sounds and contains a mixture of popular music-related grooves (the famous theme), slower more static cues (usually to accompany the slow motion running scenes) and some more abstract sonic constructions that foreshadow the *Blade Runner* score (such as the warm up scene prior to the big race).

A feature of the underscored (non-diegetic) music of *Blade Runner* is that is does not, with the exception of the end title music, use drum and bass grooves or any other type of rhythmically driving features such as rapid regular repeated notes or note patterns. As a result there is a strong ambient quality to much of the music: it is slow, motionless, lacking a strong sense of pulse or metricality. To use the words of Toop (1996: prologue np) in describing the ambient music tradition, it is "drifting or simply existing in stasis rather than developing in any dramatic fashion". These kinds of floating non-evolving musical textures fit well within the Science Fiction movie tradition because they have been coded to evoke otherworldly landscapes, space travel and futuristic technologies. One is reminded of *Alien* (1979) where Jerry Goldsmith's orchestral score often uses static textures such as held chords and slow ostinati (repeated melodic patterns); and also of *Close Encounters of the Third Kind* (1977) where the spiritual nature of the alien encounter provides occasion for sustained shimmering single-chord orchestral textures from the pen of John Williams. This is not, however, to say that these two scores are limited to ambient musical techniques. The point is that *Blade Runner* uses them more consistently.

Similarly the soundtrack of *Blade Runner* is characterised by its intensive use of ambient sound effects and atmospherics. The film sets, both exteriors and interiors, are littered with computer monitors, video screens and neon lighting from which all kinds of droning, buzzing, beeping, blipping and static noises are emitted. In addition there are many collages of sound effects that are meant to represent the background (and often unseen) mechanical and natural sounds of the cityscape. There are few scenes in the film where dialogue is not accompanied by some distinctive ambient background construction. Again this fits squarely into the Science Fiction movie tradition where sound effects are used to create imagined sounds and soundscapes. Obvious examples are the communication sounds of the robots and creatures in *Star Wars* (1977) and the mechanical sounds heard in the various interior spaces of the spaceship of *Alien* (1979).

Diegetic music

Brown describes diegetic music as coming from a "source within the diegesis – a radio, a phonograph, a person singing, an orchestra playing – and the characters within the film can theoretically hear that music" (1994: 67). Diegetic music for a film is characteristically chosen from a variety of existing recorded sources; it is not necessarily (and, in most cases, not normally) written by the composer contracted to write the underscore. In *Blade Runner* no music is credited besides Vangelis's music with the single exception of Gail Laughton's *Harps of the Ancient Temples*, which is (arguably) used non-diegetically to accompany a street scene where people on bicycles ride past a cinema and then Roy and Leon appear[1]. The implication is that Vangelis composed the other diegetic music used in the film, although this may not be the case in several instances (for example the traditional Japanese song fragments described below).

Most of the diegetic music in *Blade Runner* is orientalist, either appropriated or derived from East Asian or Arabic[2] styles. The Los Angeles street scenes of the film all have a Chinatown look about them. The oriental is othered in the narrative to reinforce the idea promoted in the script that the only people left on Earth are the dregs of humanity. To convince him to take on the blade runner assignment police chief Bryant tells Deckard: "You know the score pal – when you're not a cop you're little people". The racial and other characteristic of many of the characters are designed to reinforce this. One of the genetic scientists is Chinese (Chew); another (Sebastian) suffers from a degenerative disease. The artificial animal makers in the market are Cambodian and Egyptian. The policeman, Gaff, is Mexican-looking and uses cityspeak (a multicultural dialect of European and Asian languages). Ironically the replicants (particularly Roy and the two females) are classically Aryan looking. They are considered in the story to be superior to humans in design (stronger, more intelligent) but Bryant nonetheless refers them to in discriminatory language as 'skin jobs'.

The street scene diegetic music is designed to support this set of racial stereotypes and racial othering. A shot of an oriental woman in a giant neon advertisement is accompanied by a voice singing in traditional Japanese style to a plucked string accompaniment[3]. Although this cue first appears at the beginning of the film, prior to the meeting of Gaff and Deckard in a noodle bar, it recurs in varied form for five scenes that take place at the Bradbury building where J.F. Sebastian lives and where the climax of the film (the fight scenes and chase) takes place.

There is a significant block of Arabic-sounding music to accompany the market scene where Deckard is tracking down the origin of the artificial snake scale found in Leon's hotel room. This scene leads Deckard to Taffey's Snake Pit Bar where Zhora is performing. The music heard in the market provides the introduction to the Egyptian snake maker. It contains a prominent melodic motif played on bowed stringed instruments in octaves and a ornamental melodic line played by double-reed wind instrument (*zurka* or *zuna*) and reed flute (*nay*), backed by a synth drone and (Indian) tabla rhythmic pattern. The cue is typical of various syncretic forms of popular music found in Arab countries such as Egypt. The first piece of music heard when Deckard enters the Snake Pit Bar also has Arabic sounding melodic qualities (gapped scale and highly ornamented) but is dominated by a contemporary sounding synthetic drum groove. The next music cue to accompany the snake act is decidedly more contemporary (for the early 1980s), using a dance music groove with prominent syndrums and a less prominent trumpet (and string) melody based on a gapped oriental scale.

153

This cue continues as Deckard approaches Zhora after her performance and when they enter her dressing room.

Predictably with diegetic music, the level and definition of the music drops significantly when the door is closed. It eventually stops completely to be replaced by a non-diegetic cue (also with an influence from Arabic music). Gorbman considers that diegetic music fleshes out film space, and variables in recording, mixing, and volume levels further determine the quality, the "feel or framed/lived space in a given film" (1987:25). The treatment of the dance music cue in the bar and dressing room scenes is a good example of this process. In the subsequent scene, where Deckard pursues Zhora through the market and shoots her, further fragments of Arabic-sounding music are heard mixed in with crowd and traffic noises. A group of Hari Krishnas is also seen performing their repetitive percussion-backed chants.

Film composer Jerry Goldsmith characterises the Hollywood practice of using an amalgam of ethnic and other sources rather than authentic musical recordings:

> The ethnic-Oriental is particularly worth talking about because if we were to give the purely ethnological answer musically they [the film makers] would throw it out in a second. What is ethnic is what Hollywood has made ethnic. (quoted in Hagen, 1971: 164)

With one exception the only diegetic music cues heard in *Blade Runner* are derived from traditional Arabic and East Asian musical practices. This is the song *One more kiss, dear* heard in a café where Deckard is buying a bottle of spirits after shooting Zhora dead. The song (by Vangelis with lyrics by Peter Skellern) is composed, arranged and recorded to simulate a late 1930s/early 1940s crooning pop style. Its use, in line with the nostalgia elements of the narrative, perhaps indicates that there are nostalgia venues one can go to in 2019 to hear old popular songs. It may also be a reference to the kinds of songs used in early film noir movies and neo-noir film such as *Chinatown* (1973). The fact that it is playing languidly in the background also contrasts strongly with Deckard's agitated state of mind following the killing. This conforms to Gorbman's theory that diegetic music "has the capacity to create irony, in a more 'natural' way than non-diegetic music" (1987: 23) and Chion's characterisation of the "indifferent" power of diegetic music:

> This juxtaposition of scene with indifferent music has the effect not only of freezing emotion but rather of intensifying it ... I call this kind of music anempathetic. (1994: 8)

Non-diegetic music/ Monumentalising

The music used for the titles of *Blade Runner* begins as a series of single deep, explosive sounds probably created by recording a large bass drum with extreme 'canyon' reverb effect so that the sound echoes and sustains for a long time. A lonely single-line melody enters, played high in pitch as a synthesised bowed string sound. This slow tune is distinctive because the ending note of each phrase glissandos downwards (accompanied by the drum explosions). The use of glissandi provides a sense of other-worldliness and alienation and is exploited in other sections of the soundtrack including ambient soundscapes and more specific sound effects such as sirens.

Although we have not seen any images yet, the mournful effect sets the scene for what is to come. After four phrases of this melody, the last glissando continues further downwards and cross-fades with a spooky sound collage based on a pulsating electronic loop with bell patterns above and low sirens below. This cue accompanies the prologue text scrolling up the screen. With the first view of the Los Angeles 2019 landscape, realistic (sound effect) explosions accompany fireballs issued from giant chimneystacks. The music thus far has prepared us for the gloomy, environmental devastation of this scene. With explosions continuing, *Main Titles*, a powerful electronic orchestration of the single-line main melody first heard under the titles (but now without the haunting glissandos, and with the tune developed further) is used as the camera focuses on the Tyrell Corporation's huge mock-Mayan building, and then zooms in on the room where Leon is about to be interrogated[4]. The effect of this luscious and grandiose orchestral cue (with its brass-like melody, its rich strings arrangement and static drone-like bass) is to 'monumentalise' the landscape and immense building images. According to Huckvale:

A large orchestral sound can transform a scene or an image into something more impressive (eg more spacious, more opulent), which without music would remain mundane. (1990: 4):

The technique is also used for the music to accompany the flying vehicle scenes. When Deckard is being transported to police headquarters, the same kind of rich orchestral synthesised scoring is used. Slowly changing string section chords undulate gently, accompanied by a variety of sounds (electric piano, high bells and a celesta-like effect) doing upward and downward glissandos and arpeggios. An upward sweeping electronic sound is also used several times. All the components of the musical texture combine to create a feeling not only of grandeur but also of floating up and down. Soon after, when Deckard is being transported to the Tyrell Corporation building there is a reprise of the orchestrated *Main Titles* melody previously used with the shot of this building (as described above). This cue not only serves to create a structural link between the two shots of the Tyrell building but also works well with the flying vehicle shots. There is a similar slow and static quality: the slowly changing string section chords and drone bass that accompany the serene brass melody also invoke a floating feeling[5].

Bell symbolism

The *Main Titles* theme is not employed again until near the end of the film. It is used first in the music that accompanies Deckard's last desperate attempts to escape from Roy and when he is hanging on to a girder about to fall to his death. This version of the theme is beefed-up with dramatic brass orchestration and church-bell punctuation. The *Main Titles* theme is also the basis of the *Tears in Rain* cue used to underpin Roy's famous dying speech ("I've seen things you people wouldn't believe ... attack ships off the shoulder of Orion ..."). Here the mood is more serene but the strings and brass orchestration is nonetheless very powerfully scored. Both these cues are examples of monumentalising the drama of near death and death itself. The church bells bring an effective religious dimension to the scenes to strengthen visual imagery such as the dove that Roy releases as he dies.

Other types of bells and chimes are a feature of the score throughout *Blade Runner*. When Deckard meets Rachael for the first time at the top of the Tyrell Corporation building above the dense pollution (the only part of Los Angeles where the sun is still visible) the music consists of high ambient string chords with sparkling high bell-like sounds and a graceful descending scale-like melody. Ethereal strings chords are heard low in the mix behind their first conversation (she is not too impressed about his role as a blade runner and lets him know this). Extremely high and soft tinkling sounds (like wind chimes) are heard through this segment of the movie, symbolising the light that can only be seen at this altitude, the spark between the couple and also perhaps that fact that Eldon Tyrell is a godlike figure (the creator of replicants' brains and minds). At the point where Deckard indicates that it is too bright in the vast room to run the Voight-Kampff test, an ambient texture of electric piano, held chords (of vocal and string sounds) and high pitched wind chimes is featured, fading out as the test begins and replaced by the more quietly ominous electronic sound effects associated with the test.

It is in this scene where (part of) the cue known as *Tales of the Future* is first heard. The full cue is a texture of sustained vocal synth chords, a deep brassy bass drone, dissonant brass and string elements, high wind chimes, an instrumental melody (similar to the sound of a bassoon) and a vocal solo sung by Demis Roussos. Both the instrumental and vocal melodies possess musical qualities influenced by Arabic music. The vocal style is extremely high, ornamental, powerfully projected, with highly emotional vibrato and tone colour expressivity. The cue has dark, brooding, ominous quality but the vocals and chimes also make it ecstatic.

The cue is used on a number of occasions (in various states) to indicate some aspects of Deckard's quest to find the replicants, usually during some moment of realisation. When Deckard realises that Rachael's memories are implants from Tyrell's niece, a distant melancholic vocal melody is heard (a fragment of Roussos's vocals). It exploits the idea that memories are like voices in our heads. In the next scene, where Deckard and Gaff are searching Leon's hotel room, the chimes of the cue are used when Deckard discovers the snake scale in the bathtub. The instrumental introduction of the cue is then used to coincide with Gaff placing an origami piece he has made; and the beginning of vocal line coincides with Deckard discovering Leon's 'family' photos in a draw. Upon finding Zhora's image in one of Leon's photos (using the Esper machine) and realising a connection between the image and the snake scale, the cue is used to bridge into the market scene investigation. It is used again to underscore the scene in the dressing room when it becomes clear to the audience that Zhora realises the danger she is in from Deckard and Deckard in turn realises she is a replicant and must be destroyed.

Gorbman suggests the "two overarching roles of background music may be characterised as semiotic (as *ancrage*) and psychological (as suture or *bonding*)" (1987: 55). She borrows the term "ancrage" from Roland Barthes to indicate "anchoring the image more firmly in meaning" (ibid: 32). By accompanying these scenes about realisation or insight with the same musical cue, the scenes themselves are arguably more closely linked in the viewer's subconscious.

Piano symbolism

The piano is used symbolically in *Blade Runner* to represent memories and a hankering after former eras. When Rachael talks to Deckard about her childhood memory of spiders we hear a heavily processed piano melody, the start of the ambient piano piece titled *Memories of Green*, which underscores her stated fears that she may be a replicant with implanted memories. The processed piano sounds, reminding one of an old out-of-tune instrument, provide another level of nostalgia symbolism. But significantly we also hear sirens from the street outside the apartment mixed in with this gentle piece of music.

Deckard has a grand piano in his apartment upon which are arranged many photographs of people (presumably relatives) dressed in late 19th or early 20th century clothes. He is only seen at the piano in a scene when he is drunken and remorseful, leaning on the piano lid and striking just one note (A = 880) a few times. This diegetic sound is blended in with a non-diegetic piano-based cue (with string section chord backing) to accompany the scene. The cue prepares us for Deckard's dream of a unicorn running through a green meadow. The string section chord blends with a rich choral chord sound to accompany the unicorn images. Later, however, while Deckard is sleeping following his violent encounter with Leon, Rachael plays the same piano, appearing to respond to the sheet music on the music stand. She realises she can play the piano and although she remembers learning, she wonders whether this is an aspect of the memory implant from Tyrell's niece. The script calls for the 19th Century romantic piano composer Frederick Chopin, but what Rachael plays is a not particularly convincing Chopin imitation (and, on close inspection of a frame, the music on the music stand is not what she is playing either – it looks like a violin and keyboard *largo* in the style of Bach). The piece and the action of playing it, however, symbolise nostalgia for a previous era, the era of the childhood Rachael never had, and the romantic and romanticised era of the music and photos.

157

The pseudo romantic piano cue is heard superimposed diegetically over Vangelis' non-diegetic *Love Theme*, a jazz ballad-style tune for saxophone accompanied by a lush string section arrangement and bell-like electric piano arpeggios. This sentimental theme seems to be preparing us for a love scene to follow. It turns aggressively chromatic and dissonant, however, as Deckard finds he has to force himself on Rachael to get her to respond to his advances. The music turns sweet again as she submits.

The sound of a toy piano playing a phrase beginning with a descending major scale pattern is used to accompany the scene in JF Sebastian's apartment with Pris. Sebastian has a collection of genetically engineered walking, talking toys that he has made as companions, so it is not clear whether the toy piano is a diegetic sound (another toy) or emblematic of Sebastian's child-like personality. The phrase is repeated over and over as if emanating from an actual toy. When Roy arrives to tell Pris that Leon is dead, some related ominous sounds interrupt the toy collage. The toy piano scalic idea is then incorporated into an ambient cue to signify the momentary optimism that Roy and Pris have that they will be able to solve their limited lifespan problems if Sebastian can take them to Tyrell.

Blade Runner Blues

Blade Runner Blues is a sad and haunting improvised melody over two slowly alternating low buzzy-sounding string pad chords. The synth solo (a reedy muted trumpet sound) employs obvious blues inflections. Electric piano and synth bass interact melodically with the solo. This cue is used twice, firstly when Deckard goes to his balcony to look over the cityscape (following the scene where Rachael confronts him about her suspicions she is a replicant). The cue reflects the sadness of this reality, and the grim devastation of the city. The cue continues under the following scene where Pris is walking on the street and waiting for JF Sebastian outside the Bradbury building. The jazz-tinged blues style may also be considered as a reference to a musical style used in film noirs of the 1950s. Conomos identifies a number of classic noir films with jazz-orientated scores (2000: 82) and theorises jazz's significance in the following way:

> *Jazz was used in film noir, especially in the 1950s, to foreground the inevitability of doom. The tonality and style of jazz was not used simply to underscore or illustrate emotional, thematic and formal aspects of the narrative, but also as an integral mediating part of the audio-visual process itself, generating the desired visual and sonic atmospherics, the sturm und drang, of alienation, mystery and paranoia (Kalinak, 1992). Noir jazz does not simply exist to subserviently underscore what we see in cinema.* (ibid: 85)

Kalinak (1992: 159–181) and Brown (1994: 86–91) both detect jazz and popular music influences in David Raksin's orchestral score for *Laura* (1944), but for the most part film noir scoring is centred on the European-derived orchestral styles of composers like Steiner, Herrmann and Rozsa. Thus apart from the jazz influence of the *Blade Runner Blues* (and the diegetic popular song mentioned earlier), there is not much in Vangelis's score that could be linked convincingly to classic film noir scoring.

The second use of the *Blade Runner Blues* cue is one of the most startling musical devices in the film. When Deckard shoots three times at Zhora as she desperately tries to escape through the crowded streets, the cue (this time with a heart beat sound effect accompaniment) fades up and the street sounds disappear completely. The only other sound effects heard against the music are glass panes breaking as Zhora crashes through shop windows and a single fatal shot. The serene melancholy of the music contrasts obscenely with the desperate action and violence of the scene.

Substantial one-off cues

As JF Sebastian and Roy attempt to enter the Tyrell Corporation building, a prominent low string motif using the descending tritone interval (the so-called Devil's interval) against a wash of tam tam (large flat gong) sounds, harp glissandi and swirling pink noise, prepares the viewer for the dramatic death scene to follow. This music resumes at the beginning of the dialogue between Roy and Tyrell and forms the basis of the cue used for Roy's murder of him. It includes dramatic and forceful choral, string and brass textures which build to a monumental climax. The use of choral sounds in this way (reminiscent of music of biblical films of the 1950s and 1960s) is presumably meant to provide a religious resonance to the scene – Tyrell is, after all, Roy's 'maker', and Christian symbols, such as the dove and the nail through the hand, are involved in Roy's actions later in the film.

Tension-creating music is also used for the scene following Tyrell's death where Deckard walks into the Bradbury Building knowing Pris will be in there waiting. This spooky ambient cue is based around a sparsely recurring electric piano motif of two resonant jazz chords, the second of which is sustained to make space for the interspersal of reiterated high alarm bell sounds and low flute patterns as well as the diegetic sound effects and Japanese vocal music cue associated with the Bradbury building.

Another substantial one-off cue is one identified as *Blade Runner (End Titles)* on the sound-track CD. This is unique in the film in that it is the only music (apart from the diegetic cues used for the Snake Pit Bar performance scene) that uses a drum-groove based texture. It is based on a fast four-note ostinato that only varies with the chord changes and is further energised by drums, timpani and synth effects. This backing is used to accompany a fairly straightforward descending four-note theme that is not related in any obvious way to the other thematic ideas of the film score.

It is significant that this type of groove-based cue is used only when the narrative of the film is completed. The mood of the score throughout the film has been based largely on music that is rhythmically static and textu-rally atmospheric, even when it is dramatic or forceful in its approach.

159

Indeed, likening this cue to Vangelis' theme music for *Chariots of Fire* (1981), Stiller argues:

> *here for the first time Vangelis can write at length and as he pleases, without regard to the exigencies of dramatic action. The result is a real piece of music-not a swatch of aural wallpaper – that has a definite beginning and end and a goal-directed structure in between.* (1991: 198–9)

Sound effect-based ambient soundscapes

Throughout *Blade Runner*, the bleak exterior landscapes erupt with explosive, hissing, sucking, wheezing and whirring noises. These soundscapes are usually presented at a low volume level as background sounds to interior shots sometimes behind dialogue. Because of this they reinforce the sense of environmental devastation at a subliminal level for the viewer. The ubiquity of machine sounds in the film's soundtrack is emblematic of the absence of other life forms on earth. There are obvious sound effects associated with actions seen in the movie (such as gun shots, vehicle sounds, street scenes, computer monitors and other machines) but other sound effects used as background can be heard as more like sound collages than sound effects. In addition, sounds that might be considered as effects rather than film music are often merged with music cues. David Lynch summarises this phenomenon:

> *"There are sound effects, there are abstract sound effects; there's music, and there's abstract music,"* he adds. *And somewhere music turns into sounds, and sounds turn into music. It's kind of a strange area."* (quoted in Kenny 2000: 133)

The concept of the coherent blending of soundtrack elements, termed "mise-en-bande" by Rick Altman (cited in Buhler, 2001: 55), can be traced back to a phase of silent movie history where films were accompanied by Wurlitzer theatre pipe organs that combined orchestra-like sounds, percussion and sound effects performed by a single musician. In a way the electronic music score (composed and performed by the studio-based composer) is a modern-day revival of this practice. Compared to an orchestral score, the listener's expectations of the sound vocabulary of electronic music involves both simulations of orchestral sounds and the creation of new sounds not intended to imitate any real musical or non-musical sound sources.

The notion of electronic simulation of musical sounds and the blurring of the distinction between music and effects parallel the relationship between humans and human machines in *Blade Runner*. It is sometimes difficult to tell whether a musical sound is made by a 'real' instrument or is otherwise synthesised. The heavily reverberated bass drum sound at the start of the film is a case in point. Elsewhere, such as the use of a real saxophone for the *Love Theme*, the realness of the instrument suggests to us that even though the lovers may be replicants, their passion is human and real. Similarly, as in Holden/Leon interrogation scene, we often move seamlessly from abstract electronic non-diegetic music (the unreal) to sound effects that are diegetic (the real) or extra diegetically (the ambiguous).

As previously noted, abstract ambient sound effect collages are typically used in Science Fiction movies to define non-ordinary locations. In *Blade Runner* the sounds heard on the top floor of the Tyrell Corporation building in the early scene introducing Rachael and Tyrell have already been discussed as a music cue. Similar sounds are employed later for Tyrell's bedroom ambience just before the scene where Roy murders him. The background sounds heard in Deckard's apartment and the Bradbury building are also distinctive. Deckard's apartment features a constant low-pitched pulsating electronic oscillation and a ghostly sound similar to breathing-in with an asthmatic wheeze. This sound smoothly glissandos up a fifth and then down again over a period of three seconds. It is a loop repeated at approximately four second intervals. A very similar sound is heard in the interior of the Bradbury building. In discussing the ambiguity of the "line between the score and the sound effects" Stiller focuses on this very sound:

> We never find out what makes the hum, but it is always there, the voice of the place itself. Unlike everywhere else in the movie it radiates stability, calm and self understanding as it quietly oscillates across a fifth, tonic to dominant to tonic and back again. (1991: 199–200)

Perhaps Stiller would not have read this sound this way if he had known that "the hum" had been appropriated from Ridley Scott's earlier *Alien* (1979). It is used in that movie for a number of scenes, firstly in the spaceship hospital, where the patient is a crew member with an alien being clinging to his face; and also underpinning a conversation following the destructive acid leak from the alien after an attempt is made to cut it from the face.

The soundscape of the interior of Sebastian's apartment takes advantage of the sonic potential of all his genetic creations and mechanical toys. Chew's laboratory scene is presented with an underlying ambient soundbed of steam escaping combined with ominous low music drones and pulsating electronic loops reminiscent of warning signals. Exterior shots (and some interior shots such as Leon's hotel room) feature the sound of incessant rain. This reinforces the bleak cityscape imagery and is another reference to classic film noir mood-creation devices.

Other effective sound effects collages are associated with the two featured investigative machines (the Voight-Kampff and the Esper). The extended scene with the Esper is a complex mixture of sound effects from the environment and from the operation of the machine as well as ambient music textures designed to build up the expectation that some dramatic discovery is about to occur.

161

Conclusion

Music and sound is used to reinforce many of the particular narrative devices of *Blade Runner*. The diegetic music establishes the predominant sub-cultures of the streets of Los Angeles in 2019 as East Asian or Arabic and is complicit in the film's othering of these cultures that remain in the devastated earthly environment, now considered unfit for humans. Music and sound are used extensively to establish the ambience of particular locations in *Blade Runner*. Examples include the use of chimes and bells for the penthouse of the Tyrell Corporation building, the explosions for the opening shot of the cityscape, the traditional Japanese song used mostly with shots of the Bradbury building, the toys' sounds in Sebastian's apartment and the electronic and the wheezy background noises associated with Deckard's apartment and the interior of the Bradbury building. These sound constructions are often acousmatic in nature: "a situation wherein one hears the sound without seeing its cause" (Chion, 1994:32). Chion describes this phenomenon as "added value" as "it interprets the meaning of the image, and makes us see in the world what we would not otherwise see, or would see differently" (ibid: 34). As many of the film's sound effects collages are presented as background to whole scenes, they take on the form of ambient musical collages (at least when considered within a post-Cagean experimental or postmodern tradition of creative sound art). They provide a rich level of sonic detail to the scenes they underpin.

A case for a strong intertextual relationship between the look and the sound of the film may be made. Sobchack identifies an "excess scenography" in *Blade Runner*:

> An abundance of things to look at serves to inflate the value of the space that contains them, and emphasizes a particular kind of density and texture. This visualization of contemporary spatial experience eroticizes and fetishizes material culture, spatializing it as multidimensional and sensuous "clutter". (1988:262)

The detail in the sound track of *Blade Runner* provides a strong temporal element to the spatialising affect of the visual. Chion claims that "in the first contact with an audio visual message, the eye is more spatially adept and the ear is more temporally adept" (1994: 11). Thus the combination of the detailed sound and vision of *Blade Runner* is able to intensify the sensuous cinematic experience in an intense way.

The static rhythmic quality of many of the music cues blends seamlessly with the sound effects collages. Some of the music cues (for example the cue for Deckard entering the Bradbury building and the music cue underpinning the Esper machine scene) are constructed with the same kind of aesthetic as the effects collages through the use of drones, static held tones, melodic loops, and irregular percussive elements. Even the cues that are more convention-ally structured pieces of music (such as *Main Titles*, *Blade Runner Blues*, *Tears in Rain* and *Tales of the Future*) lack rhythmic driving qualities, evolving musical structures, and dramatic textural variation. This locates them within the ambient music tradition.

One of the main functions of the music in *Blade Runner* is to emphasise the theme of nostalgia for the past. The song *One More Kiss, Dear* and the use of the grand piano in Deckard's apartment are diegetic examples of this, but many of the main non-diegetic cues also have a nostalgic quality including *Love Theme*, *Blade Runner Blues*, and *Tears in Rain*. Even the emotionally charged *Tales of the Future*, used principally to indicate Deckard's insights in his tracking down of the replicants, is associated in some of its occurrences with the replicants' photographs. The symbolism of family photographs is central to nostalgia narrative.

The use of recurring themes to create structural links in the plot is principally done through the *Tales of the Future* and *Main Titles* cues. *Main Titles* has a monumentalising function for the shots of the enormous Tyrell Corporation building as well as the key dramatic moment of the chase on the roof of the Bradbury building. Other monumentalising cues are used to reinforce the floating sensation of the flying vehicles and the violent deaths of Zhora and Tyrell.

Bruno (1990) regards *Blade Runner* as a postmodern text, discussing its depiction of "post-industrial decay", its "hybrid architectural design", its use of simulacra (the replicant) and its pastiche of narrative styles and symbols (183–195). Music and sound in *Blade Runner* may also be considered within a postmodern context. Much of Vangelis' synthesised score is a convincing electronic simulation of the classical Hollywood orchestral score; western representations of Eastern music are composed; recordings of traditional music are appropriated; and a broad range of musical styles is employed (romantic orchestral, ambient soundscapes, abstract electronica, jazz-blues, laid-back jazz, 1940s pop, electronic dance, pseudo-Arab, Japanese and 'biblical' choral music). In this score, any sound can be music and the boundaries between music and sound effects are constantly blurred. Even the method of constructing the score through improvised layering in multi-track studio is postmodern when considered against the background of traditional methods of screen scoring. The score in fact presaged the advances of the new synchronisation technologies on the horizon (MIDI systems in 1983; hard disk editing in the early 1990s). Thus it is a score of considerable historical significance and, indeed, Prendergast considers it "one of the twentieth century's greatest achievements in sound" (2000: 312).

Notes

1. This cue may be diegetically ambiguous, although the style of the music does not suggest the locality of the street scene for which it is used.

2. Reference is made in this essay to 'Arabic music' to represent a coherent set of musical practices, some of which are specifically referred to in the description of certain cues of *Blade Runner*. This term and reference reflects Touma's contention that:

    Despite differences in their musical and aesthetic forms the peoples of the Near East and North

163

Africa, conditioned by a common history spanning over two thousand years, can be said to have a homogeneous musical culture. (1996: xvii).

3. It is unclear from the soundtrack what instrument is used.

4. The soundtrack CD issued in 1994 by Warner Music calls this fully orchestrated form of the tune *Main Titles* even though there are no titles used with it in the film.

5. The floating cue is in fact included as a central part of the *Main Titles* track on the soundtrack album, although the two section of music are never combined into the same cue in the film itself.

Chapter Nine

'I'LL BE BACK'
Recurrent Sonic Motifs in
James Cameron's *Terminator*
films

KAREN COLLINS

Introduction

In recent years, there has been a growing popular interest in Science Fiction, particularly in dystopian (or anti-utopian) visions of the future. There has been a surfeit of dystopian cinema in the past two decades or so, including remakes of *The Planet of the Apes* (2001) and *The Time Machine* (2002), as well as the *Mad Max* series (beginning in 1979), the *Robocop* series (beginning in 1987), *The Matrix* (1999), *Minority Report* (2002) etc. *Why* there is such a growing popularity of dystopia is worth exploration, but first it is necessary to ask *what* dystopia is saying. In this chapter I suggest that an exploration of the sonic aesthetic of one type of dystopia – what I will term the 'industrial-dystopia'[1] – will help us to understand what these films are communicating. Although there are many films worthy of discussion, I focus on two particularly popular dystopian films, James Cameron's low-budget *Terminator* (1984) (*T1*) and its bigger budget sequel *Terminator 2: Judgment Day* (1991) (*T2*). (NB *Terminator 3: Rise of the Machines*, released in mid 2003, directed by Jonathan Mostow without Cameron's involvement, is not considered in this analysis due to its differences from the first two interlinked films.)

The *Terminator* films represent landmarks in cinematic collaboration between sound effects and music[2]. When *T2* was released in movie theatres, the Eastman Kodak company was attempting to launch a new digital sound format, Cinema Digital Sound (CDS), a 5.1 precursor to Dolby Digital. The six channels and optical encoding of digital sound allowed sound designers not only greater creativity in producing the sounds, but also the ability to use digital sound in post-production[3]. The freedom offered by a bigger budget and new technology in both sound and visual effects meant that *T2* excelled the original *Terminator* in both achievement (winning six Academy awards) and audience (becoming one of the top twenty grossing films of all time). But the original *Terminator* was also quite noteworthy in its use of sound and effects.

This chapter explores and compares the use of various recurrent sonic and musical motifs in the first two *Terminator* films, with the intent of discovering the importance of sound as a signifier in the film. I will suggest that the sonic conventions in the films help to provide plot symmetry, create mood and reinforce settings and narrative in the films, as well as draw the two films together. I will begin with a summary of the plots, characters and settings before I explore the particular sonic aesthetics. Although there is some interesting use of diegetic music in both of the films – notably the tongue-in-cheek use of George Thorogood's *Bad to the Bone* (1982) in *T2* – I will be focussing on the non-diegetic music and the sound effects.

I. Setting the Scene: A Distinctly Dystopian Scenario

The year is 2029 and the planet has been taken over by artificially intelligent cyborgs. Humans, in a desperate attempt to destroy the machines and recapture their freedom, must fight back in a post-nuclear landscape, a world destroyed by machines that they created. A group of survivors, led by John Connor, builds a resistance movement in the underground camps to fight the machines. The machines attempt to destroy the rebel forces by sending a cyborg, a 'terminator', back in time, to 1984 (*T1*) and 1991 (*T2*). In *T1*, the cyborg's mission is to eliminate John's mother, Sarah Connor, before she had conceived the boy, and in *T2* the target is the boy himself. In both films the resistance also manages to send back a guardian. In the first film, this is the human Kyle Reese, who will father John Connor. In *T2*, it is a reconfigured terminator (T-800) model which is sent back to protect the boy Connor from the latest technology created by the machines, the T-1000 model terminator.

In *T1* Reese recounts the history of the future – his past – to Sarah. Together they struggle to survive against the threat of the T-800 terminator. Reese, mistakenly arrested for stalking Sarah, manages to convince her of his sincerity when the T-800 breaks into the police station, killing most of the police. After a long chase, Reese is killed in a final battle with the machine, played out in a factory down in the Los Angeles docks. In *T2*, Sarah has been committed to an insane asylum, sending the young John into foster care. A T-1000 model terminator arrives to kill John. The T-1000 has the power of mimicking, able to imitate most objects and lifeforms. John, with the help of a reprogrammed T-800 model sent from the future, escapes and breaks Sarah out of the institution. In an effort to prevent the future from taking the course we have seen, they travel to the desert to collect some equipment to combat Cyberdyne systems, the company that invents the intelligent computers that take over the world. After successfully blowing up Cyberdyne, there is once again a long chase and fight between the guardian and terminator, played out in a steel foundry.

There are obviously notable points of similarity between the two films, and it is worth mentioning some of the other more significant similarities. Both films start in a war zone of the future, in almost the same shot. Both films end in an industrial factory of some sort. Both films make frequent use of cars or motorcycles as cuts in the films. These similarities help to tie the films together and to create symmetry within the plots of the films themselves, but perhaps more significantly, help to create a very specific setting, enabling a very specific soundscape that supports the films' moods. The *Terminator* plots are classic dystopian scenarios, as defined by Mark Hillegas (1967: 150) nearly twenty years before *T1* came out: a cataclysmic war precedes a new state, a guardian elite (in this case, the machines) maintains power through technology, a substitution of the manufactured for the natural takes place, and then a revolt against technology. The long cinematic pre-history on which the *Terminator* draws involves the use of industrial machinery as a metaphor, and can be seen going back to Fritz Lang's *Metropolis* (1926) (see Collins, 2002). Outside of cinematic representations, as I will show, the history of the very specific sonic and visual aesthetic goes back much further.

II. Soundscaping Dystopia: Effects and Underscore

The soundscape of the future in the *Terminator* films can be described in one word: hellish. Besides the subtitle of *T2* (*Judgment Day*), the *Terminator* films make several references to Hell. In *T2*'s script (Cameron and Wisher, 1991), there are several descriptions that help to position the film as set in a kind of modern-day Hell. At one stage the setting is described as "Dante for the nuclear age". The sounds are also described in Hellish terms:

> (scene 2 EXT. CITY RUINS – NIGHT) *Same spot as the last shot, but now it is a landscape in Hell. The cars are stopped in rusted rows, still bumper to bumper. The skyline of buildings beyond has been shattered by some unimaginable force like a row of kicked-down sandcastles. Wind blows through the desolation, keening with the sound of ten million dead souls.*

> (scene 192) *With an unholy scream, like the unoiled hubs of Hell, the whole rig slides on its side at 60 mph toward the steel mill.*

The sounds are clearly crucial to creating the atmosphere of this hellish future world, as is witnessed by the mere fact that they are written into the script at several points in the films and described as such. The wind howls and whistles, and there is a hissing of steam and smoke. Bones are crunched, sonically morphed with the metallic clanking of machines. We hear the

167

foghorn-like, low groaning motif of the T-1000 repeated over mechanical sounds and constant gunfire, laser blasts, and explosions.

Even when we are in the 'present' in these films, however, there are many sonic cues that recur that are clearly of significance to the understanding and 'decoding' of the film. For instance, drones help to create suspense, doom and threat. Watch any film and low rumbling or low steady bass notes will not be harbingers of happiness (see Leeuwen, 1999: 108 and Tagg, 2000: 179). Ethereal, celestial choruses sound at key points in the film, typically during death scenes, and help to signify the transient state towards the afterlife (see Collins, 2002). There are screeching echo sounds piercing through the low bass that have a similar effect to the stabs in *Psycho* (1960) – they create a cerebral, painful and maddening type of sound. The cars, trucks, scooters and motorbikes often used as cuts in scenes help to situate the film as definitely urban, allowing for the sounding of horns, screeching of tires, and an unstable-sounding motor rumbling and revving which underlies a significant proportion of the films. It is worth looking at some of the sonic signifiers in detail to understand how they lend themselves to connotations of doom, despair, death and suspense.

III. The Theme Song and Underscore

Brad Fiedel's original score for *Terminator*, although innovative at the time, now appears outdated on account of the use of the analogue synthesiser and its dull percussion sound. Fiedel, who had once played as a keyboardist for 1980s pop band Hall and Oates, places more emphasis on tonal elements in the first film. *T2* retains the same melody, but the sound is dramatically transformed. The music, which can scarcely be separated from the effects, consists primarily of percussion, notably metal, bass and snare drums, juxtaposed with a low bass drone and sound effects, and the tonal elements are now symphonic rather than synthesised[4].

The *Terminator* theme song occurs not only during the title sequences, but also in several key points in the films. In *T1*, the theme is sped up and played on piano for the love scene, and later softened and slowed down when the hero Reese dies, towards the end of the film. It then returns for the end credits. In *T2* the theme song, as well as during title and end credits, occurs during the escape from Cyberdyne, and when the T-800 commits suicide. In other words, the theme occurs during critical moments in the film, when the 'good guys' die, when we are supposed to empathise with the plight of anguish. It is therefore apposite to explore the expressive power of the theme's main melodic motif.

The song is in D minor, and presents us with a sustained drone pedal point on the tonic. The main motif is essentially a pattern of D-E-F, with the capping note on the minor third. Although the tension created by this minor third is somewhat resolved by the leap to the more triumphant sounding fifth, the emphasis on the minor third, which is repeated throughout the theme, is crucial to the tone of the motif. Minor thirds, argues Deryck Cooke,

Figure 1. Terminator 2 theme (main motif) 1991 (Brad Fiedel).

are found throughout dramatic classical music, and commonly express "unrelieved tragedy" and "unhappy endings" (1959: 58)[5].

A similar motif – perhaps a nod to Fiedel – occurs in Don Davis's underscore to *The Matrix*, during the tense helicopter escape scene:

Figure 2. The Matrix (helicopter scene) 1999 (Don Davis).

The use of Aeolian inflections in these films (the minor sixth Bb in *Terminator*'s theme comes in the celestial choir voice) is significant. Alf Björnberg's study of Aeolian harmony in rock music found that the mode was commonly used in connection with lyrics:

> *dealing with subject matters such as historical and mythical narratives, static states of suspense and premonition, alienation in life and in personal relationships and fear of, but also fascination by, the future and modern technology and civilization.* (Björnberg, 1985: np)

Björnberg indicates a series of keywords of associations with Aeolian harmony as "vast stretches of time and space", "staticness", "uncertainty", "coldness", "grief" and "modernness" (ibid). Björnberg even goes so far as to suggest that the Aeolian mode:

> *may be seen as the musical coding of a conflict between important traits of the dominant ideology and the way in which reality is actually experienced. Faced with the growing threats affecting Western industrialized societies today: atomic war, environmental pollution, increasing unemployment the rapid dissolution of traditional social values and institutions, people in widely differing social situations, it can be argued, experience a more or less conscious distrust in the optimism of the future contained in the dominant ideology.* (ibid)

169

Aeolian modal patterns recur frequently in many 1980s and 1990s songs about the future, particularly those coupled with a sense of anxiety, perhaps exemplified best by Europe's *Final Countdown* (1986). The fact that such Aeolian inflections are common to dystopia also is further evidence to support Björnberg's contentions, and clearly invoke a similarly fateful and anguished tone in *Terminator*. Also significant in the score is the use of Phrygian inflections[6]. For instance, when the T-800 is shot through a window at the club Tech Noir in the first film, there is a motif repeated several times of D-Eb–C-D. This same I-bII-VII-I repeating four-note pattern turns up in fact in a different key in Japanese dystopia *Tetsuo: The Iron Man* (1989). In another threatening scene at the end of the film where the terminator is chasing Sarah and John in a tanker truck, there are several Phrygian patterns, for instance a repeated E-F-C-E.

The Phrygian has been called the "austere" or "severe" mode, and is often referred to as "dark", "heavy", "sombre", or "gloomy". It has also been described as "frightening and awful"[7]. William B. Kimmel has shown that Phrygian inflections are common to European death-related music, specifically as recurring elements in requiems (quoted in Rosar, 2001: 110). Acoustically speaking, the minor second has the highest felt dissonance and feels particularly unstable in the bass registers. Cooke argues that the minor second represents "unrelieved hopelessness", "hopeless anguish" and "despair" (1959: 78). Cooke here refers in particular to Brahms' *Symphony no 4 in E minor*, Op 98 (Fourth Symphony) which begins with a Phrygian minor second to emphasise grief and sorrow, written at a time when Brahms was dying (see Cooke, 1959: 77 *ff*).

It seems clear then – in western cultures, at least – that, we may associate the minor second and minor third with death, fatefulness and despair; and it is likely for these reasons that they recur in *Terminator*, as well as the other dystopian films mentioned in this section. That these elements recur in times of despair and threat, and – in the case of the minor third – the theme song, helps to build our empathy with the characters. Other non-tonal elements in the films assist in the characterisation of certain settings and emotions.

IV. Terminator Leitmotifs: Foghorn Groans and Metallic Percussion

Both *Terminator* films make use of leitmotif for the terminator characters. In *T2*, the T-1000 model takes on a foghorn-like groaning sound, which resembles the foghorn-like sound heard in the future sequences of the first film. The sound resembles a large animal groaning in pain, a low-pitch, thick warm sound with many overtones. Along with the sound of pain, it perhaps helps to signify sadness, isolation and threat through its association with foghorns, and the misty, foggy, darkness of the atmosphere one would hear a foghorn in. Ray Bradbury's short story, *The Fog Horn*, describes its sound as:

> *A cry so anguished and alone that it shuddered in my head and my body*
> *... Lonely and vast and far away. The sound of isolation, a viewless sea,*
> *a cold night, apartness.* (1983: 436)

Foghorn sounds also appear to be associated with the future through a kind of eternal quality, described by Bradbury as "the sadness of eternity and the briefness of life" (1983: 434). It is significant then that it is used in the films as either a sound *in* the future (*T1*), or a sound *referencing* the future (the T-1000 in *T2*), and as a threatening sound, helping perhaps to create a kind of future-anxiety.

The T-800 model's motifs are similar in the two films, and are essentially drum-patterns with a rhythm that is somewhere between a heartbeat and a train. This gives the feeling of a mechanical heartbeat, quick and tense. It is a powerful sound, militaristic in its percussiveness. Its propulsive repeating ostinato creates an unstoppable, inexorable feeling: it is unrelenting and merciless. As Reese tells us in the film, it will keep coming, it will stop at nothing. It is no coincidence that both terminator models should have semi-organic components to their motifs. In fact, just as humans are given some mechanical elements in the films[8], organic sounds are morphed onto several mechanical objects: lion and tiger growls and roars are substituted for the rumble of a Harley Davidson motorcycle and the force of an oncoming truck. Sound designer Gary Rydstrom wanted, as he described, to have the sounds be "demonically alive" – yet another reference to Hell (*Terminator Special Edition* DVD notes [2001]). The breakdown of the sonic barriers between organic and mechanic is perhaps an important way to subliminally drive home the movie's theme of the loss of humanity at the hands of the machines. The isolated, pained foghorn sound of the T-1000 is merely there to encourage us to recognise ourselves in the machine.

V. Industrial Motifs: The Setting

Mechanical, militaristic motifs similar to that of the T-800 occur throughout the films. The scenes are frequently set up for the sound of machinery – there are plenty of construction sites, vehicles, and factory machines helping to support, and be supported by, a regimented and repetitive percussive score. The use of metallic sound effects and percussion and deep rumbling bass helps to situate the narrative in an undoubtedly dystopian and hellish setting. If we compare the descriptions of Hell written by Milton in *Paradise Lost*, we can see clear analogies with the sonic aesthetic we have heard in *Terminator*. Milton's Hell includes the sound of cymbal-like clashing of metal on metal:

> *Against the Highest, and fierce with grasped arms*
> *Clash'd on their sounding shields the din of war*
> (1989 [edition] Book I, lines 667–668)

171

very loud percussion:

> Though for the noise of Drums and Timbrels loud
> Their children's cries unheard ...
> (ibid: 394–395)

and violent sound effects:

> With Impetuous recoil and jarring sound
> Th'infernal doors, and on their hinges grate
> Harsh Thunder, that the lowest bottom shook of Erebus
> (ibid: 376–378)[9]

Such descriptions would equally fit some of the settings in the *Terminator* films. The finale in the steel mill is a perfect analogy to Hell. It's dark, underground, in a red fiery 'cave'. There is an eerie wind, sizzling and crackling of sparks and steam, the gurgling of the oily pit, deep drones but, more in line with Milton, a very heavy metallic thumping and clanking of metal on metal. Chains rattle, rusted steel girders grate against each other and heavy sprockets grind as they turn. In fact, it is not too far a stretch to suggest that the choice of setting the endings to both of the films in some sort of factory might very well be to play up on the Hellish atmosphere of those surroundings. Metal clanks are present throughout the film but particularly in times of threat. Those sounds referred to earlier as similar to *Psycho's* stabs might easily be called 'jarring', and a thunderous low rumbling is also present in times of high suspense.

Depictions of Hell in literature and art have commonly drawn on the horrors of the contemporary times in which they were created. There are, for instance, several reasons for the recurrence of heavy, low bass sounds and thunderous rumbling common in Hell and dystopia. In nature, it is typically loud and low rumbles that represent threat: earthquakes, thunder, etc. It has been suggested, for instance, that Hell was originally fabricated from the 'unnatural' aspects of volcanoes: the reverberant rumble of a tremor, the hissing of steam from a geyser, etc. (see Hughes, 1968: 159). Homer describes Tartarus as "the pit under the earth, where there are gates of iron and a brazen doorstone" (*Iliad* 8.15)[10]. It is significant that the Greek and Roman metalsmiths Hephaestus and Vulcan kept their forge in a volcano, where the rumbling and hissing would be combined with a clanking of metal – as heard in the *Terminator* films during both the future sequences and the factory scenes.

Other than the threats of nature imposed by the gods, it is the sounds of human threat that have also been drawn into Hell and dystopia. For the ancient Greeks, this likely meant the conflict of battle, although for Milton, Bosch, Breughel or Dante the imagery seems to have been formulated also from the various torture devices used during the Middle Ages – the wheel, the rack, etc. Along with the grinding of gears, the rattling of chains, the smelting and clanking of swords and later explosives, these would have been sounds that became associated with violence and threat. Percussion is significantly associated with war. Throughout history, warriors have been known to strike their shields, and cymbals and drums were used in battle in various parts of the world. It was even said in ancient China, that whichever side made the greatest noise would win the battle (Blades, 1970: 113). In particular, the regular metronomic beating of the drums became associated with military marching (see Collins, 2002). Drums also became associated with death and Hell. Stefan Lochner's painting 'Last Judgement' (c 1435–1440) depicts demons and angels fighting for souls, demons being accompanied by kettle drums (nakers) and booming trumpets (cf Hart and Lieberman 1991: 41), and the 'End of Mankind' (1523–1526) by Hans Holbein the Younger depicts skeletons with kettle-drums, blaring trumpets, a trombone and hurdy-gurdy (ibid:113). In Medieval Christianity, "outside of the military, drumming was seen as an aberration that signalled the presence of Satan" (ibid: 40).

Death also becomes associated quite early on with metallic sounds – Thanatos wields a scythe, for instance. In Brueghel's 'Triumph of Death' (1652) skeletons chop wood, blow horns, ring bells, and attack with various metal implements. And Hell also became associated with a near-mechanical repetition. Dante's depiction of Hell, for instance, "although it contains no machines in the literal sense, is pervaded by characteristics such as endless repetition and standardised operation usually associated with the idea of the mechanical" (Abrash, 1983: 22) – reminding us of Hades: (eg Sisyphus, Tantalus): it was not so much the task, but the hopeless repetition of the task that made it Hell[11]. It is perhaps not surprising, then, that those representing threat in the *Terminator* films – the machines – are often given such metallic and percussive sounds. In fact, in interviews Cameron several times refers to the terminator models as symbols of death[12].

Metronomic percussion would take on a new significance with the coming of the Industrial Revolution, when it became the daily rhythm by which most urban dwellers lived their lives. The hiss of steam, the roar of ovens, the grinding of gears and the great repetitive thumping of the machines previously given to descriptions of Hell were now associated with the repetitive tasks demanded by the division of labour and assembly line production. It is little surprise then that the earliest cinematic depictions of dystopia made blatant references to Hell – in *Metropolis*, for instance, the workers in the factory are eventually marched straight into the mouth of Hell. Hell and the industrial dystopia, to a large extent, then, are visually, metaphorically and sonically analogous. The two have become so associated that recent depictions of Hell have begun to incorporate dystopian elements. The Hell of recent cinema has steel-girder-framed buildings or electrical pylons in blue filter[13]. The cover of the 2002 edition of Dante's *Hell* (*Inferno*) published by Penguin Books even features a photograph of drill bits.

The *Terminator* films' religious references then are clearly found not only in the narrative themes, but also in the sonic aesthetic that accompanies them. In fact, it is not too far a stretch to suggest that the sounds themselves provide sonic clues as to how we are to interpret the underlying metaphors of the films as modern day parables.

Conclusion

I have suggested here that the *Terminator* films use a very particular sonic aesthetic that helps to reinforce the narrative and plot symmetry, tie the films together, and create a specific mood and setting. This aesthetic includes the use of Phrygian and Aeolian elements, low bass sounds, urban signifiers such as machine sounds, cars, motorcycles and trains, and the use of metallic percussion. I have also suggested that this particular sonic aesthetic has become (or at least, is becoming) a convention amongst what I have termed the industrial-dystopia. Similar motifs can be found for instance in *The Planet of the Apes* (2001 version), *The Matrix* or *Tetsuo*. In other words, regimentation and mechanisation have become associated with – and used as a metaphor for – life in industrial and post-industrial urban environments. In particular, they are closely associated with the criticisms often raised in dystopian films such as *Terminator* about the loss of human control at the hands of the great 'machine' of our socio-economic system. As director James Cameron described:

> *Technology also threatens to dehumanize us. In a technical urban society we become machine-like in our responses ... from the unfeeling cop to the impersonal bureaucrat to the unsympathetic doctor. As we suppress our emotions we merge with the machines denying life.* (SE DVD notes [2001])

This sonic convention has used Hell as an archetype and very specific settings in the films lend themselves to the early associations of Hell with the forge and later, industrial production. It could be argued then that the use of this particular aesthetic essentially situates the films in a present-day secular version of Hell, albeit one without the benefit of the judgement implied by *T2*'s subtitle. And while the references may not be consciously recognised as such by the viewer, the subliminal quality of the Hellish atmosphere constructed by Cameron, Fiedel and the sound designers undoubtedly leaves an impression. It could even be suggested that the growing popularity of these films could be due to an increasing identification with this Hell-on-earth, the loss of individual power and control, and an anxiety about the future in the West.

Notes

1. By 'industrial-dystopia', I mean those dark, gritty dystopias set in near-present day which involve blue filter, mechanical motifs and a reference to human-as-machine (eg *Metropolis*, *Robocop*, *The Matrix*). Other types of dystopia would include the 'barbarian' dystopia, where humans must adapt to an absence of higher technology in often equally dark and gritty worlds (eg *Mad Max* or *Planet of the Apes* (1968)), and the 'clinical' dystopia, where

high technology has led to a very sterile police state (eg *Fahrenheit 451* (1966), *Brave New World* (1980), *THX1138* (1971), etc).

2. *T1*'s sound was by Richard Lightstone, music by Brad Fiedel. *T2* was also score by Fiedel, and the sound effects team consisted of Tom Johnson, Gary Rydstrom, Gary Summers and Lee Orloff.

3. The CDS system was quickly phased out in favour of Dolby Digital, which was compatible with analogue tracks in movie theatres, an aspect with which CDS had struggled.

4. In the first film, Fiedel used straight synthesised sounds, whereas in the second, orchestral instruments were sampled on a Fairlight and were, therefore, less obviously electronic.

5. Although Cooke has been contested by some authors, many of his ideas, while perhaps exaggerated, remain indicative of some of the basic trends in the usage of such elements.

6. I use "Phrygian inflection" as Kimmel has, to mean minor seconds used in conjunction with a minor third or minor sixth, but not necessarily both (in Rosar, 2001: 110).

7. See for instance the descriptions on:
    http://www.soundconnection.com/c.htm;
    http://www.mmissary.com/takecourage/theory5x.html,
    http://scottharlan.com/forum/htm,
    http://www.musicalheritage.com/Classical – all accessed October 2001.

    In the civil war saga *Cold Mountain*, novelist Charles Frazier describes it thus:

    He could not have put a name to it, but the tune was in the frightening and awful Phrygian mode, and when the girl's mother heard it she burst into tears and ran from her chair out into the hall.

    (http://wwchurch.uwctl.org/mountain.pdf – accessed October 2001 (See Collins, 2002).

8. See for instance the first portrayal of John Connor in *T2*, or the way Sarah is depicted becoming 'machine-like' in her hospital cell.

9. As a similar viewpoint, Dante also describes Hell as loud and booming: "Such became these foul visages of the demon Cerberus, who so thunders at the souls that they would fain be deaf" (*Inferno*, Canto VI: 32–33).

10. Greek mythology's Tartaros the Pit of c. 800 BCE.

11. This is not to say that repetition does not exist in nature, however the kind of precise and metronomic, unwavering and unchanging pulse does not. And, of course, machines are often imperfect and can err in their repetition, although our ideal of the machine is its perfect repetitiveness.

12. See, for instance, his comments in notes accompanying the Special Edition *Terminator* DVD (2001).

13. For instance, *Hellbound: Hellraiser 2* (1988) or *What Dreams May Come* (1998).

Chapter Ten

INTER-PLANETARY SOUNDCLASH
Music, Technology and Territorialisation in *Mars Attacks!*

PHILIP HAYWARD

T he title of this chapter alludes to the tradition, first developed within reggae, and now more broadly-based, of setting up a contest between (two) DJs/producers and their sound systems whose outcome is measured in terms of audiences' perceptions of the most 'deadly' – ie the most creative and effective/affective – sonic performance. In its original context this practice took forms such as successive live sets by DJs or different producers/artists featuring on opposite sides of vinyl albums (thereby inviting comparison with each other). In other spaces, other places, the soundclash has been more literally enacted. At London's annual Notting Hill Carnival, for instance, sound systems are set up opposite each other, under the Westway flyover, in the same narrow, crowded streets. Here, their pumped-up bass outputs overlap, blurring with each other at a median point, transforming into sheer noise, destabilising normal social spaces and – on many occasions – sonically facilitating and accompanying actual clashes between audiences and the police (whose own sirens have often provided an eerily appropriate dub-style treble intrusion into the unearthly din generated by the sound systems). I cite this example at some length since the soundclash, an aural contest where combatants battle with sound, is literally enacted in *Mars Attacks!*

In this sense, the use of music in film – like the example of the use of music in London's Carnival discussed above – can be understood within the framework of what Murphie refers to as a "popular music event" (1996: 21). Drawing on Deleuze and Guattari's radically original work of film theory,

A Thousand Plateaus (in English translation, 1987), he describes these as phenomena which:

> *do not only derive from certain abstract social formations (such as national states with their attendant State philosophies and State art). Such events also, in a very specific way, mark out and/or erase certain territories for social formations in the first place.* (ibid)

Equally, drawing on another (broader) framework advanced by Deleuze and Guattari themselves, the 'space opera' (to use a 1950s term) of *Mars Attacks!* can be considered as a "veritable machinic opera", wherein the "varying relations into which a color, sound, gesture, movement or position enters in the same species, and in different species, form so many machinic enunciations" (1987: 331). The machinic enunciations Deleuze and Guattari refer to here may be understood as meta-processes involving the various animate species, hard technologies and the social-cultural matrices and discourses that constitute what might be termed 'the diegesis of existence'. While Deleuze and Guattari may not have had extra-terrestrials in mind when they produced this formation, it is singularly appropriate to the representation of (biologically) inter-special conflict and difference in *Mars Attacks!* and the particular role that sound plays in this.

I. Burton/Elfman – oeuvres

For those unfamiliar with the director and his oeuvre, Burton is a former Disney animator whose first feature film was *Pee Wee's Big Adventure* (1985). He followed this up with his highly original comedy-horror feature *Beetlejuice* (1988) before going on to direct the first, dark, stylish and heavily stylised *Batman* (1989); the cult Gothic teen angst drama *Edward Scissorhands* (1990); the animation feature *The Nightmare Before Christmas* (1993) and his eponymous tribute to 1950s B-Movie director Ed Wood (1994). More recently he has directed *Sleepy Hollow* (1999) and the re-make of *Planet of the Apes* (2001). All of these films have featured original and ambitious uses of film music and soundtrack. Burton's background in animation is significant here, since (free from the restraints of aural realism iconic to a [visual] photo-realism), the animated feature film has a rich history of inventive soundtrack work and of colourful musical composition (exemplified by the work of composers such as Carl Stalling).

Like *Beetlejuice* and *The Nightmare Before Christmas*, *Mars Attacks!* features music by the prolific Hollywood composer Danny Elfman. Elfman has described working on the film as "a special treat", which allowed him to revisit and rework a series of seminal 1950s Sci-Fi film scores (quoted in Adams, 1997: np). More specifically, Elfman's score for *Mars Attacks!* takes its cue(s) from Bernard Herrmann's music for *The Day the Earth stood still* (Robert Wise, 1951)[1] (which Elfman has cited as *the* inspirational point for his career as a film composer – Elfman, 1998: 10). As subsequent sections of this chapter will argue, Elfman does not simply imitate his inspiration in

Mars Attacks! but rather reworks his source, producing a contemporary angle, modifying the affective aspect of Herrmann's 1951 score in keeping with the distinctly contemporary tone of Burton's film.

Elfman has described his general technique of reworking classic film scores in terms of a deconstruction[2]; of a 'dropping-back' through layers of film score conventions and histories to re-configure styles derived from key Hollywood composers (quoted in Adams, 1997: np). Following the model set down by composers such as Erich Korngold in the 1930s[3], Elfman's scores often utilise prominent leitmotifs, musically illustrating and enhancing key characters and themes. One of the most obvious of these is their use to introduce (and emphasise/amplify) the narrative presence of the film's hero/es. As Elfman has emphasised, *Mars Attacks!* – as a studiedly *un*-heroic film – resists such a standard approach, since the most prominent 'characters' are the scandalously amoral, anti-heroic Martian hordes. For the Martians' 'signature' sound, Elfman augmented an orchestral march sequence with high-set, choral sounds (used both texturally and rhythmically) and melodic lines played on the theremin. As discussed in Hayward (1997: 31–36), the theremin was one of the earliest musical synthesisers. Its most novel attribute was its contact-free musical interface. The instrument was played by performers moving their hands between two aerials and changing the pitch and volume of a signal. The instrument became a staple device in Hollywood cinema from the 1940s-early 1960s to signify a range of eerie and/or unearthly characters, events or moods. In this regard, Elfman's use of the theremin for the Martians' theme clearly draws on the earlier usage. Indeed Elfman has acknowledged that when writing the score for *Mars Attacks!* he frequently replayed Herrmann's film music[4].

In his attempts to produce a contemporary version of the original theremin and orchestral affect, he re-styled the original 1940s/50s instrumental role and character of the theremin. Intent on producing a contemporary sonic 'high-gloss' for his score, Elfman used the theremin – which he has characterised in terms of its trademark "rough-edged" sound (quoted in Adams, 1997: np) – as a source of melodic lines and samples. The samples enabled him to get the required theremin parts "right in tune" with his orchestral score (ibid) and, in the final version, these were combined with parts originated on the other notable early 20th Century synthesiser, the ondes martenot[5]. As he characterised it, the ondes martenot "could play any melody we wanted it to play really well ... [but] the theremin had more nastiness in the sound" (ibid). Despite Elfman's appreciation of the theremin's "nastiness", the rough edges of the instrument's sound are largely smoothed over in his score, modifying the musical/sonic affect of his sources.

The opening sequence of the film exemplifies this aspect of Elfman's revision of his reference sounds. Unlike the dissonant edge of the theremin as a sonic marker of other-worldliness in the opening sequence of *The Day The Earth Stood Still*;[6] *Mars Attacks!* opens with images of a huge fleet of flying saucers, spread out across space, approaching the Earth. These images are accompanied by a lush, harmonically integrated score where the theremin lines are a smooth melodic response to the choral melodies that precede it.

Immediately established as anthemic, by the juxtaposition of music and image (and the overt reference to previous SF film conventions), the music operates and articulates a classic process identified by Deleuze and Guattari, whereby "one ventures from home on the thread of a tune" (1987: 311). Despite this aspect, and the clear marking of the theremin-featured passages as the Martians' specific anthem; it would not perhaps be 'over-reading' this to assume that the edginess of *The Day the Earth stood still's* opening orchestral and theremin sequence was appropriate to that film's nature as an (unselfconscious) Sci-Fi/thriller produced at a time of very real (Earthly) Cold War. By contrast, the smooth stylishness of *Mars Attacks!* is threat-free, reflecting a geo-political climate where, in the mid-1990s – for the West, at least – nothing of quite the same kind was at stake and no such pronounced unease necessary. In another sense, the opening might be seen to epitomise what Marjorie Perloff has described as a key aspect of contemporary Western culture (in its postmodern phase) – its "cool Futurism" (1990: 195).

II. Whitman

If Elfman's score exemplifies a cool Futurism, inscribed, albeit prominently, within the textual planes of the film score/under-score; the nemesis of both this musical approach and the Martian hordes it signifies, is another, distinctly quirkier 1950s' sound, one significantly 'un-reworked' by the film, and directly appropriated and inserted into the narrative, soundtrack and score. The sound-presence in question – the source of the film's final, climactic clash – is Slim Whitman's 1955 recording of the Broadway show-tune standard *Indian Love Call*. For all Elfman's (previously discussed) characterisation of the odd 'nastiness' of the theremin, the instrument's lines are notably less musically distinctive and/or 'odd' in relation to *Mars Attacks!* orchestral score than the yodelling and steel guitar lines of Whitman's recordings. Indeed, it is the sonic oddness/otherness of Whitman's music and its marked difference from the smooth dissonances of Elfman's score, which produces such a deadly impact on the Martians who encounter them; causing their invasion attempt to be foiled. In this regard, the score's theremin-derived sounds are 'normal', stable and hegemonic; whereas Whitman's recording is aberrant[7].

In both the absence of any other contender, and in terms of the dramatic effect of his intervention, Whitman – or, rather, the sound of his recordings – is the principal heroic presence in *Mars Attacks!* His version of *Indian Love Call* enters the soundtrack and narrative in the final part of the film, when all seems lost, when the Martians are gleefully conquering and trashing the planet. It emerges as a significant voice and presence when a group of Martians burst into an old people's home and begin to terrorise and kill the inhabitants[8]. Finding one elderly woman unaware of their presence, a Martian carefully lines up a ray gun at her head and then pulls off her headphones as a prelude to blasting her away. However his (?) intentions are immediately undermined. As soon as the sound of Whitman's record emerges from the discarded headphones, the Martian's brain starts to boil and then explodes. As the woman and her grandson discover, Whitman's recorded music[9] has the same effect on all Martians[10]. After playing *Indian Love Call* through the streets, the duo finally arrives at a radio station and broadcast his music repeatedly. Transmitted throughout the world, deterritorialising and reterritorialising, the sound of Whitman's music obliterates the Martians and saves the planet.

In the moment of the violation of the woman's private space, the uninvited disruption of her communion with a specific sound and sound text, the film does not simply present us with an invented absurdity, it *resonates* – loops back to various (pre-Christian) cultural practices of sound and sonic association. Most particularly, the sequence invites comparison to those Papua New Guinean societies for whom certain sounds are sacred to particular groups. In these contexts, it is taboo for outsiders to simply hear the sounds of ritual instruments (such as ritual bullroarers[11]), or particular chants. What is notable in *Mars Attacks!* is that Burton does not attempt to provide us with any 'ancient' and/or (conventionally) holy sound to symbolise essential humanity but, rather, uses sounds plucked from the era and cultural context from which he derives his inspiration.

Slim Whitman was born and raised in Florida and joined the US Navy during World War Two. He took up singing and guitar playing while serving on the *USS Chilton* and began to perform semi-professionally in 1948. His highly accomplished, smoothly contoured yodelling and falsetto vocal style, and an idiosyncratic choice of material that avoided classic country music themes, secured him a deal with Imperial Records in 1949. In 1950 he became a member of the popular Louisiana Hayride, touring with a backing band named The Stardusters. During this period he developed a distinct signature sound focused on his voice and its interplay with steel guitarist Hoot Rains. The dual glissandi and frequent high pitched and soaring deliveries of these two 'voices' created an emotive, and sometimes ethereal sound that was at marked odds with mainstream country music. One of Whitman's band's signature elements was steel guitar notes sliding off into the 'infinity' of their upper register[12]. This instrumental effect, (which came to be known as 'shooting arrows'), served as a final ornament to a musical style which had a lot in common with the parallel vogue for theremin music – both styles using smooth glissandi, vibrato and upper register 'soars' for dramatic effect. Thematically, however, Whitman's best-known work differed from the theremin's association with weird and/or otherworldliness and instead had a pious 'pure' quality (drawing on his religious convictions and long-term association with the Southern Church of the Brethren). His songs evinced an (interconnected) preoccupation with natural beauty (such as waterfalls, waves, wind and rainbows), romance, verbal communication and acoustics. The 'accidental' arrangement of *Love Song of the Waterfall* gave Whitman his first US 'Top Ten' hit single in 1952. His follow-up release, a version of the standard *Indian Love Call*, also achieved similar success.

Now largely forgotten by contemporary performers, *Indian Love Call* was written by Oscar Hammerstein (music) and Rudolph Friml (lyrics) for the Broadway operetta *Rose Marie* (which premiered in 1924). The song drew upon well-established musical clichés for the representation of 'Indians' (ie indigenous North Americans) on stage and screen[13], and – "oft-parodied, almost self-parodying" (Pisani, 1998: 248) – its popularity was influential in re-inscribing these in 20th Century popular culture. These clichés – combined with a less specific exoticism – are exemplified in the song's opening (the sequence featured in *Mars Attacks!*) where, as Graeme Smith has characterised it: "the opening, descending, melody – reminiscent of the composition *Bali Hi*[14] – contrasts to the "Red Indian" pentatonic-style answer tune" (p.c. September 1997).

In its debut run, Mary Ellis and Dennis King's duet on the song rapidly established itself as a 'showstopper'. The play's narrative is set in Quebec and concerns a famous opera singer, performing in Montreal, who travels to a remote forest area to meet and assist her brother who is in hiding after killing a 'mountie' (ie mounted police officer). There she meets another mountie who – somewhat awkwardly – falls in love with her, despite his knowledge of her brother's crime. The song initially enters in the narrative as an intrusion into the Euro-Canadian milieu, as a melody, sung off-screen, echoing round the landscape, by indigenous Canadians (the 'Indians' of its title). It is subsequently taken up by the heroine, and the mountie who rapidly falls in love with her, who perform it within the narrative as a love duet[15]. This complex transaction and trans-identification of a musical-acoustic index of 'otherness' is, in Deleuze and Guattari's terms, 'inter-spe-cial'; not so much a sound *clash* here (in the narrative/diegesis) as a smooth, machinic, territorialistic acquisition.

The version recorded by Whitman in 1955 differed markedly from previous versions of the song by virtue of Whitman's particular sound and sonic spatiality, which made it more akin to his own recordings rather than previous covers of the tune. As the work of Peter Doyle has emphasised[16], North American popular music between the 1930s and 1950s, and particularly that of the cowboy/hillbilly genre(s), produced a number of explorations of complex, (pseudo-)spatial soundscapes – monaural recordings where the use of echo and reverb, together with particular instrumentations and melodic ornamentation and emphasis, produced 'impossible' spatialities – virtual acoustic spaces, impossibly 'deep', echoic and reverberative. The two Whitman tracks featured in *Mars Attacks!* exemplify the sound qualities Doyle has identified whereby:

> *the voice, often used in the falsetto range (setting it apart from 'normal' vocal performances) is always being shadowed by ever more abstracted or rarefied echoes. The steel guitar, prominently used in the arrangements, is often both echoed and reverbed to produce multiple distortions, and*

181

> *often feature heavy use of harmonics (which stands in a roughly similar*
> *relation to the usual sound of the steel guitar as the falsetto does to the*
> *standard voice).* (p.c September 1997)

Within the (actual and virtual) spaces of the recording studio, a technology – of software, hardware and bodies – dedicated to intricate fabrications of sound, continually re- and de-territorialising in search of ideal acoustic expressions; the complex cultural inscriptions of the original composition are further refracted and reconstituted. The music creates its own milieus; its own eddies and becomings.

The combination of what might be considered the technological exotica of the complex echoic and reverberative spaces, the Orientalist features of the original composition and Whitman's melodramatic delivery, produce a highly idiosyncratic recorded sound. *Indian Love Call* sounds all the more unusual in the early 2000s since Whitman's oeuvre has remained undiscovered (and thereby unrevived) by popular cultural archaeologists and has no contemporary counterparts. Fixed in a remote moment, recorded in 1952, immediately prior to the moment of rock and roll, and the very different affective spatialities of Elvis Presley's early recordings at Sun Studios[17], the sound remains the province of original aficionados, such as the grandmother featured in the film. Located there, it resides in a similar cultural era to the original alien encounter/invasion Science Fiction movies that Burton spoofs in *Mars Attacks!* (such as *The Day the Earth stood still* [1951] and *It came from Outer Space* [1953])[18] and the period during which the theremin stood as a prominent cinematic marker of aural otherness and weirdness[19]. Indeed, the use of Whitman's music and the theremin, which Burton territorialises in the film, offers a tantalising point of comparison to aspects of that previous era. While Whitman's work has often been considered as relatively isolated within the generic characteristics of (late) hillbilly music (albeit mediated by its studio experimentation); his falsetto vocal sound and the wavering tones of the steel guitar bear more than a passing relation to the (by then) well-established tradition of the theremin melody as screen score motif. Certainly, Whitman's recordings of tracks recently popularised in a hit Hollywood musical suggest a knowledge of film and film music on the part of either the artist or his producer. But, interesting as the line of conjecture might be[20], it is other factors that determine the use of the track in the film.

III. Machinic enunciations and weird auralities

Reviews for *Mars Attacks!* at the time of its original cinema release, were mixed (at best). Reviewers were, almost without exception, left somewhat puzzled by its tone. Unlike *Beetlejuice*, it was a comedy with few obvious jokes (successful or otherwise). Unlike *Edward Scissorhands*, it offered no sympathetic leading characters. Unlike *Batman*, it lacked dramatic impact or bite. In this sense it was essentially seen as self-indulgent, as a director's 'folly'. Burton's film is concerned with, and is a prime example of, 'trash-culture' – contemporary, self-conscious, glossy, high-budget trash maybe, but trash all the same. It reinvigorates the B-movie by producing a homage that sparkles with allusion and special effects of such a different order of accomplishment to their inspiration that they inhabit a different plane of affectivity. The Martians exemplify this; the inhumanity of their appearance – obviously not performed by men in suits or paper-mache mannequins – marks them out as different creations from the close-to-zero budget improvisations of films such as Burton's favourite Ed Wood production *Plan 9 from Outer Space* (1956). With their gleeful, vicious amorality the Martians are more than a match for all that the Earth's military can muster.

As previously discussed, the Martians come undone as the result of a soundclash of epic proportions. Whitman's "deeply weird, impossible spatiality" – and, particularly, his keening falsetto and steel guitar counterpoint – slices through the smoothly modulated theremin that (extra-diegetically) represents the Martians' threat and personae. They are 'outweirded' by a sonic spatiality premised on a cultural inner-space – the virtual spatiality of the mix – that is more powerful in its condensation of odd, intense, human and – arguably, *above all* – specifically *white North American* subjectivity than the malice of Outer Space embodied by the Martian hordes. Just as decisively as in its (unreconstructed) contemporary retro-Sci-Fi counterpart *Independence Day* (1996), it is the USAnians who save the human race.

Whitman's track, and, by implication, the USA hillbilly genre from which it derives, are also identified within the film as the apogee of low, *declassé* taste – as 'white trash' culture within the film's high-gloss trash aesthetic. This form is shown to be as alien to Las Vegas glitz as it is to the prim, family-orientated culture of Washington and Middle America (represented by the President and his family in the film)[21]. Whatever its studio context, Whitman's sonic assault is predicated on unfettered emotive expression, the free-fall and soar of vocal and slide guitar glissandi, echoed and refracted in the virtual space of the record's mix. In this manner, the recording resonates with the emotive cries of a marginal cultural tradition unpasteurised by postmodernity. In terms of dominant tastes (even in the eclectically pluralist early 2000s), the track and the tradition are so ultra-'trashy' that they represent the 'wickedest', 'deadliest' sounds on offer. The trebles hit places where the bass doesn't even register.

In terms of the formation offered by Deleuze and Guattari (1987), Whitman's music, for the Martians at least, represents "the cutting edge of deterritori-alisation" (ibid: 348). Indeed, in a phrase that could almost have been scribbled by a Martian invader into her/his spaceship's log as the full realisation of her/his imminent annihilation hit home, the music

> *invades us, impels us, drags us, transpierces us. It takes leave of the earth,*
> *as much in order to drop us into a black hole as to open us to a cosmos.*
> *It makes us want to die.* (ibid)

Set against Elfman's highly polished score, where even the (treated, combined) theremin and carefully crafted musical dissonance has an exemplarily contemporary sheen, the rawness and emotion of Whitman's track provides a musical and cultural noise that not only kills Martians within its fiction but also deterritorialises more broadly, unravelling the generic context into which it intrudes.

But despite the centrality of Whitman's recording to the narrative, it is another track, Tom Jones' evergreen MOR[22] standard *It's Not Unusual* (originally recorded in 1965), which precedes the narrative's transformation into a duel of musical/metaphoric oppositions. In a series of sequences depicting Martian attacks, the film shows us Jones on-stage in Las Vegas, providing a spirited rendition of the Vegas 'anthem'. As the song's title and lyrical refrain has it – and constantly re-states – "It's not unusual". Within the film, the song and its sounds represent normality. On a deeper level, that of musical-historical association, it also represents another stability, that of the pop music mainstream. Bursting on-stage, the Martians stop the number in mid-flow and shoot-up the club, unmoved and unaffected by Jones and his band's performance.

Established and inscribed within the film as an exemplar of musical normality, the song is positioned in polar opposition to Whitman's tune, which enters minutes later. What Burton's film offers here is a set of refrains and territorialisations. The Martians' refrain(s), territorialisations and deterritorialisms are signified in the (extra-diegetical) musical score and, specifically, in the theremin themes. These work off an identifiable tradition, laden with the affect and significance of *The Day the Earth stood still* (etc) and are, in a sense, given and unproblematic – clearly understood as aurally emblematic of alienness. Jones's track, hoary, respectable (and even rehabilitated as acceptable kitsch through its 1987 reworking and re-release[23]), represents the territory invaded by the Martians. The song's lyrical hook, even when sung with Jones's deep-throated passion, simply emphasises terrestrial normality. Jones, in Murphie's terms, represents the perception of the pop star as ideal "despotic" subject, occupying a "smooth space" (1996: 19), transcending the time/spaces of 1965/1995 consistent and virtually unchanged. But his despotism is only derived from, and inscribed within, "certain abstract social formations" (ibid).

With the arrival of the (*necessarily* extra-terrestrial) Martians, the certainties destabilise. Previously inscribed (and maintained) territories are contested anew. In terms of the film's sequential flow, the soundclash between Whitman and the Martian invaders skews away from the (up-to-then) linear narrative, moving into a battle of refrains which struggle to impose *their* territories, *their* orders of affectivity, upon the film's plot (and the USA, as represented). To mix genre references, Whitman's music bursts into the narrative like an aural cavalry emerging over the (narrative) horizon. It also recalls a motif from the fantasy/horror genre, that of a hidden, primeval force unleashed from its confines to combat evil and save the day. In this sense, Whitman's recording and its trademark sonic spatialities are *mythic*, as deeply historical – within the surface of 1990s late-period postmodernism

– as they are deeply weird. In this way, Burton's flatly hysterical film twists into the mythic and lifts its narrative into a more complex self-reflexive text, cued by and premised on a soundclash framed within histories and discourses of sound technologies, their musical application and their affectivity. The difficulty with this, of course, is that this aspect is 'unreadable' on the purely narrative level, invisible in terms of mis-en-scene, but clearly apparent in its audio track.

Burton and Elfman's collaboration on *Mars Attacks!* produces a film whose impact and complexity *have to be heard*. Its critical under-recognition reflects the manner in which – even in the age of spectral-mixing, THX sound and film composer-as-celebrity – soundtracks are still under-engaged with. Being Hollywood, rather than the avant-garde, the film's sonic accomplishment has a particular enablement, permitted and facilitated by the film's nature as a big-budget, idiosyncratic 'spoof', premised on Burton's prior bankabil-ity. In this, the film offers a notable example of innovative contemporary postmodernism and emphasises one of Attali's premises, that sound and noise have a constant ability to destabilise and de- and re-territorialise. In this manner, in terms of Deleuze and Guattari, the film's conclusion – apparently facile in terms of the *sturm und drang* of the conflict which dominates the film – can be read as a clear aural resolution, a gleeful attempt to (globally) reterritorialise. Having performed its function, with all the Martians apparently dead, Whitman's music disappears from the film's diegesis and soundtrack. The final act of reconsecration of space, normality and stable musical aurality is provided by Jones, who off-stage, in the natural landscape, launches into *It's Not Unusual* anew, accompanied – in classic musical film fashion – by off-screen accompaniment. The star-as-des-pot – and with him, all other normality – is re-instated. The film thereby performs a classic narrative closure that, as in many Hollywood genres, only just manages to cram its genies back into their box[24]. Its sounds echo, re-sound and, in the context of 1990s multi-product packaging, re-group and resignify on the soundtrack CD[25]. Here, sheered from their (visual, dialogic) narrative, their soundclashes can be eternally replayed; eternally evocative of the "forces of chaos" (Deleuze and Guattari, 1987: 312) (terres-trial or otherwise) which provided the big dimension to the human condition; precisely that quality that Jones's reassuring refrain tries to banish to the dark edge of existence so playfully enacted and defeated in Burton's film.

Thanks to Peter Doyle, Jon Fitzgerald, David Horn and Graeme Smith for their assistance with research for this chapter. Also thanks to Andrew Murphie for his perceptive comments on an earlier draft and to Rebecca Coyle for various assistances.

Notes

1. Discussed in Hayward (1997: 38–39).
2. Understood in the conventional rather than Derridean sense.
3. For a discussion of Korngold and the classic Hollywood film score in the 1930s see Kathryn Kalinak (1992: 66–110).

4. Elfman has stated that:

    [with] *the theremin thing... I went and listened to* The Day the Earth stood still *to make sure. Sometimes I do something and I need to hear the source and go, "God, have I just done that?" And it's really tricky, especially when you are dealing with the theremin. You start doing an octave* [slide] *on a theremin and it's like, "Whoa! I better put on* The Lost Weekend *and then go quick* [and check]. (quoted in Adams, 1997: np)

5. Although I have been unable to verify the connection, Elfman appears to have followed the lead of composer Howard Shore in this regard since Shore employed the unusual combination of Lydia Kavina on theremin and Cynthia Miller on ondes martenot in his soundtrack to Tim Burton's earlier film *Ed Wood* (1994).

6. Discussed in Hayward (1997: 38–39).

7. This is a curious twist, in many ways, since *Indian Love Call*''s opening yodelling sequence is more akin to classic uses of the theremin in its melodic leaps and oddness than Elfman's smooth 1990s' substitution.

8. Whitman's music is fleeting introduced in an earlier scene when the old woman returns to her room in the retirement home and treats her Whitman LP as a cherished comfort and secure cultural reference point.

9. Along with *Indian Love Call*, the film also features a brief sequence of Whitman's yodelling extracted from his recording of the Jimmy Wakeley and Lee White composition *My Lassoo to the Sky* (1957).

10. As Peter Doyle has pointed out, there is a 'metaphysical' precedent for this in the 1980s radio series 'Riders Radio Theatre', produced by the group Riders in the Sky, as a homage to 1930s cowboy radio shows. Ranger Doug used to defeat the baddies with a 'yodelling secret weapon' (p.c. September 1997).

11. An instrumental device which, when whirled round the head on a string, produces a deep roaring noise.

12. This apparently occurred by accident. According to one account, during live performance of a song entitled *Love Song of the Waterfall* (written by Bob Nolan, leader of the Sons of the Pioneers):

    Hoot overshot a note sending it soaring skyward. Slim asked Hoot after the show, "what happened out there"? Hoot said, "I missed it". Slim liked what he heard and said, with a wry grin, "Well, miss it again!" They soon worked this unusual new sound into his songs. (http://personal.riverusers.com/~flash/swliner.html)

13. See Michael Pisani (1998) for detailed discussion of these.

14. From the Rogers and Hammerstein musical *South Pacific*.

15. The composition was recorded (at least) twice in 1925, with versions by the Paul Whiteman Orchestra and Leo Reisman. The tune also experienced a major revival in popularity following its appearance in the 1935 MGM musical version of *Rose Marie*, performed by the highly popular film musical performers Jeanette MacDonald and Nelson Eddy. This version was released as a successful single in 1936. Further versions followed, by Artie Shaw and his Orchestra (1938) and by Ann Blyth and Fernando Lamas in the 1954 Hollywood remake.

16. See Peter Doyle's unpublished PhD thesis, 'Spatiality in Pre-Stereo Popular Music Recording' (2001) Macquarie University, Sydney.

17. Such as the immense, dramatic spatialities of *Heartbreak Hotel* (1956) which marked both something of a zenith of such sound explorations and the end of an era, with rock music overwhelming and eschewing such approaches from then on.

18. As a tribute to the latter, sound designer Randy Thoms sampled the death ray sounds from Stevens' film and used them for the Martians' rays in *Mars Attacks!* While I can find no evidence that the process inspired the use of Whitman's music in Burton's film, it is

somewhat of an apposite coincidence that Harry Lindgren and Gene Garvin produced their ray sounds by recording notes played on electric guitars and running them backwards and distorting them. Steel guitarist Noel Boggs has been attributed as the originator of the source notes.

19. See Philip Hayward (1997: 28–53) for further discussion.

20. Research and documentation on this area is scant and, in this sense, unproven.

21. The film pointedly features Jones exclaiming 'What the hell's that?' when he hears it broadcast over the radio for the first time.

22. MOR – Middle of the Road – a term which refers to mainstream music tastes.

23. Which marked Jones's return to the UK/USA Singles charts after a ten-year absence.

24. It has often been observed, for instance, with regard to film noirs, that it is not the femme fatale's eventual submission to patriarchy/marriage, or alternatively her demise, which we remember. Rather it is her power and glamour within the (temporarily) 'suspended solution' of the narrative.

25. *Music From the Motion Picture Soundtrack 'Mars Attacks!' – Music by Danny Elfman*, Atlantic Records, 1996.

Chapter Eleven

MAPPING *THE MATRIX*: Virtual Spatiality and the realm of the Perceptual

MARK EVANS

N otions of spatiality have been present in film soundtrack analysis since the 1980s, with more systematic analysis coming in the 1990s. Despite this, rapid advances in the technology of film spatiality, specifically the development and widespread adoption of 5.1 discrete channel surroundsound, have not been matched by academic enquiry in the area. The deficiency has been both theoretical and pragmatic. This chapter seeks to redress this paucity by critically examining sonic spatiality within *The Matrix* (1999) and applying the analysis to new, broader theoretical frameworks (thereby expanding notions of sonic spatiality in film soundtrack studies). However, before proceeding with this enterprise it is necessary to refer to the role of music in *The Matrix* and its relation to the main focus of the chapter. As many of the contributions to this anthology have demonstrated, music is a key conveyor of impressions in SF films (as in cinema in general). Don Davis's score for *The Matrix* is no exception. The film's score uses a blend of electronic and orchestral elements to produce textural and atonal passages appropriate to the technological settings and events that unfold. The score primarily provides a complement to the narrative that *overarches* the discrete sound environments that are the focus of my exposition. Discussions of musical passages are therefore integrated within analyses of the film's separate audio realms. (For further discussion of Davis's score see UGO, 2002.)

Theorising the Spatial

Film sound spatiality has often been analysed according to the three 'spaces' proposed by Doane (1980: 166) that are involved in cinematic construction. Firstly, there is the space of the diegesis – a virtual space constructed by the film, with no physical limits. The opening of *Contact* (1997) illustrates this both visually and sonically as the camera is seemingly propelled away from the Earth into the furthest regions of outer space. Simultaneously the soundtrack presents an audio-collage that, in part, traces a history of recorded sound. It moves from current stereophonic surround sound to basic stereo, to mono music broadcasts, to simple talkback, finally arriving at crackly pronouncements of war. After (though historically and chronologically before) this, the film plunges into silence. The diegesis, represented by the 'place' of the camera, has reached the furthest sound waves emitted from the Earth and passed through them. Humankind has had no bearing on this place, and although the diegetic space of the film to this point has been expansive (both historically and physically), it now becomes infinite.

The second cinematic space is the visible space of the screen. This is a measurable, fixed space. The visual limitations of this space are obvious, yet these can be exploited for various effects. For example, the opening of *Man In The Moon* (1999) sees Kaufmann (Jim Carey) appearing randomly around the edges of the frame, in a sense peering back through the screen space to see if the audience is still there. Delineation of screen space, and movement within it, is assisted in the surroundsound environment by the use of the left, centre and right speakers.

The final space identified by Doane (ibid) in the cinematic situation is the acoustical space of the cinema. Here sound is not exactly framed, but rather envelops the spectator/listener. Indeed, as Stilwell has characterised, Doane uses a "metaphor of the womb in describing film sound, a 'sonorous envelop' surrounding the spectator" (2001: 171). If this was the case two decades ago, then the implementation of 5.1 channel surroundsound has only advanced the distinctness and comfort of the 'womb'. Not only is the spectator enveloped by the sound, they are positioned within the soundtrack, thereby taking a more biased or privileged position within the diegesis. There is now an auditory point-of-view that is as powerful as camera positioning. Examples of this positioning abound in contemporary film, from the simple identificatory position along the pianist-protagonist of *Shine* (1996) as he has his breakdown on stage, to the complicated, liminal audience positions induced in *Fight Club* (1999) to reflect Jack's mental disorder.

Soundtrack has become increasingly important in construction of the three cinema spaces outlined by Doane. Developments in sound technology have provided greater definition to these spaces and allowed filmmakers greater licence in their visual projections of the diegetic world and the spaces encompassed by it. This chapter will go on to argue however, that these technological and professional developments in soundtrack construction have also created new spaces within cinematic experiences[1]. These new spaces require new understandings from the audience in regards to spatial readings of texts and they also warrant greater deconstruction from those areas of the academy devoted to sonic relationships within film. For all their innovation, these spaces are still reliant on the signifying practice of film. As Doane has noted:

> Nothing unites the three spaces [outlined above] but the signifying
> practice of the film itself together with the institutionalization of the
> theater as a type of meta-space which binds together the three spaces, as
> the place where a unified cinematic discourse unfolds. (1980: 167)

The notion of a place where these conceptual and physical spaces meet is integral to the discussion that follows. However, Stilwell usefully deconstructs this place in terms of object/subject positioning:

> While vision creates a 'there', locating an object in space separate from
> (though obviously in relation to) one's own subject position, sound creates
> a 'here', or rather a 'there' + 'here': two points in space, the object and
> the subject, both separated and connected by the vibrating medium which
> transmits the sound. We create a geography of sound with our subject
> position always at the centre; to make an analogy to the visual, it is our
> 'point of audition'. (2001: 173–174)

While it is somewhat contentious that our subject position is "always at the centre", the formation of a geography of sound provides a paradigm by which to map the new sonic landscape. Part of mapping this terrain involves not only acknowledging the physical landmarks – represented by the more quantifiable screen and cinema spaces – but also considering the imaginary landscapes. That is, those spaces – diegetic and virtual – that are experienced within the 'place' of cinema, yet exist in less tangible, identifiable form.

Perceptual Geography

In acknowledging the existence of a less tangible, more conceptual space within film soundscapes, Stilwell proposes that it extends further than the individual elements of the soundtrack, even beyond the theoretical constructions used to describe them (eg the diegetic) (ibid: 185fn12). She argues that such a space is alluded to by some of the terminology employed to analyse film sound: *voice*over, *under*score, *back*ground etc (ibid). Thus, in addition to Doane's three established spaces, this chapter follows Stilwell's proposal, nominating 'perceptual geography' as a fourth spatial area. This fourth space is a perceptual reality, formed from our necessity to 'hold' all the elements of the film 'together'. It is conceptual in that it is a purely mental space, constructed from the various stimuli of the film, but particularly from the sonic elements. However, it is perceptual in that it is the moment of insight, the place of understanding, the perception of how the filmic world intersects with the real world. Thus it would appear that such a 'perceptual geography' is a key element in the Science Fiction film, since the SF cinema requires viewers to immerse themselves within a foreign realm, a world made believable through the constructions of film yet removed from the physical realm of the cinema auditorium. Perceptual geography becomes the space where the actual world of the cinema meets the abstract world of the film. This space is further complicated, and necessitated, in *The Matrix* (1999).

In order to illustrate perceptual geography in *The Matrix*, it is necessary to extend Doane's model of diegetic space somewhat (the argument being that the film actually constructs several separate realms in which the diegesis of the film unfolds.) These realms are discrete, and are skilfully crafted in order to destabilise the viewers' actual spatial experience. Thus the place of perceptual geography becomes crucial in tying together the worlds of the film, and bringing them into the physical auditorium space of the theatre. In order to illustrate the different diegetic worlds created, a brief narrative synopsis is necessary.

The Matrix Revealed

Set in the future (sometime after 2199), *The Matrix* revolves around the classic Sci-Fi theme of human verus machine. In an age when machines rule the Earth and humans are merely 'farmed' for the electricity they produce, a small band of rebels (who have been freed from machinic slavery), search for a way to defeat the matrix. The matrix itself is a computer program that simulates the everyday life experiences of humans, that is, it makes those being farmed believe they are actually living real lives in a world (unsurprisingly) similar to contemporary society. The rebels, prophetically promised a saviour, scour the coding of the matrix for the one who can deliver them from slavery. Ironically, they have the power to free (select) individuals from the sweeping robotic farms, in the hope that eventually that individual might free them all. The classic Biblical imagery is enhanced when Neo (Keanu Reeves), is freed and brought aboard the rebel ship. There he is trained and educated in the workings of the matrix, and the 'miraculous' powers he possesses within it. His mentor and rebel leader, Morpheus, firmly believes he is the one to deliver humanity from the evil of intelligent technology.

Mapping the Diegetic Worlds

Given the tension throughout *The Matrix* between real-life and simulation, between human and machinic, the following diagram attempts to graph the different diegetic realms created, and indicate their relationship to the other cinematic spaces articulated by Doane.

The first realm created is the matrix. As noted above, it is an electronic city, comprised entirely of digital data. It is a representation of contemporary society as we know it[2]. This realm is controlled and regulated by machines. Being a computer program it is feasible that elements of this realm, although having the appearance of permanence (eg buildings), can in fact be altered instantaneously. Freed humans can insert themselves back into the matrix, but they remain subject to the rules of the matrix as set by the ruling machines. Communication in this world is digital, with movements and variations within the matrix reflected in the coding of the program. The second realm is the simulated matrix, called 'The Construct' – a computer program designed by humans to replicate the 'real' matrix (itself a simulation of reality). This realm is also entirely digital yet communication here is

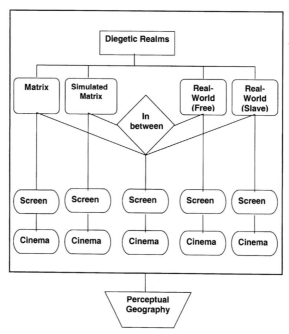

Figure 1. Cinematic Spatiality in The Matrix.

largely oral. This realm is where Morpheus trains Neo for 'missions' into the matrix. The realm designated as real–world (free) is the third diegetic realm created in the film. This is the realm of the Nebuchadnezzar – the spaceship, or perhaps more aptly the (space)ship, where the rebels live. Despite the technology present – and relied on – for survival, this realm remains organic and oral. The fourth realm is the real-world (slave). This is a farm for humans where bodies are maintained in pods and harvested by machines. This, we are told, is the actual state of the world after the war between humans and machines. It is in this realm that humans are fed – digitally – the signals that make them believe they are living in the matrix. The final realm established has been designated as 'in-between', a virtual world that largely exists to connect the other realms. Most clearly heard in the opening scene of the movie as code blips over the screen, it is a world operated by freed humans, yet largely controlled by the machines. The entry and exit points to this world are telephonic.

All of these realms are inter-related with various networks existing between them, yet it is the specific differences between them that allow tension and drama to be created throughout the film. As indicated in Figure 1, part of this tension is the reconciliation of these realms within a perceptual geography. The audience is called upon to not only establish an understanding of these realms and how they are represented, but also to relate them to their current subject positioning. These realms must necessarily interact with perceptions of reality held by the audience member, thereby constructing a new, virtual space that combines their cinematic experience of these realms with their own subjective perceptions of their world. The soundtrack becomes pivotal in constructing cues and motifs that define the separate realms of the film and enhance the space of perceptual geography.

Philip Brophy has argued that film sound:

> *generates sonic effects which* symbolise and simulate the territorial sense of space *that governs both the fictional [diegetic world] and the actual [listening/viewing experience]* ... [The film] *Colors... deals with territorial sound and demarcated space, where the presence and flow of sound shapes all forms of cinematic space (symbolic, actual, dramatic, cultural, musical) throughout the film.* (1991: 100 – emphasis added)

Part, then, of mapping *The Matrix* involves extracting those sounds and sonic effects that the sound designer (Dane Davis) uses to govern the realms of the film. As with *Colors* (1988), the film deals in part with demarcated spaces, with spaces constricted both physically and virtually. Augmenting the sonic binaries established by Brophy, we can see the interplay of diegetic worlds, and their impact on the perceptual geography of the viewer/audience.

Realm	Matrix	Simulated Matrix	Real-World (Free)	Real-World (Slave)
Control	Computer	Human	Human	Computer
Domain	City (inside/ outside)	Virtual	(Space)Ship	Human farm
Ambience	Digital (blips) Heightened	Heightened	Organic throb, subdued	Mechanical, electric
Contact	Digital signal	Oral	Oral	Digital signal
Mobility	Walking/cars	Physical	'Space' travel	Denied
Voice	Measured, deep, mechanical	Restrained, 'normal'	Frantic, expressive, emotive	None
Depth	Large (reverb, distance)	Changeable	Enclosed, dry	Vast (confined)
Music	Production, Orchestral	Production, Orchestral	Orchestral	Orchestral
Temporality	Controllable	Controllable	Fixed, constant	Fixed, constant

Figure 2. Sonic Components Of Diegetic Worlds.

Figure 2 highlights the similarities and differences in sound construction between the various realms of *The Matrix*. As would be expected there is significant crossover between the two matrix realms as well as the two realms devoted to the real world. Yet there are differences as well, largely attributable to who controls the realm. In those controlled by computers the soundscape is noticeably digital, full of electronic effects sounds and atmospheres. Foley sounds, particularly those created through mechanical processes, are heightened, while vocal intonation, where present, is measured, subdued and somewhat digitised. Curiously, the realms controlled by computers contain the largest sonic depth fields. Considerable reverb has been added to the sound mix to convey the vastness of these realms, in both cases producing an ironically expansive sound canvas, given that both realms represent the enslavement of humankind. Conversely, the realms controlled by humans are more organic, enclosed, and utilise oral communication with all its expressive and emotive connotations.

(Dis)locating the body and the voice

Mary Ann Doane has noted that:

> Just as the voice must be anchored by a given body, the body must be anchored in a given space. The fantasmatic visual space which the film constructs is supplemented by techniques designed to spatialize the voice, to localize it, give it depth, and thus lend to the characters the consistency of the real. (1980: 164)

This notion is reversed in *The Matrix*, for the voice is freed from the body. Indeed, it is the body, literally anchored into the portal chair, which is immovable and stripped of vocality. In light of this, spatialisation and localisation of the voice are manipulated to lend the characters the consistency of the 'unreal'. Clearly reified from their actual bodies, the voices mutate into representation. Vocality within the matrix is measured, deep, purposeful and somewhat mechanical. Classically the 'voice without body' in the cinema is the artificial voice of the computer (eg Hal in Kubrick's *2001* [1968]), yet human voices take on the 'bodyless' role when they enter the matrix realm. When apostate Cyphus turns on his colleagues, unplugging their bodies, we see the death of the voice. What adds power to this scene is the healthy voice, seemingly 'unfairly' terminated without right of reply. As Switch pleads, "No, not like this – not like this". Doane points out however, that:

> The voice-off is always submitted to the destiny of the body because it belongs to a character who is confined to the space of the diegesis, if not to the visible space of the screen … Its efficacity rests on the knowledge that the character can easily be made visible by a slight reframing which would reunite the voice and its source. (ibid: 168)

Such reframings are impossible for characters entering the matrix. They are entirely disengaged from their bodies. Yet some simulation, or simulacrum, of the human body is frequently required in Science Fiction films. Indeed, vocal representation, albeit artificial, is uncommon without some degree of anthropomorphism[3]. Doane noted back in 1980 that it was uncommon for computers to be given both mobility and a simulacrum of the human form (175fn2). This is no longer the case, with a long list of Sci-Fi films (the first two *Terminators* [1984; 1991] amongst them) predating *The Matrix*.

Notably, it is the voice of Agent Smith that posits him most clearly as a virtual construct. His throaty, legato speech, with non-organic accent, signifies sonically his displacement from human reality. More than that, it highlights his power, given that he is often involved in prophetic announcements based on signals from elsewhere in the matrix. Yet Agent Smith's vocality also becomes his prison. Able to move through the matrix effortlessly, Agent Smith is confined by his inability to express himself, seen most clearly in the interrogation of Morpheus where he 'disconnects' himself from the matrix in order to 'connect' himself with Morpheus. His desire for a degree of humanness (particularly vocal expression) is played against Neo's quest for greater digitisation at the same point in the movie. Interestingly, Neo's dialogical impact decreases rapidly from the beginnings of Morpheus's rescue through to the end of the film, when he himself 'becomes' digital.

For the audience holding these spatial disconnections together, release does not come until the concluding scene of the film. Initially the disorientation continues with a voice-off from Neo over images of matrix coding and another trace program. Finally we see Neo, talking to the computers directly via telephone. Although clearly 'within' the matrix at this point, Neo remains curiously outside it – through his direct and untroubled interaction with the computers. The dislocation is finally over with the voice and body finally reunited, the "voice ... frequently returned to the body as a form of narrative closure" (Doane, 1980: 168).

"Did you hear that?" – Establishing an In-Between

The film opens with green computer code falling down the screen. Non-diegetic orchestral sound swells as 'THE MATRIX' is spelt out, the appearance of each letter accompanied by a fuzzy electronic splash. The letters then shoot offscreen with appropriate left and right spectral mixing. The scene cuts to a lone cursor flashing in the top left of the screen. The assumed beep of the cursor is split to the background left and right, creating plenty of space for the dominant telephone ringing in the centre channel. The answering of the phone begins a totally off-screen conversation between Trinity and Cyphus. Although speaking of the "one" and developing the character of Morpheus, the voice-off contributes more than narrative information. This contribution lies more in the nature of the voice-off[4], a tool which:

> deepens the diegesis, gives it an extent which exceeds that of the image, and thus supports the claim that there is a space in the fictional world which the camera does not register. ... The voice-off is a sound which is first and foremost in the service of the film's construction of space and only indirectly in the service of the image. (Doane, 1980: 167)

Thus it is that spatiality is fabricated in *The Matrix*. Once again various letters

195

and characters start scrolling with tinkling electronic sounds providing a sense of movement. It is here that the rear speakers come in, building the sound, and the space of this in-between world flows out to encapsulate the audience. "Did you hear that?" Trinity asks Cyphus, effectively alerting the audience to the changing sonic scenario. We have become a participant in the in-between world, no longer removed from the action, no longer an observer but a listener. Visually, a phone number trace program begins to lock in numbers from the scrolling characters. The numbers morph into blazing green bars that fuzz and 'live' electronically, breathing electricity through the sound mix. From a distant hollow they move forward on the screen, ultimately sliding off-screen to the left and right. The sound of the bars shoots past the audience, down to the rear speakers where they dissipate into silence. Displaced from our in-between world, we, the audience, have entered the realm of the matrix.

Having been drawn into the matrix sonically, it is not surprising that the emphasis on the audible continues to guide the viewer/listener. Of immediate prominence are the heightened sounds (especially Foley elements of the soundtrack) in the matrix realm. Outside scenes involve police radios mixed to the right rear (background). This, combined with reverb of the soundscape, creates a large spatial area, embodied by the deserted city street. In one sense this is a real soundscape, yet in another it is 'super-real' due to the depth, volume and clarity of sounds present.

During the first fight scene (which prepares and accustomises the audience for those to follow) the orchestral music is mixed to the rear, with many of the action sounds coming from the centre. The body movements of Trinity (when performing jujitsu) start in the rear speakers and are propelled to the forward speakers, creating a spatial 'whoosh' that adds power (and a degree of unpredictability) to the scene.

The soundtrack has been slowed down in the floating kick scene, which utilised new 'bullet-time' technology in order to match the vision. Both sound and visual are malleable. The sound envelope for the kick contains a strong attack that quickly trails off during the mid-air suspension of Trinity, only to build sharply for the final release, which coincides with the moment of impact.

Bullets shot can be heard from the front speakers, yet ricochets can be heard in the rear (particularly left). Thus the viewer here is positioned with Trinity, the bullets are bouncing off walls behind her and, once she secures the gun shell casings, can be heard dropping in the rear speakers as she (and the audience) move forward past them.

During the chase that ensues, Trinity and the Agent jump between two buildings, accompanied by a deep sound – resembling the slow, leaden sound of the bullet-time sequence. When police officers make same jump they receive a light, trebly, quiet sound, clearly positing them as lesser participants in the matrix realm. As the rooftop chase continues, footsteps can be heard in the front speakers with a frantic, stabbing brass motif being kept to the rear. Trinity ultimately jumps an 'impossible' distance between two buildings, during which a (moving) police siren on the street swells to be loudest in the middle of the jump (ie when Trinity is over the middle of the street). Again the audience is positioned with Trinity, the siren fading off as she lands. The immense depth to the matrix realm is necessary, in part, to offset the characters' ability to manipulate time and space. That is, they need an unnaturally vast realm to operate within lest they appear omnipotent. This is especially true for the Agents, who possess even more manipulatory power than the humans. It is the sonic spatiality of the film that assists the creation of this vastness, as well as simultaneously contributing to its believability.

'Welcome to the Real World'

The human slave farm occupies a more fantastic realm. In this one, the human and the machinic are in direct tension, the battle between them played out sonically as well as visually. It is a realm both fantastic and frightening, marvellous and morbid. A constant wet-slap sound (encased in echo and reverb) figures prominently in the rear speakers. It is at once mechanical and biotic. It is combined with a variety of energy sounds, flashes etc, as well as various electronic and machinic noises (both on and off-screen). The deep reverb employed across the soundtrack reflects the enormity of the farm.

Airlock cords that pull out of Neo's body are heard both front and rear, revealing the positioning of the cords and the audience's positioning along-side Neo. A 'heavenly' choral piece enters the soundtrack as Neo looks out over the field of entombed humans. This, combined with the main orchestral rhythmic motif, creates an extremely otherworldly ambience for this human apocalypse. Freed from the energy harvesting connections, Neo is released down a long slimy tube. The soundscape thins inside this delivery tube. Paradoxically, the more enclosed soundscape represents the newfound freedom attained by Neo – a similar technique as used aboard the Nebuchadnezzar. The heavenly choral motif returns as Neo is rescued, 'saved' from the liquid pool in order to become the saviour himself.

Throughout *The Matrix* the audience is called upon to understand the boundaries of the different realms, and establish their relationship to these worlds. In all cases, the soundtrack is pivotal to the creation and maintenance of these realms, with all being constructed around certain spatial principles that both support the narrative and legitimise future sonic development. These sonic (particularly spatial) elements are thus essential in constructing the perceptual geography necessary for the audience to make sense of the film in relation to their own world. The realms created either become real or abstract, yet what problematises the spatiality of the audience is the realisation that what is real in the movie is abstract in actuality, and visa versa. Thus the most realist soundscape in the movie occurs during the dinner between Cyphus and Agent Smith, yet, ironically this is the embodiment of the artificial matrix world. The sonic reality of the audience is directly

197

confronted by the sonic (non)reality presented in the soundtrack, enabling the development of a perceptual geography within the viewer, a space of resistance and tension, a place where the aural conditioning of the viewer can be constantly challenged and reconfigured. Ultimately, for the audience of *The Matrix*, the "difference between the dream world and the real world" (Morpheus) has become sonically unstable, providing the film with its most original inflection of the genre.

Notes

1. For example, the spectral mixing processes utilised in contemporary music production have largely been overlooked in film sound analysis. That 'production' or 'needle-drop' music contains its own spatial elements within its 'mix' – more so with the development of 5.1 channel mixing of music – necessitates its being considered within the spatial qualities of the film and soundtrack more generally. The audience positioning from these deliberate spatial decisions can be as pronounced as that within film. As Théberge notes:

   The multitrack recording process allows for the sound of the drums and cymbals to be spatially separated in the stereo mix, thus creating an artificially enhanced, spatialisation of the rhythmic structure of the music itself. The sound of the voice and other instruments and, ultimately, the listener are placed within this spatial/rhythmic field. (2001: 14)

2. Indeed, all city footage and outdoor location work was shot in Sydney, Australia.

3. *Star Wars* (1977) is perhaps the best example of this with C3PO constantly drawing attention to his human qualities.

4. Metz argues that sound is never "off"; a voice-off is still audible (see Doane, 1980: 166).

ABOUT THE AUTHORS

Melissa Carey is a BA (Hons) graduate in music composition from Southern Cross University, Lismore. Her current research interests include film music and audiovisual composition.

Karen Collins recently completed her PhD at the University of Liverpool on industrial music's appropriation of dystopia, and is currently researching video game sound.

Rebecca Coyle is program leader in Media Studies at Southern Cross University, Lismore. She edited the anthology *Screen Scores: Studies in Contemporary Australian Film Music* in 1998 and completed a PhD thesis on music in contemporary Australian feature films in 2002.

Mark Evans is a lecturer in Contemporary Music Studies at Macquarie University, Sydney. His PhD thesis analysed contemporary Christian music in Sydney and he is co-editor of *Perfect Beat – The Pacific Journal of Research Into Contemporary Music and Popular Culture*.

Michael Hannan is a composer, performer and music researcher. He is Head of the School of Arts at Southern Cross University, Lismore.

Philip Hayward is professor of Contemporary Music Studies at Macquarie University, Sydney and co-editor of *Perfect Beat – The Pacific Journal of Research Into Contemporary Music and Popular Culture*.

Shuhei Hosokawa is an associate professor in the Department of Humanities and Social Sciences at the Tokyo Institute of Technology. He has published several books on popular music and popular culture in Japanese.

He also contributed to Philip Hayward's anthology *Widening the Horizon* (1999).

Associate Professor **Neil Lerner** (Davidson College, North Carolina, USA) has published several essays on film music, including studies of Aaron Copland, Virgil Thomson, *The Birth of a Nation* and *High Noon*.

Rebecca Leydon is an associate professor of music theory at the Oberlin Conservatory, Oberlin, Ohio. Her writings on music and image appear in *Music Theory Spectrum*, *Perspectives on New Music*, *Music Theory Online* and *Popular Music*.

Paul Théberge is Canada Research Chair in Music and Interdisciplinary Studies at the Institute for Comparative Studies in Literature, Art and Culture at Carleton University, Ottowa.

Nabeel Zuberi is a senior lecturer in the Department of Film, Television and Media Studies at the University of Auckland. His books include *Sounds English: Transnational Popular Music* (2001) and he is currently working on a book about South Asian diaspora media.

BIBLIOGRAPHY

Abrash, M (1983) 'Dante's Hell as an Ideal Mechanical Environment', in Erlich, R.D and Dunn, T.P (eds) *Clockwork Worlds: Mechanized Environments in SF*, Connecticut (USA): Greenwood Press

Adams, D (1997) 'Tales from the Black Side: An Interview with Danny Elfman', *Film Score Monthly* – http://www.filmscoremonthly.com/articles1/elfman.html – accessed January 1997

———— 'The Sounds of the Empire: Analyzing the Themes of the *Star Wars* Trilogy', *Film Score Monthly* v4n5

Adams, P (1979) 'The dangerous pornography of death' *The Bulletin*, 1/5

———— (1993) 'Promiscuous power of popular music' *The Australian* 'Weekend Review', 16–17/10

Akiyama, K (1974) *Nihon no Eiga Ongakushi I* ['History of Japanese Film Music I'], Tokyo: Tabata Shoten

Allighieri, D (2002) *Hell*, London: Penguin Classics

Altman, R (1998) 'Reusable Packaging: Generic Products and the Recycling Process' in Browne, N (ed) *Refiguring American Film Genres: Theory and History*, Berkeley and Los Angeles: University of California Press

Anisfield, N (1995) 'Godzilla/Gojiro: Evolution of the Nuclear Metaphor', *Journal of Popular Culture* v29

Appadurai, A (1996) *Modernity at Large: Cultural Dimensions of Globalization*, Minneapolis (USA): University of Minnesota Press

Appollonio, U (ed) (1973) *Futurist Manifestos*, London: Thames and Hudson

Ascheid, A (1997) 'Speaking Tongues: Voice Dubbing in the Cinema as Cultural Ventriloquism', *The Velvet Light Trap* n40, Fall

Attali, J. (1985) *Noise: The Political Economy of Music*, Minneapolis (USA): University of Minnesota

Barajas, V (2000) 'GYPSY (of a strange and distant time): an interview [with Justin Hayward]', *Outre Magazine* – http://www.bluegypsycamp.com/vince/jh-outre.html – accessed July 2003

Barbour, D. H (1999) 'Heroism and Redemption in the Mad Max Trilogy', *Journal of Popular Film and Television* v27 n3, Fall

Barron, B and L (1989) Liner notes to *Forbidden Planet* sountrack, MGM

Bazelon, I (1975) *Knowing the Score: Notes on Film Music*, New York: Arco

Beard, W (2001) *The Artist as Monster: The Cinema of David Cronenberg*, Toronto: University of Toronto Press

Belton, J (1992) '1950 Magnetic Sound: The Frozen Revolution', in Altman, R (ed) *Sound Theory, Sound Practice*, London and New York: Routledge

Berk, M (2000) 'Analog Fetishes and Digital Futures' in Shapiro, P (ed) *Modulations: A History of Electronic Music, Throbbing Words on Sound*, New York: Caipirinha Productions

Berkwits, J (nd) 'Sound Space: *Destination Moon*' *SciFi.com* n213 – http://www.scifi.com/sfw/issue213/sound.html – accessed May 2003

Björnberg, A (1985) 'On Aeolian Harmony in Rock Music', paper presented to the Third International Conference of IASPM, Montreal – http://www.theblack-book.net/acad/papers/other.html – accessed July 2001

Blades, J (1970) *Percussion Instruments and their History*, London: Faber and Faber

Bond, J (1998) 'Watch the Record Stores, Please: How the Score to *Close Encounters of the Third Kind* Finally Got the Album It Deserves', *Film Score Monthly* v3n4

Born, G and Hesmondalgh, D (eds), *Western Music and Its Others: Difference, Representation, and Appropriation in Music*, Berkeley, Los Angeles and London: University of California Press

Boss, J.E (1999) 'Godzilla in the Details', *Strategies* v12n1

Bouzereau, L (1998) 'An Interview with John Williams', liner notes for *Close Encounters of the Third Kind: The Collector's Edition Soundtrack*

Bowlt, J. E (1976) *Russian Art of the Avant-Garde: Theory and Criticism*, New York: Viking

Bradbury, R (1983) 'The Fog Horn', in *The Stories of Ray Bradbury Volume One*, London: Grafton Books

Broeske, P (1982) 'George Miller Interview', *Films in Review* v33n8, Oct

Brophy, P (1991) 'The Architecsonic Object: Stereo Sound, Cinema and *Colors*' in Hayward, P (ed) *Culture, Technology and Creativity*, London, John Libbey and Co./Arts Council of Great Britain

————— (1998) 'Picturing Atonality, Part 1: Birth of the Monstrous', *The Wire* n168 – http://media-arts.rmit.edu.au/Phil_Brophy/SCRTHSTartcls/AcademyPeril.html – accessed April 2003

————— (ed) (1999) *Cinesonic: The World of Sound in Film*, Sydney: Australian Film Television & Radio School

Brown, J (2000) 'Bartók, the Gypsies, and Hybridity in Music', in Born, G and Hesmondalgh, D (eds)

Brown, R (1994) *Overtones and Undertones: Reading Film Music*, Berkeley (USA): University of California Press

Browne, N (1998) 'Preface' in Browne, N (ed) *Refiguring American Film Genres: Theory and History*, Berkeley and Los Angeles: University of California Press

Bruno, G (1990) 'Ramble City: Postmodernism and *Blade Runner*', in Kuhn, A (ed)

Buhler, J (2000) '*Star Wars*, Music, and Myth', in Buhler, J, Flinn, C and Neumeyer, D (eds) *Music and Cinema*, Hanover (USA): Wesleyan University Press

————— (2001) 'Analytical and Interpretive Approaches to Film Music (II): Analysing Interactions of Music and Film', in Donnelly, K (ed)

Bukatman, S (1997) *Blade Runner*, London: British Film Institute

————— (2002) 'The Artificial Infinite: On Special Effects and the Sublime' in Kuhn, A (ed)

Burman, M (1997) 'Making Music for Forbidden Planet', in Boorman, J and Donahue,

W (eds) *Projections 7: Film-makers on Film-making*, London and Boston: Faber and Faber

Bush, R (1989) 'The Music of *Flash Gordon* and *Buck Rogers*', in McCarty, C (ed) *Film Music 1*, New York and London: Garland

Byers, T (1990) 'Commodity Futures', in Kuhn, A (ed)

Byrd, C (1997) 'The Star Wars Interview: A New Talk', *Film Score Monthly* v2n1

Cameron, J and Wisher, W (1991) *Terminator 2: Judgment Day* (screenplay) – http://www.screentalk.org – accessed February 2002

Caputi, J (1988) 'Seeing Elephants: The Myths of Phallotechnology', *Feminist Studies* v14n3

Carlsson, S (ed) (nd) 'Sound Design of Star Wars' – http://www.filmsound.org/star-wars/ – accessed August 2003

Carroll, N (1998) 'The Future of Allusion: Hollywood in the Seventies (and Beyond),' in his *Interpreting the Moving Image*, Cambridge: Cambridge University Press

Cartmell, D (ed) (2000) *Classics in Film and Fiction*, London: Pluto Press

Chadabe, J (1997) *Electronic Sound: the Past and Future of Electronic Music*, New Jersey: Prentice Hall

Chapman, J (1999) 'A bit of the old ultra-violence' – *Clockwork Orange*, in Hunter, I.Q (ed) *British Science Fiction Cinema*, London: Routledge

Chion, M (1994) *Audio Vision: sound on screen* (ed & trans Gorbman, C), New York: Columbia University Press

Chute, D (1982) 'The Ayatolla of the Moviola', *Film Comment* v18n4

Clarke, F. S, and Rubin, S (1979) 'Making *Forbidden Planet*', *Cinefantastique* v8n2/3, Spring

Clifford, J (1988) *The Predicament of Culture: Twentieth-Century Ethnography, Literature, and Art*, Cambridge (USA): Harvard University Press

Collins, K (2002) 'The Future is Happening Already: Industrial Music and the Aesthetic of the Machine' (unpublished PhD thesis, University of Liverpool)

Collins, P and Blair, D (1989) *Australian English – The Language of a New Society*, Brisbane: University of Queensland Press

Conomos, J (2000) 'Sonic Darkness: Notes Towards an Aesthetic of Jazz in the American Film Noir', in Brophy, P (ed) *CINESONIC: Cinema and the Sound of Music*, Sydney: Australian Film, Television and Radio School

Cooke, D (1959) *The Language of Music*, Oxford: Oxford University Press

Corbett, J (1994) *Extended play: Sounding off from John Cage to Dr. Funkenstein*, Durham (USA) and London: Duke University Press

Cox, A (2001) 'The Mimetic Hypothesis and Embodied Musical Meaning', *Musicae Scientiae* v5n2

Coyle, R (ed) (1998) *Screen Scores: Studies in Contemporary Australian Film Music*, Sydney: Australian Film Television and Radio School

Crane, D (2000a) 'In Medias Race: Filmic Representation, Networked Communication, and Racial Intermediation' in Kolko, B.E, Nakamura, L and Rodman, G.B (eds) *Race in Cyberspace*, New York and London: Routledge

———— (2000b) 'A Body Apart: Cronenberg and Genre', in Grant, M (ed) *The Modern Fantastic: The Films of David Cronenberg*, Westport (USA): Praeger

Cranny-Francis, A (1988) 'The Moving Image: Film and Television', in Kress, G (ed) *Communication and Culture: An Introduction*, Sydney: University of New South Wales Press

Cumming, N (1997) 'The Subjectivities of *Erbarme Dich*', *Music Analysis* v16n1

Davis, A.Y (1998) 'Afro Images: Politics, Fashion, and Nostalgia' in Guillory, M and Green, R.C (eds) *Soul: Black Power, Politics, and Pleasure*, New York: New York University Press

Deftereous, F (1998) 'Do Humans Dream in Negative Strips?' – http://scribble.com/uwi/br/dreamstrips.html – accessed March 2003

Deleuze, G and Guattari, F (1987) *A Thousand Plateaux*, Minneapolis: University of Minnesota Press

Dery, M (ed) (1994) *Flame Wars: The Discourse of Cyberculture*, Durham (USA) and London: Duke University Press

Diederichsen, D (2002) 'Digital Electronic Music: Between Pop and Pure Mediality: Paradoxical Strategies for a Refusal of Semantics' in Van Assche, C (ed) *Sonic Process: A New Geography of Sounds*, Barcelona: Actar/Museu d'Art Contemporani de Barcelona

Doane, M (1980) 'The Voice in the Cinema: The Articulation of Body and Space' in Weis, E and Belton, J (eds) (1985) *Film Sound: Theory and Practice*, New York: Columbia University Press

Donnelly, K (1998) 'The Classical Film Score Forever? *Batman*, *Batman Returns* and Post-classical Film Music', in Neale, S and Smith, M (eds) *Contemporary Hollywood Cinema*, London and New York: Routledge

———— (ed) (2001) *Film Music: Critical Approaches*, Edinburgh: Edinburgh University Press

Durwood, T (1977) *Close Encounters of the Third Kind: A Document of the Film*, Kansas City (USA): Ariel Books

Elfman, D (1998) 'Foreword', *Gramophone Film Music Good CD Guide* (3rd Edition), London: Gramophone Publications

Engel, C (1996) 'Language and the Music of the Spheres: Steven Spielberg's *Close Encounters of the Third Kind*', *Literature/Film Quarterly* v24n4

Enns, A (2001) '"The Mutated Flowers of Hiroshima": American Reception and Naturalization of Tôhô's Godzilla', *Popular Culture Review* v12n2

Entman, R and Seymour, F (1978) '*Close Encounters of the Third Kind*: Close Encounters with the Third Reich', *Jump Cut* v18

Eshun, K (1998) *More Brilliant Than the Sun: Adventures in Sonic Fiction*, London: Quartet Books

Fancher, H and Peoples, D (1981) *Blade Runner* (screenplay) - http:/scribble.com/uwi/br/script_19810223.txt – accessed February 2003

Feisst, S (1999) 'Arnold Schoenberg and the Cinematic Art', *The Musical Quarterly* v83n1, Spring

Flanagan, G (1983) 'A Conversation with Brian May: Interview', *Cinema Score* n11/12, Fall/Winter

Flinn, C (1992) *Strains of Utopia: Gender, nostalgia and Hollywood film music*, Princeton (USA): Princeton University Press

Fox, T (1977) 'The *Star Wars* War: II: Star Drek', *Film Comment* v13n4

Freud, S (1919) 'The Uncanny', in, Freud, S *The Standard Edition of the Complete Psychological Works of Sigmund Freud*, London: Hogarth Press

Gabbard, K (1982) 'Religious and Political Allegory in Wise, Robert *The Day the Earth Stood Still*,' *Literature Film Quarterly* v10n3

Gabo, N and Pevsner, A (1976) 'The Realistic Manifesto, 1920' in Bowlt, J.E (ed) *Russian Art of the Avant-Garde: Theory and Criticism*, New York: Viking

Garcia Espinosa, J (1983) 'For an Imperfect Cinema', in Chanan, M (ed) *Twenty-five*

Years of the New Latin American Cinema, London: British Film Institute and Channel Four Television

Gibson, R (1985) 'Yondering: A Reading of *Mad Max Beyond Thunderdome*', *Art & Text* n19, Oct/Dec

Gill, J (1995) *Queer Noises: Male and Female Homosexuality in Twentieth-Century Music*, London: Cassell

Gilliam, B (1999a) *The Life of Richard Strauss*, Cambridge: Cambridge University Press

————— (1999b) 'A Viennese Opera Composer in Hollywood: Korngold's Double Exile in America', in Brinkmann, R and Wolff, C (eds) *Driven Into Paradise: The Musical Migration from Nazi Germany to the United States*, Los Angeles and London: University of California Press, 1999

Gilroy, P (2000) *Against Race: Imagining Political Culture beyond the Color Line*, Cambridge (USA): Harvard University Press

Gioa, T (1988) *The Imperfect Art: Reflections on Jazz and Modern Culture*, New York: Oxford University Press

Gold, L (1997) 'An Egocentric and Convoluted History of Early "Filk" and Filking' – http://www.geocities.com/Area51/Dimension/3511/filkhist.html – accessed July 2003

Gorbman, C (1987) *Unheard Melodies: Narrative Film Music*, Bloomington, (USA): Indiana University Press

————— (2000) 'Scoring the Indian: Music in the Liberal Western', in Born, G and Hesmondalgh (eds)

Greenwald, T (1986) 'The Self-destructing Modules Behind the Revolutionary 1956 Soundtrack of *Forbidden Planet*', *Keyboard* v12n2, February

Gross, L (1995) 'Big and Loud', *Sight and Sound* v5n8

Grünberg, S (2000) *David Cronenberg: Entretiens avec Serge Grünberg*, Paris: Cahiers du Cinéma

Guokas, J (1996) 'Blade Runner: Tee-Vee or Not Tee-Vee' – http://scribble.com/br/brtv.html – accessed February 2003

Hagen, E (1971) *Scoring for Films*, USA (no city given): E.D.J. Music

Hall, S (1982) 'Action speaks louder than words', *The Bulletin* v101, 12/1

Handling, P (ed) (1983) *The Shape of Rage: The Films of David Cronenberg*, Toronto: General Publishing Co. Limited

Hargus, B.B (1997) 'Interview with John F. Szwed' – http://www.furious.com/perfect/sunra2.html – accessed August 2002

Harley, R (1998) 'Creating a Sonic Character: Non-Diegetic Sound in the Mad Max Trilogy' in Coyle, R (ed)

Hart, M, and Lieberman, F (1991) *Planet Drum: A Celebration of Percussion and Rhythm*, New York: Harper Collins

Hayward, P (1997) 'Danger Retro-Affectivity! The Cultural Career of the Theremin', *Convergence* v3 n4, Winter

————— (1999) 'The Cocktail Shift: Aligning Musical Exotica', in Hayward, P (ed) *Widening the Horizon – Exoticism in Post-War Popular Music*, Sydney: John Libbey and Co/Perfect Beat Publications

Heble, A (2000) *Landing on the Wrong Note: Jazz, Dissonance and Critical Practice*, New York and London: Routledge

Hendershot, C (1997) 'The Atomic Scientist, Science Fiction Films, and Paranoia: *The Day the Earth Stood Still, This Island Earth*, and *Killers From Space*', *Journal of American Culture* v20n1, Spring 1997

Hillegas, M (1967) *The Future as Nightmare: H.G. Wells and Anti-Utopians*, New York: Oxford University Press

Homan, S (1997) 'Terra Incognita: The Career of Charlie McMahon' in Neuenfeldt, K (ed) *The Didjeridu: From Arnhem Land to Internet*, Sydney: John Libbey & Co./ Perfect Beat Publications

Honda, I (1994) *Godzilla to Waga Eiga Jinsei* ['Godzilla and My Film Life'], Tokyo: Jitsugyôno Nihonsha – http://scribble.com/uwi/br/br-misog.html – accessed February 2003

Huckvale, D (1990). '*Twins of Evil*: an investigation into the aesthetics of film music', *Popular Music* v9 n1

Hughes, R (1968) *Heaven and Hell in Western Art*, London: Weidenfeld and Nicolson

Hunter, I.Q (1999) 'Introduction: the strange world of the British science fiction film' in Hunter, I.Q (ed) *British Science Fiction Cinema*, London: Routledge

Hutchinson, I (1978) 'Brian May interview', *Cinema Papers* n17, Aug/Sept

Ifukube, A (1951) *Ongaku Nyûmon* ['Introduction to music'], Tokyo: Kaname Shobô

Ifukube, A (1953 [1999]) *Kangengakuhô* (2 vols) ['Orchestration'], Tokyo: Ongakunotomosha

———— (1959) 'Ainuzoku no Ongaku' ['The music of the Ainu'], *Ongaku Geijutsu*, December

———— (1971) 'Romanshugi no Hitei Aruiwa Koretono Ketsubetsu' ['Denying or breaking away from Romanticism'], *Ongaku Geijutsu*, June

Inoue, H (1994) *Kenshô Godzilla Tanj: Shôwa 29 nen Tôhô Satsueijo* ['Examining the Birth of Godzilla: Tôhô Studio in 1954'], Tokyo: Asahi Sonorama

Jakubowski, M (1999) 'Music: Science Fiction in Classical Music' in Clute, J and Nicholls, P (eds) *The Encyclopedia of Science Fiction*, London: Orbit

Jameson, F (1983) 'Postmodernism and Consumer Society', in Foster, H (ed) *The Anti-Aesthetic: Essays on Postmodern Culture*, Seattle: Bay Press

Jones, L (1967) *Black Music*, New York: Morrow Paperback Editions

Kalinak, K (1992) *Settling The Score*, Madison (USA): University of Wisconsin Press

Karlin, F (1994) *Listening to Movies: The Film Lover's Guide to Film Music*, New York: Schirmer Books

Kart, L (2000) 'The Avant-Garde, 1949–1967' in Kirchner, B (ed) *The Oxford Companion to Jazz*, Oxford and New York: Oxford University Press

Kawamoto, S (1994) *Ima hitotabino Sengo Nihon Eiga* ['Recollecting the Postwar Japanese Movie one more time'], Tokyo: Iwanami Shoten

Kendall, L (1997) 'Did You Know There's No Theme for Han? A Look at the *Star Wars* Scores in Terms of the Movies and What Makes Them Work (Or Not Work)', *Film Score Monthly* v2n1

Kenny, T (2000) *Sound for Picture: The art of sound design in film and television* (2nd ed) Vallejo (USA): Mix Books

Kibby, M and Neuenfeldt, K (1998) 'Sound, Cinema and Aboriginality' in Coyle, R (ed)

Kibe, Y (1997) *Ifukube Akira: Ongakuka no Tanjô* ['Akira Ifukube: The Birth of a Musician'], Tokyo: Shinchôsha

King, N (1984) *Abel Gance*, London: British Film Institute Publishing

King, N and Guilliatt, R (1999) 'The Max Factor' in *Good Weekend*, 18/12

Knight, A (2002) *Disintegrating the Musical: Black Performance and American Musical Film*, Durham and London: Duke University Press

Kobayashi, A (1998) *Ifukube Akira no Eiga Ongaku* ['Akira Ifukube's Film Music'], Tokyo: Waizu Shuppan

———— (2001a) *Nihon Eiga Ongaku no Kyosei Tachi I* ['The Giant Stars of Japanese Film Music I'], Tokyo: Waizu Shuppan

———— (2001b) *Nihon Eiga Ongaku no Kyosei Tachi II* ['The Giant Stars of Japanese Film Music II'], Tokyo: Waizu Shuppan

Kozloff, S (2000) *Overhearing Film Dialogue*, Berkeley and Los Angeles: University of California Press

Kuhn, A (ed) (1990) *Alien Zone: Cultural theory and contemporary science fiction cinema*, London: Verso

———— (ed) (2002) *Alien Zone II: the spaces of science fiction cinema*, London and New York: Verso

Landon, B (2002) 'Diegetic or Digital? The Convergence of Science-Fiction Literature and Science-Fiction Film in Hypermedia' in Kuhn, A (ed)

Larson, R (1985) *Musique fantastique: A Survey of Film Music in the Fantastic Cinema*, Metuchen (USA) and London: Scarecrow Press

Lerner, N (2001) 'Copland's Music of Wide Open Spaces: Surveying the Pastoral Trope in Hollywood', *Musical Quarterly* v85n3, Fall

Lincoln Collier, J (2001) 'Tcherepnin, Alexandr', *The New Grove Dictionary of Music and Musicians* v25

Lubow, A (1977) 'The *Star Wars* War: I: A Space *Iliad*', *Film Comment* v13n4

Maddox, G (1985) 'Marketing *Mad Max 3*', *Encore*, August

Manvell, R and Huntley, J (1957) *The Technique of Film Music*, New York: Communication Arts Books

Matessino, M (1997) Liner notes to *Star Wars: A New Hope* (RCA)

McBride, J (1997) *Steven Spielberg: A Biography*, New York: Simon and Schuster

Middleton, R (2000) 'Musical belongings: Western Music and Its Low-Other', in Born, G and Hesmondalgh, D (eds)

Miller, D (1991) 'Primitive Art and the Necessity of Primitivism to Art', in Hiller, S (ed) *The Myth of Primitivism: Perspectives on Art*, London: Routledge

Milton, J (1989 edition) *Paradise Lost*, London: Penguin Classics

Minawa, I (1995) 'Interview', in the CD booklet to *Godzilla's Sound Effects* (Toshiba-EMI)

Morphett, T (1984) '*Mad Max* and the Vigilantes', *Quadrant*, March

Musolf, P (1998) *Gojira to wa Nanika* ['The Godzilla Question'], Tokyo: Kôdansha

Neale, S (1990) 'Questions of Genre', *Screen* v31n1, Spring

———— (2000) *Genre and Hollywood*, London: Routledge

Nelson, A (2002) 'Introduction: Future Texts', *Social Text* v20n2, Summer

Nepier, S.J (1993) 'Panic Sites: The Japanese Imagination of Disaster from Godzilla to Akirra', *Journal of Japanese Studies* v19/2

Nicoll, J (1985) 'When will he come in from the cold?', *Metro*, n68, November

Nishimura, Y (1990) *Kurosawa Akira: Oto to Eizô* ('Akira Kurosawa: Sound and Vision'), Tokyo: Tatsukaze Shobô

Noriega, C. A (1996) 'Godzilla and the Japanese Nightmare: When *Them! Is U.S.*', in Broderick, M (ed), *Hibakusha Cinema: Hiroshima, Nagasaki and the Nuclear Image in Japanese Film*, London and New York: Kegan Paul International

Omura, K (1992) 'Sakuhin no Tokuchô to sono Kôzô' ['The Characteristics and Structure of Ifukube's Work'), in Sagara, Y (ed) (1992) *Ifukube Akira no Uchû* ['The Universe of Akira Ifukube'], Tokyo: Ongaku no Tomosha

Palmer, C (1990) *The Composer in Hollywood*, London and New York: Marion Boyars
———— and Marks, M (2001) 'John Williams', in Sadie, S (ed) *The New Grove Dictionary of Music and Musicians*, London: Macmillan

Paulus, I (2000) 'Williams Versus Wagner Or An Attempt At Linking Musical Epics', *International Review of the Aesthetics and Sociology of Music* v31n2

Peary, D (1984) 'Directing Mad Max and The Road Warrior – An Interview with George Miller by Danny Peary' in Peary, D (ed) *Omni's Screen Flights/Screen Fantasies: The future according to Science Fiction Cinema*, New York: Dolphin/Doubleday & Co
———— (1988) *Cult Movies 3: 50 More of the Classics: The Sleepers, The Weird & The Wonderful*, New York: Simon & Shuster

Perloff, M (1986) *The Futurist Moment: Avant-Garde, Avant Guerre, and the Language of Rupture*, Chicago and London: University of Chicago Press
———— (1990), *The Futurist Moment*, Chicago: University of Chicago Press

Pinch, T and Trocco, F (2002) *Analog Days: the invention and impact of the Moog synthesizer*, Cambridge (USA): Harvard University Press

Pisani, M (1998) '"I'm an Indian Too"', in Bellman, J (ed) *The Exotic in Western Music*, Boston: Northeastern University Press

Pollak, A (1985) 'Outrage in the Outback', *City Limits* 18–24/10

Pollock, D (1983) *Skywalking: The Life and Films of George Lucas*, New York: Harmony Books

Powers, O. D (1997) 'Interactions between composers and technology in the first decades of electronic music, 1948–1968' (unpublished DoA dissertation, Ball State University)

Prendergast, M (2000) *The Ambient Century: From Mahler to Trance – the Evolution of Sound in the Electronic Age*, London: Bloomsbury

Rhodes, C (1983) 'Review of *Forbidden Planet* soundtrack', *Computer Music Journal* v7n1, Spring

Rodley, C (ed) (1992) *Cronenberg on Cronenberg*, Boston: Faber and Faber

Rosar, W. H (2001) 'The *Dies Irae* in *Citizen Kane*: Musical Hermeneutics Applied to Film Music' in Donnelly, K.J (ed)

Rubey, D (1978) 'Star Wars: Not So Far Away', *Jump Cut* v18

Saini, T (1996) 'Eye Disbelieve' – http://scribble.com/uwi/br/tinku/ – accessed February 2003

Sammon, P (1996) *Future Noir: The Making of Blade Runner*, London: Orion Books

Sardar, Z (2002) 'Introduction' in Sardar, Z and Cubitt, S (eds) *Aliens R Us: The Other in Science Fiction Cinema*, London: Pluto Press

Schafer, R. M (1967) *Ear Cleaning: Notes for an Experimental Music Course*, Don Mills (Canada): BMI Canada
———— (1977/1980) *The Tuning of the World: Towards a Theory of Soundscape Design*, Philadelphia: University of Pennsylvania Press

Schatz, T (1993) 'The New Hollywood', in Collins, J, Radner, H and Preacher, A (eds) *Film Theory Goes to the Movies*, New York and London: Routledge

Scheurer, T (1997) 'John Williams and Film Music Since 1971', *Popular Music and Society* v21n1

Scott, S (no date) 'Is *Blade Runner* a Misogynist Text?' – http://scribble.com/uwi/br/br_misog.html – accessed April 2003

Shapiro, J. F (2002) *Atomic Bomb Cinema*, London and New York: Routledge

Smalley, D (1997) 'Spectromorphology: Explaining Sound Shapes', *Organised Sound* v2n2, August

Smith, J (1998) *The Sounds of Commerce: Marketing Popular Film Music*, New York: Columbia University Press

Sobchack, V (1988) *Screening Space: The American Science Fiction Film*, New York: Ungar Publishing Company

————— (1999) *Screening Space: the American Science Fiction Film* (2nd ed) New Brunswick (USA): Rutgers University Press

Solman, G (2002) 'Fancy Math', *Film Comment* v38n4

Sontag, S (1965) 'The Imagination of Disaster', *Critical Commentary* n42v8

————— (1975) 'Fascinating Fascism', *The New York Review of Books* v22n1

Spielberg, S (1977) *Close Encounters of the Third Kind*, New York: Dell

————— (1980) *Close Encounters of the Third Kind: The Special Edition*, New York: Dell

Stilwell, R (2001) 'Sound and Empathy: Subjectivity, Gender and the Cinematic Soundscape' in Donnelly, K (ed)

Stiller, A (1991) 'The Music in Blade Runner', in Kerman, J (ed) *Retrofitting Blade Runner: Issues in Ridley Scott's Blade Runner and Philip K. Dick's Do Androids Dream of Electric Sheep?* Bowling Green (USA): Bowling Green State University Popular Press

Stoner, D (1986/1987) 'Maurice Jarre Scoring Session for *Mad Max Beyond Thunderdome*' in *Cinema Score*, Special n15, Winter/Summer

Szwed, J.F (1997) *Space is the Place: The Life and Times of Sun Ra*, Edinburgh: Payback Press

————— (2000) *Jazz 101: A Complete Guide to Learning and Loving Jazz*, New York: Hyperion

Tagg, P (1983) *'Nature' as a Musical Mood Category*, Gothenburg (Sweden): International Association for the Study of Popular Music

————— (2000) *Kojak: Fifty Seconds of Television Music*, New York: Mass Media Music Scholars' Press Inc

Takeuchi, H (ed) (2000) *Honda Ishirô Zenshigoto* ['The Complete Works of Ishirô Honda'], Tokyo: Asahi Sonorama

————— and Yamamoto, S (eds) (2001) *Tsuburaya Eiji no Eizô Sekai* ['The Visual World of Eiji Tsuburaya'], Tokyo: Jitsugyôno Nihonsha

Tanaka, T (ed) (1983) *Tôhô Tokusatsu Eiga Zenshi* ['The Entire History of Tôhô Science Fiction Film'], Tokyo: Tôhô

————— (1998) *Denshi Ongaku in Japan 1955–1981* ['Electronic Music in Japan, 1955–1981'], Tokyo: Asupekuto

Taylor, C (1998) *The Mask of Art: Breaking the Aesthetic Contract – Film and Literature*, Bloomington and Indianapolis (USA): University of Indiana Press

Taylor, T (2001) *Strange Sounds: Music, Technology and Culture*, New York and London: Routledge

Telotte, J (1990) 'The Doubles of Fantasy and the Space of Desire', in Kuhn, A (ed)

————— (1995) *Replications: A Robotic History of the Science Fiction Film*, Urbana and Chicago: University of Illinois Press

————— (2001) *Science Fiction Film*, Cambridge: Cambridge University Press

Toop, D (1996) *Ocean of Sound: Aether Talk, Ambient Sound and Imaginary Worlds*, London: Serpent's Tail

Torgovnick, M (1990) *Gone Primitive: Savage Intellects, Modern Lives*, Chicago and London: University of Chicago Press

Torry, R (1991) 'Politics and Parousia in *Close Encounters of the Third Kind*', *Literature/Film Quarterly* v19n3

209

Turner, G. W (1972) *Good Australian English and Good New Zealand English*, Sydney: Reed Education

UGO (2002) 'The Music of Matrix: Exclusive interview with Don Davis, composer of *The Animatrix* and *The Matrix* trilogy. – http://www.ugo.com/channels/music/features/thematrix/dondavis.asp – accessed May 2003

Unattributed (1956a) 'Forbidden Planet', *Time* v67n4, 9/4

———— (1956b) 'Music of the Future', *Time* v68n1, 2/7

———— (1959) 'Music of the Future?', *Mademoiselle* n50, December

———— (1979) 'Production Report: *Mad Max*', *Cinema Papers*, May/June

Vale, V and Juno, A (1993) *Re/Search #14: Incredibly Strange Music, v1*, San Francisco: Re/Search Publications

———— (1994) *Re/Search #15: Incredibly Strange Music, v2*, San Francisco: Re/Search Publications

———— (1994) 'Interview with Bebe Barron', in Vale, V and Juno, A

Van Assche, C (ed) (2002) *Sonic Process: A New Geography of Sounds*, Barcelona: Actar/Museu d'Art Contemporani de Barcelona

Van Leeuwen, T (1999) *Speech, Music, Sound*, London: Macmillan

Venkatasawmy, R, Simpson, C and Visosevic, T (2001) 'From Sand to bitumen, from bushrangers to "bogans": Mapping the Australian road movie', *Journal of Australian Studies* n70

Vincent, R (1995) *Funk: The Music, The People and The Rhythm of The One*, New York: St. Martin's Griffin

Waksman, S (1999), *Instruments of Desire: The Electric Guitar and the Shaping of Musical Experience*, Cambridge: Harvard University Press

Watkins, G (1988) *Soundings: Music in the Twentieth Century*, London and New York: Schirmer Books

———— (1994) *Pyramids at the Louvre: Music, Culture and Collage from Stravinsky to the Postmodernists*, Cambridge and London: Harvard University Press

Weheliye, A.G (2002) '"Feenin": Posthuman Voices in Contemporary Black Popular Music', *Social Text* v20n2, Summer

White, J (1985) *Black Leadership in America 1895–1968*, London and New York: Longman

Wiener, N (1948) *Cybernetics*, New York: J. Wiley

Williams, L (1991) 'Film Bodies: Gender, Genre, and Excess', *Film Quarterly* v44n4, Summer

Williams, T (1983) 'Close Encounters of the Authoritarian Kind', *Wide Angle* v5n4

Wilmer, V (1992) *As Serious As Your Life: John Coltrane and Beyond*, New York and London: Serpent's Tail

Wood, R (1986) *Hollywood from Vietnam to Reagan*, New York: Columbia University Press

Worby, R (2000) 'Cacophony' in Emmerson, S (ed) *Music, Electronic Media and Culture*, Aldershot (UK): Ashgate

WuDunn, S (1997) 'Tomoyuki Tanaka, the Creator of Godzilla, is Dead at 86', *New York Times* 4/4

Yearwood, G. L (2000) *Black Film as a Signifying Practice: Cinema, Narration and the African-American Aesthetic Tradition*, Trenton (USA) and Asmara: Africa World Press

Yoshimoto, M (2000) *Kurosawa: Film Studies and Japanese Cinema*, Durham (USA) and London: Duke University Press

Index